THE MEMOIRS OF
JOHN ADDINGTON SYMONDS

THE MEMOIRS OF

JOHN ADDINGTON SYMONDS

EDITED AND INTRODUCED BY

PHYLLIS GROSSKURTH

RANDOM HOUSE

NEW YORK

Library of Congress Cataloging in Publication Data
Symonds, John Addington, 1840–1893.
The memoirs of John Addington Symonds.
Includes index.
1. Symonds, John Addington, 1840–1893—Biography.
2. Authors, English—19th century—Biography.
3. Homosexuals, Male—England—Biography.
I. Grosskurth, Phyllis.   II. Title.
PR5523.A425   1984   828'.809[B]   84-42676
ISBN 0-394-54085-9

Manufactured in the United States of America
9   8   7   6   5   4   3   2

Contents

Illustrations

All photographs reproduced by kind permission of Bristol University Library except where indicated

Between pages 80 and 81

A painting of John Addington Symonds, 1853
Sophie Girard
Mrs Sykes ('Auntie')
The drawing room at Clifton Hill
Clifton Hill House
John Addington Symonds at Harrow
Dr Vaughan, *c.* 1860 (National Portrait Gallery)
John Addington Symonds with Dr Symonds and Charlotte
Maribelle
Edith

Between pages 144 and 145

John Addington Symonds, 1864
Catherine North
John Addington Symonds with his daughter, Margaret
Janet Symonds
'My mother's alpine garden' by Margaret Symonds
Boys with sculpture
Catherine Symonds

Foreword

Some years ago, rummaging in a second-hand book shop in Broad-stairs, I chanced upon a copy of H. F. Brown's 1895 biography of John Addington Symonds. I was about to embark on a doctoral dissertation, and had been considering exploring Symonds's writings as representative of the attitudes and preoccupations of nineteenth-century literary criticism. I bought the book, took it back to my hotel and sat up most of the night reading it. Why, I kept wondering, did Brown – only two years after Symonds's death in 1893 – choose to write a biography of Symonds comprised largely of excerpts from Symonds's autobiography, rather than simply publish the auto-biography? I began work on my thesis and although I was far more preoccupied with tracking down Symonds's articles in periodicals, I continued to be haunted by the question of the autobiography, particularly as Symonds's critical writings are unusually subjective. My supervisor, Professor Geoffrey Tillotson, suggested that Brown – in nineteenth-century fashion – might have cut out snippets from the autobiography and then tossed what he didn't use into the wastebasket. But I was in the grip of a compulsion to unearth everything about the man that I could possibly find. I placed an inquiry requesting information about Symonds's unpublished papers in *The Times Literary Supplement* and, much to my astonishment, I shortly received a letter from the Librarian of the London Library, Mr Stanley Gillam, informing me that he had possession of the manuscript of Symonds's memoirs.

Mr Gillam later explained to me how the London Library happened to own the memoirs. When Symonds's literary executor, Horatio Brown, died in 1926, he bequeathed the document to the London Library with instructions that it was not to be published

9

for fifty years after his death.* In 1926 the Librarian of the London Library was Charles Hagberg Wright and the Chairman of the Committee was Sir Edmund Gosse.

In a letter to the Librarian, dated 21 December 1925, Brown expressed his appreciation to Wright and Gosse for consenting to accept custody of Symonds's autobiography – 'and other papers'. He informed Wright that he would receive 'a green card-board box, tied with strings, measuring at most 6 inches by 12 inches by 18 inches and labelled "J. A. Symonds' Papers" '. The box, Brown continued, would contain 'the Autobiography which Symonds was anxious to have preserved, the Diaries and his letters (of which I have made great use already) and my letters which he kept, will probably be destroyed on my death'. This last phrase is puzzling. Did Brown mean that his own letters or his letters *and* Symonds's letters and diaries would 'probably be destroyed'? The instructions in Brown's will, dated the day following the letter to Wright, are startling:

> As to literary papers, I have already deposited in perpetuity in the London Library my large collection of transcripts from the Venetian Archives. I am endeavouring to get the British Museum to accept custody of J. A. Symonds' Autobiography, with an embargo of 50 years, against publication. There is a dark green cloth covered book tied with string which contains autographs which might prove of some value, Gladstone, Rhodes, Swinburne, Hardy, Curzon, Roseberry, T. E. Brown, Ruskin, etc. This might be kept for dispersal. The rest had better be destroyed. It is the safest and simplest way.

But there is a further instruction to Brown's trustees and executors:

> I desire that a green card-board box tied with strings and labelled 'J. A. Symonds' Papers', bequeathed to the London Library . . . shall be handed to the London Library on my death. . . .

One can only assume that the main body of the will, including the intention to bequeath the manuscript to the British Museum, had been drawn up before the arrangement had been made with the London Library. Why did Brown alter his plans? And what papers, precisely, did he leave to the London Library?

Brown died on 19 August 1926. In the minutes of the Committee

---

*See Appendix 2.

of the London Library for 11 April 1927, with Sir Edmund Gosse in the chair, there is the following brief comment:

> It was proposed and seconded that the gift of the Ms. autobiography of John A. Symonds should be accepted, and that a notice should be placed on the Ms. that it is not to be opened by the Librarian or any other person without leave of the Committee.

Any additional papers found with the memoirs are printed as appendices. Although the memoirs specify that some personal letters will be left with them, there is only one; nor, unfortunately, have we the diaries or valuable holograph letters from distinguished people mentioned in Brown's will.

In 1949 the green cloth box was opened for the first time when Symonds's daughter, Dame Katharine Furse, requested permission to read the memoirs. Then in 1954 a sub-committee of the Committee of the London Library – in view of 'the more liberal climate of 1954' – recommended 'that it would be obscurantist, and out of keeping with the Library's tradition and its duty to its members and to scholarship at large, if access to the manuscript, with due safeguards, was longer denied to *bona fide* scholars'. Curiously enough, Rose Macaulay (who was a member of the sub-committee), in a letter written a fortnight after the sub-committee's report, expressed misgivings about the advisability of the eventual publication of the memoirs (*Last Letters to a Friend*, 1962).

The manuscript is a lengthy document, far too long to make its publication in entirety practicable. Consequently, I have cut roughly one-fifth of the text – not to the detriment of the original, I believe. The omitted passages are confined mainly to Symonds's execrable poetry and to self-conscious nature descriptions quoted from his own letters. Now that the embargo is lifted, interested scholars may, if they wish, obtain permission from the Librarian to read the original document in full.

In the main the narrative flows freely and is fairly easy to read. I have left in their original form the idiosyncrasies of Symonds's spelling. Some of the key incidents – the Vaughan affair and Symonds's initial reactions to his marriage, for example – are heavily scored and rewritten. There is a good deal of marginalia, particularly pertaining to Symonds's later clinical investigations into the pathology of homosexuality. I have made note of the marginalia and the textual changes which seemed significant.

From the outset I decided not to encumber the narrative with a ponderous freight of footnotes. My principle has been to document those references where fuller explanation would illuminate or explicate the text. It seemed more necessary, for example, to include a note for a minor nineteenth-century literary figure than for a major Renaissance painter. I frequently found that what struck me as requiring explanation might appear insultingly naïve to some readers – but almost all editing is marked by a degree of whimsicality. Symonds's own footnotes and textual emendations are placed at the bottom of the relevant page; the explanatory references can be found at the end of the volume.

Above all, I wish to express my gratitude to Mr Gillam for his unfailing kindness and help during our long association. For background material I am indebted to the three volumes of Symonds's collected letters edited by Robert Peters and Herbert Schueller.* I have also consulted P. L. Babington's *Bibliography of the Writings of John Addington Symonds*† for information about Symonds's poetry. Ian Storey has translated and traced the sources of the classical quotations. (Mr Storey, incidentally, was amazed by Symonds's knowledge of the more arcane regions of classical literature.) Professors Beatrice Corrigan and Walter Bauer generously provided me with translations of the Italian and German quotations. Douglas Matthews and Jean Elliott did invaluable research for me in the London Library and the British Museum. Richard Giles kindly permitted me to examine Symonds's annotated copy of *Leaves of Grass*. Many of my friends and colleagues have patiently and generously answered my innumerable queries. I wish to thank the Headmasters of Clifton College and Harrow School; Peter Allen; Timothy D'Arch Smith; Desmond Conacher; J. B. Conacher; John Gross; Robert Harney; H. Montgomery Hyde; Robin Jackson; Trevor Lloyd; John Lynen; Steven Marcus; Mavor Moore; David Newsome; Sybil Pantazzi; F. E. L. Priestley; Dr Vivien Rakoff; Mrs Douglas West and William Whitle. Cynthia Good, Philippa Simpson and Mary Atkinson were responsible for various stages of the typescript. Finally, I could not have undertaken the task of editing the manuscript without a research grant from the Canada Council.

Phyllis Grosskurth

*To be referred to subsequently as *Letters*.
†To be referred to subsequently as Babington.

Introduction

During the latter part of the nineteenth century, John Addington Symonds (1840–93) was regarded as one of the major English men of letters. His reputation was based on an extraordinarily impressive literary productivity: frequent reviews in the leading periodicals, studies of Dante and the Greek poets, travel books, volumes of poetry, and collections of essays. Above all, he was distinguished for his seven-volume *Renaissance in Italy*. Symonds has never been given sufficient credit for producing the first *Kulturgeschichte* in English – except by scholars of the period, who do not hesitate to compare it with Burckhardt's *History of the Renaissance in Italy*.

With the passing of the years his reputation has faded and many people have the vague but mistaken impression that he was associated with the aesthetes of the *fin de siècle*. As a reading of his *memoirs* will reveal, such an association, with its emphasis on art for art's sake, would have been an anathema to him.

By an ironical twist of fate Symonds has been rescued from neglect by the revelations in a work which he knew would be impossible to publish during his lifetime – namely, his frank account of the difficulties encountered by a homosexual in the nineteenth century. In the past few years there has been a marked change of attitude towards homosexuality. This therefore seems a propitious moment for the publication of Symonds's memoirs. Symonds himself was deeply concerned about the 'education' of the public regarding homosexuality. We may not be much more 'educated' about the causes and nature of homosexuality than the public was in Symonds's day, but at least we are by and large more tolerant. As a consequence, the memoirs are not likely to be approached with the salacious curiosity they once might have elicited, but rather with the interest due to a historical document, or – more important – a record of profound personal suffering.

The reasons why people write autobiographies are varied, complex and contradictory, but two major motivations seem general: the conviction that one's self and one's life are unique, and the belief that no one but the writer is in a position to tell the undistorted truth about himself. Sometimes the writer feels compelled to set straight a record he is persuaded was misunderstood during his lifetime. Rousseau, for example, believed that he had been vilified largely because people failed to understand his uniqueness and judged him by conventional standards. But is a man ever in a position to see himself dispassionately? And is it in his power to manipulate his readers' reaction to his will? In that great baroque scene at the opening of the *Confessions*, Rousseau stands grandiloquently before God and man, confident that his account of his purity of heart will win for him eternal veneration. Nevertheless, the response of one of his admirers, Mme de Bouffler, would have utterly startled him. After a horrified perusal of the book, she wrote to the King of Sweden, 'The mad avowal of all his vileness strikes me as an act of providence which has forced this infamous man to snatch off his own hypocritical mask.'

There is no question that Rousseau's somewhat naïve candour made future autobiographers wary about throwing discretion to the winds. Certainly nineteenth-century English autobiography is characterized by an inhibiting reticence. Where Rousseau felt he had nothing to apologize for, De Quincey felt obliged to bend the knee to propriety. Of his less than exemplary life, he commented:

> I trust that it will prove, not merely an interesting record, but, in a considerable degree, instructive. In *that* hope it is that I have drawn it up, and *that* must be my apology for breaking through those restraints of delicate reserve, which, for the most part, intercept the public exposure of our errors and infirmities.

To a post-Freudian generation, the autobiographies of Mill, Newman and Ruskin are as interesting for what they fail to say as for what they do tell us. J. Ashcroft Noble, one of the most enthusiastic proponents of the 'anagogical truth' revealed only by autobiography, had to admit ruefully that 'to expect [the autobiographer] voluntarily to reveal that which would expose him to execration or contempt is simply to expect a moral impossibility' (*Impressions and Memories*, 1895). 'That I,' said Trollope, 'or any man should tell everything of himself I hold to be impossible. Who could endure to own the doing of a mean thing? Who is there who has done?' (*An Autobiography*, 1883).

John Addington Symonds's *Memoirs*, then, are unique in the history of the genre during the nineteenth century. Unlike Ruskin, he could not indulge in writing 'frankly, garrulously, and at ease; speaking of what it gives me joy to remember at any length I like ...' (*Praeterita*, I, V). Symonds wrote of incidents which were painful for him to evoke; and he recalled relationships which were still bittersweet – but then he could speak freely about them because he was confident that they would not be made public until long after his death.

The conviction of his uniqueness and his compulsion to describe himself had long smouldered in his mind. As early as 1863, while still wrestling with the truth of his own nature, he wrote to a friend:

> I have often thought that, if I lived to do nothing else, I should write Confessions which would be better for the world to read than Rousseau's and not less interesting. I sometimes think that I am being trained for this.

Nearly thirty years later – in 1889 – Symonds, then in his fiftieth year, put aside all other work to pour himself finally into his memoirs. Incidentally, it is curious that Symonds should have chosen the term 'memoirs' for, strictly speaking, a memoir is a record of events whereas Symonds's work is both an account and a justification of his life, and an interpretive analysis of his temperament. It seems probable that he was following the example of Count Carlo Gozzi, the eighteenth-century Venetian nobleman and playwright whose memoirs he had recently translated. In the Preface to this translation, Symonds anticipated his readers' reaction to Gozzi's unrestrained candour by explaining that this was 'the candour of a cleanly heart'. Nevertheless, he had felt obliged to remove 'those passages and phrases which might have caused offence to some of my readers'. In the Preface to Cellini's *Autobiography* which Symonds also translated, he ventured a sly poke at Victorian hypocrisy: 'I hold him for a most veracious man,' he said of Cellini. 'His veracity was not of the sort which is at present current. It had no hypocrisy or simulation in it.'

Of the effect of these works on his own approach, Symonds wrote to his friend Graham Dakyns:

My occupation with Cellini and Gozzi has infected me with their Lues Autobiographica; & I have begun scribbling my own reminiscences. This is a foolish thing to do, because I do not think they will ever be fit to publish. I have nothing to relate except the evolution of a character somewhat strangely constituted in its moral and aesthetic qualities. The study of this evolution, written with the candour & the precision I feel capable of using, would I am sure be interesting to psychologists & not without its utility. There does not exist anything like it in print; & I am certain that 999 men out of a thousand do not believe in the existence of a personality like mine. Still it would be hardly fair to my posterity if I were to yield up my vile soul to the psychopathical investigators.

I do not know therefore what will come of this undertaking. Very likely, I shall lay it aside, though the fragment is already considerable in bulk & curious in matter − & I feel it a pity, after acquiring the art of the autobiographer through translation of two masterpieces, not to employ my skill upon such a rich mine of psychological curiosities as I am conscious of possessing.

This may appear rather conceited. But it is not so. I speak as an artist, who sees 'a subject of which he is confident'. *Infin del corti* [to make a long story short] I believe I shall go forward, & leave my executors to deal with what will assuredly be the most considerable product of my pen.

You see I have 'never spoken out'. And it is a great temptation to speak out, when I have been living for two whole years in lonely intimacy with men who spoke out so magnificently as Cellini and Gozzi did.

(*Letters*, III, p. 364)

As this letter suggests, the actual writing of the autobiography was in large measure therapeutic. The compulsion to unburden himself must have been very great indeed if he believed that the manuscript would be locked away until many years after his death. How could he envisage any other alternative since the legal penalty for sodomy at the time he was writing was two years' hard labour?*

Symonds emphasizes that the primary value of an autobiography is that, despite an inevitable degree of self-deception, the subject

*For a full account of the legal penalties see H. Montgomery Hyde's *The Other Love* (1970).

16

reveals how he appeared to himself. The figure conveyed by these memoirs is that of a tormented hero, and he was confident that anyone who read his story 'must acknowledge that it possesses the dignity of tragic suffering' (page 183).

He evinces occasional startling insights and, for want of an appropriate psychological vocabulary, he makes an impressive attempt to formulate one. In a pre-Freudian age, he is singular in his awareness of the importance of formative childhood experiences:

> According to my conception of such a work, the years of growth are the most important, & need the most elaborate analysis. . . . It is a fascinating canvas, this of *Lebensschilderung*, for a man who has been hitherto so reticent in writing, and who is so naturally egotistical & personal as I am.

Convinced as he was, however, of the congenital bias of his nature, it never crossed his mind that an infantile trauma might have been responsible for his condition. Any such event would certainly have been deeply repressed. A distinguished psychiatrist has drawn to my attention the significance of Symonds's two memories of his mother: the first a terrifying experience of driving with her in a carriage when the horses suddenly bolted downhill; the second her death. The combination of the two – the fear engendered by the violent rocking from side to side within an enclosed space, and a young child's later bewilderment at the mystery of death – might well have left him with deep psychological scars. But Symonds simply relates the two incidents, adding only that he can remember feeling no grief over his mother's death.

As a genre, the *Memoirs* are a hybrid, falling somewhere between literature and a psychological case history. A reader may experience a sense of frustration because if Symonds had not been preoccupied with an obsessional theme, he might have produced a work of art of the first order. Undoubtedly the finest section is the account of his childhood, with its vivid – almost Proustian – recollection of early sensations. It is a present remembrance of times past which evokes a former self co-existing with his present self in that multiple awareness which Wordsworth describes in *The Prelude* as 'two consciousnesses'. The narrative flows easily, with scarcely an erasure, as he dwells affectionately on a time which was undoubtedly the happiest of his life. This is followed by the abrupt contrast of the miserable years at Harrow. The Vaughan episode, bizarre and dramatic, makes compelling reading. His coverage of the period after his marriage is a sort of gallimaufry, containing far less concrete detail, a good deal of extraneous and disparate material (such as tedious nature descriptions from his letters) and long repetitive quasi-essays on his religious and philosophical beliefs. He seems indifferent to the clutter and contingency of everyday life. If one encounters Symonds only through his *Memoirs*, the overriding effect is that of a man tortured and tormented by his sexual obsession. He is not concerned with rendering his life as a *gestalt*, a rich composite of perceptions of the external world blended with personal reflection. An autobiography consisting chiefly of cogitation and self-analysis presents as distorted an imprint as one which only describes things seen and done. The latter part of the work is less sharply focused because his life had become so multifariously compartmentalized. It develops into an overt *apologia pro vita sua*, special pleading which, however justified, could have been more effective if he had not launched into polemicism. One has the impression that Symonds was growing restive with the project. A predictable conclusion might have been an acceptance that his suffering had some meaning in it – that it increased the range, the depth and the awareness which one expects from a process of development. The ending, however, is abrupt and unexpected. After a discussion of the inner conflict experienced by a man of his propensity, he concludes, 'The quarrel drives him into blowing his brains out, or into idiocy.'

There was a reason for the wavering organization of the latter part of the work. When he undertook the memoirs in 1889, he continued writing steadily and feverishly for eighteen months. Then it was obviously sharply cut off in the midst of a fervid discussion of the miseries suffered by homosexuals. Clearly a good deal of marginalia was added later. These comments allude to the large number of clinical studies of the psychopathology of homosexuality which Symonds had apparently been reading while engaged in the composition of the *Memoirs*. When he had undertaken the work he had been under the impression that his case was unique. 'It has been my destiny to make continual renunciation of my truest self, because I was born out of sympathy with the men around me, and have lived a stifled anachronism' (page 218). However, his reading revealed that he was only one among thousands of others. Unlike Rousseau, he could no longer say, 'I am made unlike anyone I have ever met.'

18

Symonds may have had ambivalent feelings about such a discovery, but at least they galvanized him into practical action.

In 1883 he had published privately ten copies of a pamphlet entitled *A Problem in Greek Ethics*, a treatise on homosexuality among the Greeks. Now, in 1891, he turned to a topic of more immediate concern, writing a pamphlet called *A Problem in Modern Ethics*, which also was printed privately and distributed among fifty selected individuals. Significantly, on the title page it is described as being 'Addressed Especially to Medical Psychologists and Jurists'. Its contents include an historical survey of homosexuality, various modern theories as to its cause, and a concluding section dealing with suggested amendments in legislation. This work ought to be read in conjunction with the *Memoirs*. In the notes he added later to the original manuscript, Symonds mentions that among the vast amount of reading he had done of studies by modern investigators, he was familiar with the work of J. L. Casper, Carl Liman, P. Moreau, B. Tarnowsky, R. von Krafft-Ebing, Cesare Lombroso and K. H. Ulrichs. In the *Memoirs* he does not differentiate between the relative validity of their respective theories. The reason is clear: if there was no possibility of publication within the foreseeable future, nothing could be gained from a polemical attack on these writers.

With the exception of Ulrichs, all these men, in Symonds's view, were disseminating dangerous theories. In discussing each of the theories in turn, his tone is dispassionate, and he conveys a confidence in his ability to demolish unscientific 'scientific' investigators. In turn he attacks Krafft-Ebing's theory that inverts had inherited morbid predispositions; Tarnowsky's conclusions which were garnered from the most debased elements of society; and Moreau's inability to separate himself from the prevailing prejudices of his time. In a note appended to the section on Krafft-Ebing, he includes a letter from 'a man of high position in London'. The tone and sentiments, with the constant reference to 'comrades', sound suspiciously like Symonds himself. (Suspicion is fortified by his ingenuous reference to 'a treatise entitled "A Problem in Greek Ethics" composed by an Englishman in English'.) In a discussion of the plight of the tormented invert who is condemned both by legal and social sanctions, the writer echoes the passage at the conclusion of the *Memoirs*:

19

In some cases the nerves give way altogether: mental alienation sets in; at last the wretch finds in a madhouse that repose which life would not afford him. Others terminate their unendurable situation by the desperate act of suicide. How many unexplained cases of suicide in young men ought to be ascribed to this cause!

The longest section is devoted to Ulrichs, of whom Symonds thoroughly approved because he shared his conviction that homosexuality is innate. (This, too, could be interpreted as a case of special pleading since Ulrichs himself was a homosexual, a fact Symonds neglects to mention.) He adds the following case (which he relates in the *Memoirs*) to substantiate Ulrichs's theory of *Urnings* (homosexuals):

> A relates that, before he was eight years old, reveries occurred to him during the day, and dreams at night, of naked sailors. When he began to study Latin and Greek, he dreamed of young gods, and at the age of fourteen, became deeply enamoured of the photograph of the Praxitelian Erôs in the Vatican. He had a great dislike for physical contact with girls; and with boys was shy and reserved, indulging in no acts of sense.

The pamphlet was also useful to Symonds as a means of commenting on Whitman's famous letter of 1890 written to him to denounce the implications Symonds was drawing from Whitman's poetry, particularly from 'Calamus'.* While the *Memoirs* are infused with his admiration of Whitman there is no reference to his long struggle to persuade Whitman to commit himself categorically. But here Symonds very skilfully and subtly suggests that in actual fact Whitman's 'treatment of comradeship, or the impassioned love of man for man' was unique in modern literature – was, indeed, closely akin to Symonds's own espousal of 'adhesiveness'.

Finally, Symonds used the pamphlet as a plea for more enlightened legislation to replace the prevailing harshness of the British law; he preferred a legislation modelled on the Code Napoleon and the *Codice Penale* of 1889. One could wish that he had addressed himself more specifically to the current situation. Comments in his letters indicate that he was deeply disturbed by the Cleveland Street scandal and the Criminal Law Amendment Act which made homosexual acts punishable by up to two years' hard labour; while he

---

*In all probability he received the letter after he had abandoned work on the *Memoirs*.

speaks vaguely in the *Memoirs* about the dangers to which homosexuals were exposed, it would have been remarkably interesting to us if he had given us some candid views on specific issues and events. (One can assume that all his letters on these subjects have not been recovered.)

An even more important incursion into the practical field than the pamphlet was the initiation of his collaboration with Havelock Ellis in 1890, a project which eventually emerged as *Sexual Inversion*, the first volume in the series *Studies in the Psychology of Sex*. Symonds felt that if an impeccable scientific figure could be persuaded to join him in writing a book on the subject, there was at last a very real possibility of presenting his views to the public openly. The two men never met, but fortunately there is extant a fascinating interchange of letters between them. Symonds's part in the collaboration was largely confined to the historical aspects, but he was also responsible for contributing a large number of case histories (including his own).* He gathered these by means of a questionnaire which he based on his studies of Krafft-Ebing's methods. In 1893, while the book was still in process of completion, Symonds died suddenly in Rome. By the time Ellis reorganized their material, it was clear that he would have difficulty in finding an English publisher. As a result, the study first appeared in 1896 in Germany, where it was acclaimed as the pioneer work Symonds believed it was destined to be. He would have been disturbed, however, if he had known that Ellis would postulate the view that homosexuality was a congenital aberration. In England, the trial of Oscar Wilde had taken place between Symonds's death and the appearance of the German edition of *Sexual Inversion*. Brown and the Symonds family became alarmed at the scandal an English edition might cause. When it was finally published in England in 1897, Brown attempted to buy up the entire edition, but a number of copies managed to slip through the net.

One can imagine Symonds's horror if he had lived to witness the Oscar Wilde scandal. If he had lived even until 1900 he might have been one of the few early readers of Freud's *Interpretation of Dreams* (he had sent details of many of his own dreams to the Society for Psychical Research). And if he had lived even longer he would have become familiar with Freud's theory that homosexuality was the

*See Appendix 1.

21

expression of an infantile fixation, a neurosis frequently caused by an early trauma. Freud, it will be remembered, wrote a compassionate letter to the troubled mother of a homosexual, but he never deviated from his view that the condition was basically neurotic. Symonds would have found it difficult to challenge Freud in the way he demolished Krafft-Ebing, Moreau and Tarnowsky; but he would have found it unpalatable to accept that his own propensity was not innate.

In reading the *Memoirs* one is aware of a certain superiority of tone when Symonds speaks of his own proclivities. Again and again he emphasizes the purity of his relationships, his attitude towards his partners as 'comrades', the help and guidance he was able to proffer his sexual partners. In his friendships among the lower classes he obviously idealized himself as a pioneer of true democracy. Although he indulged in numerous passing affairs, his aim was always to establish a relatively permanent relationship. He is either decorous, discreet or evasive in discussing his actual practices. He is careful to dissociate himself from voluptuaries like Marzials and Lord Ronald Gower. The question might well be raised: if he is to be exonerated from blame, why can he not extend the same tolerance to inverts like Marzials and Gower?* Again, *A Problem in Modern Ethics* provides the explanation. In the epilogue he divides inverts into five categories:

1. Forced abstinence from intercourse with females, or *faute de mieux*
2. wantonness and curious seeking after novel pleasure
3. pronounced morbidity
4. inborn instinctive preference for the male and indifference to the female sex
5. epochs of history when the habit has become established and endemic in whole nations.

Apparently Marzials and Gower belonged to 'those individuals who amuse themselves with experiments in sensual pleasure, men jaded with ordinary sexual indulgence, and indifferent voluptuaries'. Symonds, on the other hand, would appear to belong with those

*In a letter of 1893 he relates that at Venice he made Gower 'acquainted with my working friends, & he tells me that it has been to him a revelation of the untold wealth of happiness lying close to people of his kind – undreamed of by them' (*Letters*, III, p. 825).

men who 'behave precisely like persons of normal sexual proclivities, display no signs of insanity, and have no morbid constitutional diathesis to account for their peculiarity'.

Nevertheless, the *Memoirs* occasionally contain puzzling comments. In Chapter 15, concerning his religious development, Symonds states:

> I have allowed myself to be an innovator, taking the principles of human sympathy and self-respect as my guides. At only one point have I come into collision with conventional morality; and on this point I have felt it to be both *my right and duty to act as I thought best.* [page 250; my italics]

Despite the sense of his essential integrity and the importance he attaches to giving free expression to his emotions, at times an uneasy or melancholy note infuses his rhapsodizing. Speaking of his literary career (page 239), he comments, 'Trying to evade the congenital disease of my moral nature in work, work had drained my nerves and driven me to find relief in passion.' Even when away from the confining atmosphere of England, he was incapable of successfully compartmentalizing his role as a *litterateur* from his happy gambols among the Alpine peasants, 'a contrast,' he says, 'which acted somewhat unwholesomely upon my moral temperament' (page 238). But the most poignant expression of his feelings breaks forth in a long passage on page 266:

> Alas, while writing this, I must perforce lay the pen aside, and think how desolate are the conditions under which men like me live and love. Into comradeship itself does not our abnormal nature introduce an element of instability, even as it distorts marriage? Something remains amiss, unsatisfied, ill-correlated in each case.

His apologia for his condition was that it was utterly natural to him and as noble as a Greek passion. Yet the frequency with which he uses the words 'abnormal', 'morbid', 'unwholesome' suggests a growing suspicion that he might be some kind of monster. Despite all his protestations of the purity of his own feelings, there is an undercurrent of disgust about sex. The curious poem 'Phallus Impudicus' (page 177) is infused with morbid horror. Undoubtedly such fears were implanted in him by his moral and social upbringing; yet while he rhapsodizes over the Graubünden world into which he escaped – a utopia which has strong overtones of Morris's *News from Nowhere* – he never managed finally to escape from himself.

23

No reader of these *Memoirs* can fail to be puzzled by his attitude to his work. The manner in which he lists his extensive works is dull and perfunctory. There is a certain pride, undoubtedly, in what he has achieved. (Note his childlike delight in being elected to the Athenaeum.) His *Renaissance in Italy* and *Shakespeare's Predecessors in the English Drama* are still highly regarded. But he expresses no passionate involvement or delight in his work. Only in his poetry did he feel able to express himself freely; but here his critical faculty must have been entirely in abeyance because he seemed incapable of recognizing how deplorable most of it was. We must never forget that this is an autobiography, and what he presents, as he himself emphasizes, is his own version of himself. His involvement in Greek and Italian culture, he asserts, both stimulated and irritated his imagination.

> The underlying preoccupation of my life has been a tyrannous emotion, curbed and suppressed for the most part, but occasionally indulged with spasmodic violence. Literature takes the second place; and for this reason, although I have persevered in it for solace and escape from fretting care, I have never been able to regard it very seriously.

He had a large number of friends, many of whom have testified to his enchanting companionship, but the solipsistic atmosphere of this work gives no evidence of this side of his nature. There is no reference, for example, to friends like Edmund Gosse who shared his proclivities. Apart from his lingering descriptions of his sweethearts – and even they are somewhat shadowy figures – the only person who is depicted in any depth is his father. At any rate, we are given a vivid impression of Symonds's preoccupation with him; but it cannot be said that we are left with any clear idea of what Dr Symonds was really like. The early part of the *Memoirs* has this in common with Mill's *Autobiography*: in both the figure of the father plays a dominant role. Kindly but undemonstrative and remote, Dr Symonds seemed all that the sickly boy could never be. It is startling to find Symonds writing twenty years after his father's death that he saw his father as representing the apex of the Symonds line while he regards himself as a symbol of its inevitable decline.

Dr Symonds epitomized respectability, rectitude and, above all, power – particularly as it manifested itself in his ability to ruin Vaughan. Unlike Mill, Symonds obviously had a very real affection for his father. But his feelings were undoubtedly ambivalent towards a figure who acted in every sense as his super-ego. The frequency with which Symonds speaks of his father, his idealization of him, and his inability to humanize him suggest a rather peculiar relationship. His candid admission of his relief when his father died is reminiscent of the tears the younger Mill shed on encountering Marmontel's account of his reaction to his father's death.

Given the social attitudes of the time, Dr Symonds, it seems to me, should not be faulted for his attempts to cope with his son's sexual proclivities. More questionable is the part he played in the unfortunate Vaughan incident. Some people have suggested that his sadistic hounding of Vaughan was monstrous, an attitude I find difficult to share. Should he have ignored the whole business? Should he have given him a severe warning and let it go at that? Like Caesar's wife, a prominent clergyman in the eyes of most Victorians should have been above reproach. Surely one must view the whole incident within the context of its time.

Others have suggested that Symonds's own behaviour was reprehensible. But, as he himself suggests, a degree of transference was at work. Aware of his own bias, he unconsciously used Vaughan as a means of catharsis and confession. Nor must one forget the agitated and bewildered state of mind he was in at the time. But he never felt easy about his contribution to Vaughan's disgrace. His numerous justifications are enough to indicate this. It is significant that this particular section contains more erasures and changes than any other part of the manuscript.

After my biography of Symonds appeared I received a number of letters from former Harrovians (a large number, incidentally, from clergymen) expressing scepticism about the truth of the episode, particularly since I was unable to find any corroborative evidence of Symonds's version. It seems improbable to me that anyone could doubt the story after reading Symonds's account. It is rather interesting that Dr Vaughan left express instructions in his will that no biography of him was ever to be written. It is strange that Symonds retained the material dealing with the case during his lifetime but wanted it destroyed at his death. Such evidence would have been invaluable to substantiate his case.

One of the most intriguing and puzzling aspects of Symonds's life was his marriage. Repeatedly he contradicts himself. On various occasions he makes the following comments about it: it was a happy and successful relationship; he should never have married – and certainly not a woman like Catherine; if she had been more interested in sex, he might have developed into a 'normal' man; the very fact that she found sex distasteful was fortunate since it left him free to indulge his natural tastes. Probably he held all these views.

But what was Catherine really like? Symonds makes a single cryptic reference to her temper which she often vented on him. Even after they moved permanently to Switzerland, it is clear that Catherine was an ever-present, sometimes peevish presence to remind him that his past and its responsibilities still shackled him. It is probable that his frequent solitary excursions to Venice were as much to escape domesticity as to embrace the delights of his favourite city.

Symonds reveals little more than Trollope's dismissive statement in his autobiography: 'My marriage was like the marriage of other people, and of no special interest to anyone except my wife and me.' One might speculate, What interests did they share, what did they talk about? The two sections from Catherine's diary are extremely interesting. The first could have been written by a romantic school-girl, but she was twenty-nine when she wrote it; the second is written by a sadly disenchanted woman. Why, one wonders, did she allow these highly personal outpourings to fall into her husband's hands? How can one avoid the suspicion that his total silence about her is an indication that he simply never really looked at her? A photograph taken of her in middle age reveals more than anything he has to say. The eyes gaze into the distance, sad, grave and preoccupied. The taut crooked mouth has its hint of a smile cracked by a droop at the corners. According to her grandchildren, she developed into a remote, formidable old lady.

Symonds wrote, 'Those who lived nearest to me in everyday existence had no conception of my sexual troubles.' But surely Catherine possessed the bitter knowledge that there were others whose company he preferred to her own? The pencilled letter he wrote to her on his deathbed is chilling in its absence of any affection:

My dearest Catherine

There is something I ought to tell you, and being ill at Rome I take this occasion. If I do not see you again in this life you remember that I made H. F. Brown depositary of my printed books. I wish that legacy to cover all Mss Diaries Letters & other matters found in my books cupboard, with the exception of business papers. I do this because I have written things you could not like to read, but which I have always felt justified and useful for society. Brown will consult & publish nothing without your consent.

Ever yours

J A Symonds

You are ill at Venice & I have fallen here.

(*Letters*, III, page 839)

There is ample evidence that Symonds was an affectionate father, yet his only reference to his daughters is the crisis their births caused in his marital situation. On page 181 he records the exact date on which he met Norman Moor. Immediately after this he mentions his daughter Madge's birth but leaves a space as he has obviously forgotten the date.

All this is to suggest that the *Memoirs*, invaluable as they are, do not give us a complete picture of the man. Can we say the same of H. F. Brown's biography written only two years after Symonds's death? In *Love in Earnest* Timothy D'Arch Smith has quoted letters and argued persuasively that Brown would have preferred to have published the memoirs *in toto* but was prevented from doing so out of delicacy for the feelings of the family. Nevertheless, in the manuscript there are comments by Brown in the margin which suggest that he was adhering to Symonds's wishes, based on his view that the time was not propitious for its publication. Frankly, I believe the publication of Brown's biography was a regrettable decision. If he could not speak the truth, there was no necessity for any sort of publication. By the omission of all reference whatsoever to homosexuality, Symonds's whole reason for writing the autobiography was distorted. The general impression left by the filleted version is that of a man tormented by religious doubts, a sort of Arthur Hugh Clough. Consequently, certain distinguished scholars have seen his condition as symptomatic of the general malaise of the period, and what religious doubts he had have been exaggerated beyond all reality.

The memoirs were, as Symonds repeatedly insists, undertaken initially to help others as unfortunate as himself. As his investigations broadened, he began to realize that there were far, far more people in the same position than he had originally imagined. In a sense this seems scarcely credible, yet friends such as Graham Dakyns, Roden Noel and F. W. H. Myers must have seemed to belong to a different category from himself since they were able to experience passion for a woman.

I have suggested that the evocation of memory – as in so many autobiographies – was in large measure therapeutic. One rather puzzling aspect of the memoirs is their curious admixture of candour and evasiveness. If he were writing primarily for himself – or for posterity – why could he not be entirely frank? Possibly Victorian prudery had something to do with it. Yet what are we to make of the following statement (page 193), 'This boy, whom I will call Norman, though that was not his real name, played a considerable part in my life for the next few years'? Since Norman *was* his real name, could Symonds actually have been naïve enough to believe that he was protecting him? He has no compunction about naming other people. The reader cannot help being struck by the inconsistency of style throughout the work. There are times when casual references to people and events reflect the tone of an intimate letter.

Like all autobiographers, Symonds assumed that eventually his memoirs would fall into the hands of the ideal reader. Such a reader would find his life as fascinating as he regarded it; such a reader would find his temperament and his interests of absorbing interest. In its most basic sense, such an autobiography is a plea for love.

Preface

It would be difficult to say exactly why I have begun to write the memoirs of my very uneventful life. The most obvious reason for my doing so, perhaps, is that I have been to a large extent occupied during the last three years with the autobiographies of Benvenuto Cellini and Carlo Gozzi, both of these personal histories. I have translated them into English and sent them to press, acquiring in the process certain opinions with regard to the method of self-portraiture and considerably adding to the interest which I always felt for this branch of literature. Other and more important reasons – more important in their bearing on my psychological condition and the anxiety problem of the coming years – will reveal themselves to those who read the ensuing chapters.

Carlo Gozzi called his memoirs 'useless', and published them (as he professes) from motives of 'humility'. Mine are sure to be more useless than his; for *I* shall not publish them; and it is only too probable that they will never be published – nobody's humility or pride or pecuniary interests being likely to gain any benefit from the printing of what I have veraciously written concerning myself.

That I have a definite object in the sacrifice of so much time and trouble upon a task so useless and so thankless, will not be doubted by those men who understand the nature of human indolence, and who are also able to estimate the demands made upon the industry of a fairly successful writer in his forty-ninth year.

Without vanity, I may affirm that the author of *Renaissance in Italy* and *Studies of the Greek Poets* has had to refuse lucrative offers and to postpone labours of remunerative literature for many months, in order to produce this piece of sterile self-delineation. My object is known to myself. But it is not one I care to disclose in set phrases. Someone, peradventure, will discover it; and if he is a friend, will shed perhaps a tear at the thought of what these lines have cost me – if he is a scientific student of humanity will appreciate my effort to be sincere in the dictation of a document – if he be but a fellow creature will feel some thrill of pity, and will respect the record of a soul which has still to settle its accounts with God.

A life without action seems to fall naturally into three main sections. The first of these comprises childhood, boyhood and adolescence. The second extends over early manhood, when habits are formed and character is fixed. The third exhibits the mature man in his development and in possession of his faculties.

I propose therefore to divide my memoirs into three unequal parts. The first part will be concerned with my life from birth in 1840 to 1864 when I married and took leave of Oxford. The second part will deal with the years 1864–1877. The third will be devoted to my intellectual, emotional and religious experience – partly retrospective and partly confined specially to the period which I have spent in residence at Davos Platz. What cross-divisions and subdivisions I shall introduce into these main sections, I am unable to foresee. It is the peculiarity of an autobiography, which consists of self-delineation, and is not determined by the narration of salient events, that the third of these parts should be resumptive of the earlier and to a large extent a commentary on the past.

Palazzo Gritti
S. Maria Zobenigo
Venice
May 1889

When I read the book, the biography famous,
And is this then (said I) what the author calls a man's life?
And so will some one when I am dead and gone write my life?
(As if any man really knew aught of my life,
When even I myself I often think know little or nothing of my real life,
Only a few hints, a few diffused faint clews and indirections
I seek for my own use to trace out here.)

(Walt Whitman, 'Inscriptions' from *Leaves of Grass*)

Chapter One

Childhood, 1840–51, 7 Berkeley Square, Bristol

I was born on 5 October 1840 at 7 Berkeley Square, Bristol. Here I lived until June 1851, when our home was changed for Clifton Hill House. This section of my autobiographical notes will be confined to recollections of the first ten years of my life.

I cannot say that I have a distinct memory of my mother. She died of scarlet fever when I was four years old, and she had been always too weak in health to occupy herself energetically in the household. Those who knew her intimately were unanimous in saying that she combined rare grace and beauty of person with singular sweetness of character and distinguished mental endowments.

The one thing which I can clearly remember about her is that we were driving alone together in my father's carriage (a chariot with glass windows at the front and sides, drawn by two horses) down a steep hill by Cornwallis Terrace to the Lower Crescent, when the horses plunged and broke into a gallop. Her fright must have made a deep impression on me. I can still see a pale face, a pink silk bonnet and beautiful yellow hair. These have for background in my memory the glass windows of a coupé and the red stone walls overhung with trees which embanked the garden of Cornwallis Terrace. I do not know now whether the road has been altered. It is long since I walked there. But the instantaneous flash of that moment on my brain persists as I describe it.

I can also remember the morning of my mother's funeral. We children were playing in our nursery with the tin soldiers and clumsy wooden cannon painted black and yellow. These were on the floor beside us. We were dressed in black. The nurses took us away to my grandmother's house in the Lower Crescent.

This is all I recollect about my mother. I have been told that my name was the last upon her lips when she was dying. But my father never spoke to me much about her, and only gave me a piece of her hair.

He sometimes took me with him to her grave. This was in the Arno Vale Cemetery, high up upon a grassy hillside, where harebells and thyme blossomed in the short turf of a down. A plane tree spread its branches over the tomb; and the flat stone which marked her resting place was enclosed by iron railing. My father took jealous care that these railings should be over-rioted with ivy, roses and clematis, growing in unpruned luxuriance. He wished to withdraw the sacred spot from vulgar eyes. I could not see inside it. It was our custom to pluck leaves from the plane tree and the creepers, and to return in silence to the carriage which stood waiting by the gate. These leaves, gathered from my mother's grave, were almost all I knew about her, all I had of her. I used to put them into a little book of texts called *Daily Food*[1] which had belonged to her, and which I read every night, and still read at all hours of the day in the year 1889. It was Auntie who gave me this little amulet in the year 1854.

I cannot pretend that I greatly desired to have a clearer notion of my mother, or that I exactly felt the loss of her. It was all dreamy and misty to my mind. I did not even imagine what she might have been to me. Sometimes I thought that I was heartless and sinful because I could not want her more. But this was foolish, because I had never really felt the touch of her. My father showed no outward sign of grief, and said nothing. He was only more than usually reserved on these occasions, and inspired me with a vague awe. Death was a mystery, into which the mother I had never really known was now forever drawn away from me.

I doubt whether the following is worth reading. But, since it is the first event of which I seem to have a distinct recollection, I must do so. My sister Charlotte, younger than myself by two years short of two months, was christened at St George's Church, Bristol. So far as I can now recall it, the building is of pseudo-Graeco-Roman architecture, rectangular in the body, faced with a portico; and surmounted with a nondescript Pecksniffian spire in the bastard classic style. Of its internal arrangement I remember nothing definite.

And yet I seem to see this picture vividly – an area of building, dim, grey, almost empty; a few people grouped about in my immediate neighbourhood; tall enclosed pews of a light yellow colour round the groups; something going on at no great distance to our left, which makes the faces turn in that direction, looking backwards; myself dressed in white, with a white hat and something blue in the trimmings of it, half standing, half supported, so as to look over the rim of the pew. This is what I remember, or think I remember, of my sister's christening.

It is surely impossible to be certain whether these very early memories, definite as they may be and not improbable, are actual impressions of scenes left upon our senses, or whether they are not rather the product of some half-conscious act of the imagination working reflectively upon what has been related to the child.

About another of these recollections I have not the same kind of doubt. I was in the nave of Bristol Cathedral during service time, lifted in my nurse's arms and looking through the perforated doors of the organ screen, which then divided nave from choir. The organ was playing and the choristers were singing. Some chord awoke in me then, which has gone on thrilling through my lifetime and has been connected with the deepest of my emotional experiences. Cathedrals, college chapels, 'quires and places where they sing'[2] resuscitate that mode of infancy. I know, when I am entering a stately and time-honoured English house of prayer, that I shall put this mood upon me like a garment. The voices of choiring men and boys, the sobbing antiphones and lark-like soaring of clear treble notes into the glook of Gothic arches, the thunder of the labouring diapasons, stir in me that old deep-centred innate sentiment.

So it is with another of my earliest experiences. When I was still a little child, my father began to take me with him on his long drives into the country. After jolting through the city streets, we broke away at his quick travelling pace into unknown regions of field and wood and hedgerow, climbing the Somersetshire hills, threading their deep lanes and bosky coombs, passing under avenues of ancient parks, halting at low-roofed farmhouses. Then I used to leave the carriage and wander for a while alone in fairyland, knee-deep in meadowsweet and willow-herb, bruising the water-mint by shallow brooks, gazing at waterlilies out of reach on sleepy ponds, wondering why all about me was so strangely still and who the people were who dwelt there. The hush of sickness and expected death sobered the faces of the men and women who received my father; he was often very thoughtful when he left their homesteads and we journeyed back in silence. It used to be late in the evening generally when we returned from these excursions. Twilight added to the mystery of the unknown, the shadow of the unintelligible sorrow I had felt. The shimmer of moonlight blending with late sunset upon boughs of wild roses or spires of foxglove or hyacinths in ferny hedges – a sallow western sky seen from the healthy heights of Mendip or of Dundry – the heavy scent of clematis or privet when the air is hot and moist in June – the grey front of lonely farm buildings flanked by yew trees – the perfume suddenly distilled from limes and laurels through darkness at some turning of a road – such things have always brought the feeling of those solemn evenings back. I used often to fall asleep in the carriage, and woke up startled by a carter's shout as we swept onward, or by the glare of the city lamps when we broke at last away from the country roads and rattled over the pavement of the city streets.

I had no love for my birthplace, 7 Berkeley Square. I am distinctly aware of the depressing effect produced upon me by the more sordid portions of this town house – especially by a dingy dining room and a little closet leading through glass doors into a dusty back garden. The garden had one miracle, however, to ennoble it. That was a cherry tree which clothed itself in silver beauty once a year, *maugré* the squalor which surrounded it. I ought also not to forget that our back windows looked out on Brandon Hill, from which a glorious prospect over city, river, meadow, distant hills and wooded slopes could then be gained.

The front door of our house was fairly well proportioned and surmounted with a pediment, boldly hewn of Bath stone, grey and mossy. I felt a particular affection for this pediment. It had style. The limes and almond trees and bright berries of the mountain ashes in the square garden were also a great consolation. But certain annuals – escholchia, Virginia, stock and minor convolvulus – have always remained unpleasantly associated with the forlorn, ill-cared-for flowerbeds. I found some difficulty in conquering my dislike for the nasturtium on account of the innumerable earwigs which its gorgeous trumpet blooms concealed. On the other hand, certain dusky-green and brownish-pink hawk moths, fluttering about the limes on summer evenings, seemed to me like angels from a distant land.

36

Trifling as these matters are, they indicate the spontaneous development of powerful instincts. My long exile in the High Alps has been rendered more than tolerable by the fact that nothing which man makes can wholly debase the mountains of Graubünden. Simplicity and purity and wayward grace in natural things, strength and solidity and decent form in things of art, were what my temperament unconsciously demanded.

The sense of meanness which annoyed me in our house afflicted me far more keenly in the Chapel of the Blind Asylum, where we attended service twice on Sundays. The bastard Gothic lancets, dead grey, rough-cast walls and ugly painted woodwork of that paltry building gave me absolute pain. It suffocated my soul and made me loathe evangelical Protestantism. Most of all, at night, when gas lamps flared in open jets upon the sordid scene, I felt defrauded of some dimly apprehended birthright.

It is significant, in this respect, that two tales made a deep impression at this period on my mind. One was Andersen's story of the ugly duckling. I sympathized passionately with the poor bird swimming round and round the duck-puddle. I cried convulsively when he flew away to join his beautiful wide-winged white brethren of the windy journeys and the lonely meres. Thousands of children have undoubtedly done the same, for it is a note of childhood, in soul destined for expansion, to feel solitary and debarred from privileges due to them. The other was a kind of allegory, called 'The Story Without An End', translated, I think, by Lucie Duff Gordon from the German.[3] The mystical, dreamy communion with nature in wild woods and leafy places took my fancy, and begat a mood of *Sehnsucht* nostalgia which became habitual.

My sisters and I were riding one day upon a rocking-horse, which stood in the landing of the attic floor. I was holding onto the tail, I remember, a little anxious lest the tuft of grey horsehair should suddenly give way and precipitate me backwards, as it often did. We were screaming out in chorus Scott's lines upon the death of Marmion:

> With dying hand, above his head,
> He shook the fragment of his blade,
>   And shouted 'Victory!' –
> 'Charge, Chester, charge! On Stanley, on!'
>   Were the last words of Marmion.

Suddenly I ceased to roar. A resolve had formed itself unbidden in my mind: When I grow up, I too will be an author.

I was a very nervous child and subject to many physical ailments, which made me no doubt disagreeable to the people round me. It seems that I suffered from a gastric fever soon after my birth, and this left me weak – liable to recurrent attacks of diarrhoea and non-retention of urine. Being sensitive to the point of suspiciousness, I imagined that I inspired repugnance in others; and my own condition not unfrequently made me noisome to myself. My constitutional dislike of squalor had to suffer severe mortification. I became unreasonably shy and timid. In connection with these childish illnesses, and what follows about night terrors, it is proper here to say that I had an elder brother, John Abdy Stephenson, who only lived seven months, and died of cerebral inflammation. He had been preceded by twin sons, premature and stillborn. My elder sister Mary Isabella was born in 1837, the twins in 1838, John Abdy Stephenson in 1839, myself in 1840. There is every reason to suppose that my mother's constitution at this time was inadequate to the strain of childbirth and that she transmitted a neurotic temperament to certain of her children.

At night I used to hear phantasmal noises, which blended terrifically with the caterwauling of cats upon the roof. I often lay awake for hours with my fingers in my ears.

I fancied there was a corpse in a coffin underneath my bed, and I used to wake up thinking it had risen and was going to throw a sheet over me.

Lights seemed to move about the room if I opened my eyes in the dark. I feared them; but I was fated to stare and follow them about, until I either sank back hypnotized, or rushed from the bed and sat in my night-shirt on the staircase. Yet I did not dread the dark so much as the light of a rush-candle burning in a perforated cylinder of japanned metal, which cast hideous patterns on the roof and walls of the nursery.

When I slept, I was frequently visited with the following nightmare. I dreamed that we were all seated in our well-lit drawing room, when the door opened of itself just enough to admit a little finger. The finger, disconnected from any hand, crept slowly into the room and moved about through the air, crooking its joints and beckoning. No one saw it but myself. That was the horror. What would happen if it should touch me or any other person present, I never discovered, for I always woke before the catastrophe occurred.

My father, thinking, I suppose, that I needed to be looked after, took me to sleep with him in his own bed. He added to my terror by talking in his sleep. I remember one especially grim night, when I woke up and saw a man seated by the bed and talking with my father earnestly in a low voice about some case of fever. I did not miss a word, though all I can now recall of the conversation related to the swollen blackness of the patient's tongue.

In some way or another – perhaps by listening to the dismal sermons of the Blind Asylum – I developed a morbid sense of sin, and screamed at night about imaginary acts of disobedience. My aunt or my father, hearing me sob and cry, left their chairs in the drawing room and tried to reassure me.

I was persuaded that the devil lived near the doormat in a dark corner of the passage by my father's bedroom. I thought that he appeared to me there under the shape of a black shadow, skurrying about upon the ground, with the faintest indication of a slightly whirling tail.

When the cholera was raging in the year 1848, I heard so much about it that I fell into a chronic state of hysterical fear. Some one had told me of the blessings which attend ejaculatory prayers. So I kept perpetually mumbling: 'Oh, God, save me from the cholera!' This superstitious habit clung to me for years. I believe that it obstructed the growth of sound ideas upon religion; but I cannot say that I ever was sincerely pious, or ever realized the language about God I heard and parroted.

Apropos of the cholera in Bristol, this scene comes before me very clearly now. Whether it is the memory of fact or vision, I cannot say. We were returning from Clevedon in an open carriage. I noticed men stirring up great bonfires of tar barrels at the corner of a street near the quays. When I asked my aunt what they were doing, she replied that they were burning the infection in the air. After this, I thought of the cholera as a tangible substance capable of passing into our bodies from the air.

Burglars entered my father's house in Berkeley Square one evening while a dinner party was going forward. They carried off considerable booty from my aunt's and sisters' wardrobe and trinket boxes. It appeared that they had worked their way through the attic windows from an adjacent house which was empty at the time. We could see the marks of their dirty, clumsy hands upon the staircase wall next morning. I then made the mental reflection that people who were afraid of robbers could never have seen visions or dreamed nightmares. These men did not affect my imagination disagreeably. So far as I thought about them at all, I sympathized with their audacity and felt my curiosity aroused. Neither then nor afterwards did I fear anything so much as my own self. What that contained was a terror to me. Things of flesh and blood, brutal and murderous as they might be, could always be taken by the hand and fraternized with. They were men, and from men I did not shrink. I always felt a man might be my comrade. Dreams and visions exercised a far more potent spell. Nigh to them lay madness and utter impotence of self-control.

These childish terrors, of which I have written thus much, were stimulated by the talk of our head nurse, a superstitious country woman. She was not exactly kind in her ways with us and used to get drunk at times. Then she would behave strangely and threaten us children. I lived in fear of her. Sarah's theory of discipline may be illustrated by the following anecdote. We were passing some weeks of the summer at an old inn on Kings Weston Down – a very delightful place for children with a swing suspended from the bough of a huge elm tree, breezy downs where mushrooms grew and blueberries were plentiful, a farmyard, an old park hard by and shady copses of arbutus and juniper to wander in. Indoors the furniture was deficient; I found it difficult to fall asleep in a stiff armchair covered with black horsehair and prolonged I do not know how into a makeshift bedstead. Sarah sat beside me working in the evening light, prodding the pillow and mattress at intervals with her needle, under the impression that she could frighten me into slumber.

A very superior being to Sarah Jones was Mrs Leaker, head nurse in the family of my cousins the Nashes. She had much to do with fostering and ennobling my sense of the supernatural. Mrs Leaker had been born and bred in a Devonshire village on the sea coast. She claimed gypsy blood and belonged to a family of smugglers. So at least she told us. Her physiognomy and complexion, and the legends with which her head was stored, accorded with this account of her ancestry. She was a great reader of good literature, and had the plays of Shakespeare and the history of our old English wars by heart. Sitting round the nursery fire, we used to make her tell us stories. It was easy then to pass from Shakespeare and the landing

of Monmouth in the west to eerier traditions of the countryside –
haunted churches, whose windows burned at night before a tempest
– East-Indiamen from Bristol firing distress guns in the offing – the
parson leaving his pulpit and the seamen stealing off to join the
wreckers – the avenue to the old hall, up which a phantom lord
rode in his chariot drawn by six black horses, holding his head upon
his knees – the yeoman belated on Dartmoor, following a white
rabbit, which disappeared when he arrived at home and found his
only daughter dead in bed there – the wild carousings of smugglers
in their caves and murderous conflicts with coastguards-men – the
wicked gentlemen who sat up days and nights at play, deep to
their knees in scattered cards, losing fortunes and sallying forth to
exchange shots upon a Sunday morning. Ghosts naturally took a
large place in these legends. But Mrs Leaker had a special partiality
for presentiments and warnings. She knew the dream of Lord Camer-
ford before his duel, and the clasp of a fiery hand upon Lady
Tyrone's wrist and the bird which fluttered against the window of
Lord Lyttleton at Hagley. Tales like these she related in the twilight
with intense conviction of their truth and with a highly artistic sense
for the value of vagueness.

To sum up this chapter of the spiritual terrors of childhood, I
may mention some literature which took hold of my imagination.
We had a book of old ballads in two volumes, illustrated by Maclise[4]
and other draughtsmen. The pictures to 'Glen Finlas', the 'Eve of St
John' and 'Kempion' made me feel uncomfortable. But I think that
Marley's ghost in one of Dickens's tales – was it done by
Cruikshank?[5] – bit deeper. The most impressive books of all were
not illustrated. These were a series of articles on spectral illusions
in Chambers's[6] *Miscellany*, and a translation of a German collection
of murder stories – by some name like Feuerbach.[7] It is certain that
I ought not to have had access to these scientific or semi-scientific
sources. They worked potently and injuriously on my brain. But
books abounded in our house and I was naturally drawn to literature. I used even to examine the atlases of pathological anatomy in
my father's cupboards, and to regard the skeletons of man and beast
with awful joy.

Our family consisted of my father, my aunt Miss Mary Anne
Sykes and my three sisters, Edith, Mary Isabella and Charlotte. I
cannot recollect any bond of friendship between me and my sisters,
though we lived together in amity. One touch of sympathy brought

41

me closer to Maribella than the others. When I began to learn arithmetic I could not understand the simplest sums. She noticed me crying over a sum in long division, and with great gentleness and kindness helped me through the task.

My hair was light and fell in curls over my shoulders. This I have been told; but it survives in my memory owing to the following incident. I was walking with Edith and Maribella in Berkeley Square, pacing up and down the pavement before our house. I took it into my head to promenade with my eyes shut and my hands clasped behind my back. The result was that I ran up against a lamp-post, and fell half-stunned to earth with the concussion. My sisters hastened to the spot and while they were lifting me, the long fair curls upon their arms attracted my dazzled eyesight.

We used to go to children's parties together. On these occasions I was reputed to have brought some confusion on my elder sisters. Once, when I thought I was being neglected at table, I pointed to a cake and said, 'I never ask, but I point.' At another party, impatient of waiting for supper, I asked the mistress of the house, 'Lady, when are you going to help?'

My aunt was sometimes very kind, sometimes very irritable, but always amusing. She lost my confidence and a good portion of my sympathy by an act of thoughtless want of sympathy. I collected curiosities; and among them was a stuffed kingfisher on which I doted – probably because it reminded me of *The Boy and the Birds*.[8] At any rate I used to take it to bed with me. It so happened that my aunt went to stay at the house of her uncle Admiral Sykes in Wilton Crescent, and there she met a French lad who was also fond of curiosities. When she came home, she induced me, sorely against my will, to give up the kingfisher, and sent it to her new acquaintance. I have rarely suffered such distress of mind as the loss of this stuffed bird and the sense of my aunt's injustice caused me.

My grandmother Sykes played a considerable part in our young lives. She was a handsome old lady with strongly marked features and a great air of blood and breeding. This contrasted strangely with her material and social surroundings. She had become a Plymouth Sister[9] and held the most innocent amenities of life for sinful. Her house in Cornwall Crescent, or the Lower Crescent, had nothing in it to rejoice the eye except flowers to which she was devoted. Yet it never impressed me with a sense of squalor. The perfume of potpourri in a blue Chinese bowl and of Tonquin beans exhaling from drawers and workbasket gave distinction to the rooms, and the old lady's stately person rendered it impossible to regard any of her possessions as beneath the dignity of a gentlewoman. Nevertheless all objects of taste and luxury, all that delights the sense, had been carefully weeded out of the grim bare dwelling. And what company my grandmother kept! It was a motley crew of preachers and missionaries, tradespeople and cripples – the women dressed in rusty bombazine and drab gingham – the men attired in greasy black suits with dingy white neckties – all gifted with a sanctimonious snuffle, all blessed by nature with shiny foreheads and clammy hands, all avid for buttered toast and muffins, all fawning on the well-connected gentlewoman whose wealth, though moderate, possessed considerable attractions and was freely drawn upon.

I often went to stay with my grandmother when circumstances – generally some infectious ailment in our nursery – made it desirable that I should be away from home. So I had plenty of opportunities for studying these strange people and appreciating the marvellous figure which that formidable old lady, aristocratic to the backbone and terribly ill-tempered, cut among them.

Heavy teas like those described by Dickens were a frequent occurrence, after which the Chadband[10] of the evening discoursed at a considerable length. Then followed prayers, in the course of which a particularly repulsive pharmaceutical chemist from Broad Mead uplifted his nasal voice in petitions to the Almighty which too often, alas, degenerated into glorification of the Plymouth Sect at Bristol and objurgations against the perverse members of other religious bodies. My grandmother came in for her due share of fulsome flattery under the attributes of Deborah and Dorcas.[11] My father was compared to Naamon, who refused to bathe in Jordan[12] – Jordan being Bethesda, or the meeting house of the Plymouth Brethren.

Sometimes I was taken to Bethesda, which brought no healing to my soul but seemed to me a pool of stagnant pietism and turbid middle-class Philistinism. This chapel did not, however, afflict me so grievously as the Blind Asylum. Partly perhaps because I knew it less, and it always had a kind of novelty. Partly because nothing which my grandmother touched was wholly commonplace or sordid. I think too that I was even then capable of appreciating the ardent faith and powerful intellect of George Muller[13] who preached there, and who founded the celebrated orphanage at Horfield near Bristol.

My grandmother naturally made a strong point of family prayers. She delighted in the Lamentations Of Jeremiah, the minatory chapters of the prophets and the Apocalypse. In a deep sonorous voice, starting with a groan and rising to a quaver, she used to chant forth those lugubrious verses which began or ended with '*Thus saith the Lord!*' I remember hearing nothing of the Gospel or the love of Christ for the whole human race either in the readings from scripture or in the extemporary prayers which followed. She concentrated her attention on the message to the chosen people, with a tacit assumption that all who lived outside the Plymouth fold were children of wrath.

She had one redeeming quality of great price. That was her love of flowers. The public garden of the Lower Crescent flourished under her assiduous care; and the small plot therein which was her own particular property abounded with old-fashioned plants – grape hyacinths and double primroses, auraculas and polyanthuses and oxlips, *Pyrus japonica* and ribes and gum cistus with its papery stained petals, and heavy-scented jessamine and burly cabbage roses.

Bred in the deer park and pleasances which surround Albyns Hall, built by her ancestor Sir Robert Abdy in the reign of King James I, she retained an affection for nature which gloomy religion did not forbid her to indulge.

Her married life had been embittered by the lingering illness of my grandfather. He died of consumption, after trying all the doctors of the spas of England. The poor man used to be bled, cupped, blistered and bathed in vinegar, after the method of those days. One humorously pathetic saying of his survived in my aunt's memory: 'I cannot tell, girls, how I caught this cold, unless it was through not going to bed in my boots.' During his lifetime there was no lack of money, and after his death a handsome competency remained to his widow. But she believed that a great and terrible crime had been committed during his last hours, which defrauded her and his three daughters of the larger portion of his fortune. My great-grandfather Sykes had been a Navy-agent, and prospered during the long war with Napoleon. He left his business to his sons. My grandfather, finding himself at the point of death, had a deed prepared which was intended to dissolve the partnership and enable him to bequeath by will his share in the joint capital. This deed only awaited his signature when my great-uncle Admiral Sykes demanded to be introduced alone into his brother's sickroom. He wanted to speak on business of importance, and would not suffer the wife to be present at the interview. When he left the room my grandfather had died, the deed was not executed, and the interest in the Navy agency passed to him. Certainly Admiral Sykes became a very rich man, while my grandmother remained far poorer than she had a right to expect. It is to be hoped that the foul play ascribed to my great-uncle had no foundation in fact. It certainly rested on no proof. But the circumstances of his brother's death and his own subsequent behaviour, which was harsh and ungenerous, lent colour to the dark suspicions. Looking back upon the past, known to me only by hearsay, I absolve him of the guilt of fratricide – even of such comparatively innocent fratricide as the puffing out of the last flame of life in an expiring candle. It would have been assuredly better if Admiral Sykes had fulfilled his dead brother's intentions, as though the deed of separation had been legally executed. Instead of that, he claimed his full rights of inheritance, and bred a hatred in the proud soul of my grandmother which proved disastrous to the interests of her own descendants. But for the facts which I have related, I might in the natural course of events have succeeded to a fortune of some £500 a year upon the death of Admiral Sykes in 1857.

My grandmother was a thorough Abdy, subject to chronic insomnia and irritable to the highest degree. She lived alone with two servants in a tolerably large four-storied house. She slept upon the second floor and no one was allowed to inhabit the third. When I was there, I occupied a bedroom next the drawing room on the first floor. There was no living creature except a cat and cockroaches in the house below me. Between me and the servants slept the imposing old lady in her solitude. And the whole habitation during the long night hours resounded to my fancy with the doleful litany of *Thus saith the Lord: Woe woe to the ungodly*. It may be imagined how prolific of nightmares number 14 Lower Crescent was for me!

Many of my mother's relations used to visit us at this time. Among these I must give the first place to my aunt Isabella. She was a beautiful and highly gifted woman, accomplished in language, endowed with remarkable facility for art. She sang with true feeling and painted with the skill of Prout.[14] There was genius in all she did and said, a felicity of aptitude for culture. I am not exaggerating. Many of her watercolour drawings remain to show that I am

speaking the truth. Such a nature could not thrive in the grim
environment of Mrs Sykes's home. A mutual attachment between
her and John Sterling[15] came to nothing. Disappointed in her affections and galled by the uncongenial society of Plymouth Brethren,
she imprudently accepted the offer of a certain Dr Harpur Gamble.
The marriage was unhappy and condemned her to a miserable life
in Upper Charlotte Street, Fitzroy Square, London. Her husband
was sincerely attached to her. But he was jealous, quarrelsome,
suspicious, violent, cross-tempered, out of humour with the world
in which he had failed to win position. She died young of slow
consumption, unalleviated by the comforts of tranquillity and home-
happiness.

Colonel Abdy, retired from the Indian Service, was a frequent
inmate of 7 Berkeley Square. His lonely, cadaverous, dyspeptic form
remains impressed upon my memory; and how he used to bolt his
food still fills me with a shudder. He had a trick of rhyming proverbs,
three of which I have retained and found to some extent serviceable.
The first was:

> Change not a clout till May be out:
> Change not in May, change not in one day.

There is the philosophy of clothing in the *demi-saison*. The second
ran thus:

> If you eat till you're cold, you'll live to be old.

I have never fathomed the depth of wisdom contained in this apho-
rism. But I suppose it means that people who rise from hearty meals
with a diminished sense of surface heat are in a healthy condition —
their vital forces being absorbed in the assimilation of food, not
wasted upon any feverish process. The third was extremely appli-
cable to the squeamish stomachs of fastidious childhood:

> What does not poison fattens,
> And what does not fatten helps to fill.

It is singular that Colonel Abdy should have passed into a little
kinsman's consciousness and have passed out of it again, leaving no
memory but that of a lean gaunt voracious man and these three
homely proverbs.

John Abdy,[16] now Regius Professor of Law at the University of
Cambridge, at that time an undergraduate, was our frequent play-
fellow. He let us children climb over him and pull him about, always

ready for a game or romp. It is mainly owing to a little incident with him in one of our after-luncheon rampages that I can remember the drawing room at Berkeley Square. I happened to press heavily with my hand upon a sensitive part of his body. He gave an involuntary start; the armchair in which he was lounging between the window and the fireplace, the piano at the opposite end of the room and a copy from a Madonna by Vandyck which hung over it, swim into distinctness when I recall that contraction of the long kindly young man under the momentary pang I gave him.

In the same way, a very trifling occurrence brings James Byron, my mother's first cousin, before me. He was a gigantic fellow with a huge copper-coloured face – good-natured like a giant, but subject to sudden fits of passion. We called him Goliath of Gath; and one day leaning from the drawing-room window above my favourite pediment of the front door, I screamed this nickname after him as he was walking down the square. He looked up with a not unnatural scowl of irritation. The background of trees to his burly figure, the moss-grown Bath-stone of the pediment, the windowsill where I was sprawling, and the angry face of the good-tempered Titan, were photographed upon my brain. Later on, when I first went to Harrow, James Byron was very kind to me. He used to drive down from London in a Hansom, take me to dine at the King's Arms, talk to me about our kinsman Lord Byron, and press a sovereign into my hand when we said Goodbye. I followed his cab with grateful eyes, as it sped backward on the London road.

One of the families with whom we were intimate during the period of my childhood, and who still exercise an influence over my life – though each member of the same has long since died without posterity – bore the name of Sisson. They came from Cumberland, where their ancestors had been settled as small country gentry in the neighbourhood of Penrith for many generations. At the time when I first knew them the father had died. An old bed-ridden mother, two brothers and three sisters, were living together in a house on the Lower Crescent. Neither of the brothers had any business or occupation. The sisters were past the age of marrying. They lived comfortably upon the produce of their farms and other property in Cumberland. But it sufficed to spend a couple of hours in their society to be aware that some mysterious doom hung over them. This doom was madness.

The bed-ridden mother was also imbecile. She used to sit propped up with pillows in the middle of a huge mahogany four-poster, her weazened wrinkled face surrounded with the double frills of an exquisitely white mobcap. Her complexion was of a dark amber yellow; hair white as snow; eyebrows coal black, bushy above little restless beady brown eyes. She had no teeth; and her jaws kept incessantly moving and mumbling between the beaked nose and the pinched chin, which seemed as though they were always vainly trying to touch. A well-developed moustache and beard of glossy black completed the singular appearance of this old lady. I used to be lifted up to sit beside her on the bed; and when she stretched her skinny trembling arms out and kissed me with her bearded toothless mouth, it was the utmost I could do to keep from screaming. All the same, I was not exactly afraid of her, even when she asked me sudden questions about people and things in the remote past of her life, or followed persons with her eyes about the room, whom I could not see, and sometimes spoke to them in tones of angry irritation, and then smiled in a sickly satisfied way and fumbled with her hands upon the counterpane. One of her children was always present during these interviews; and the ancient dame, witch though I thought her, had always some little present ready to be handed to me when I left her.

The affairs of the family were managed by the eldest sister and the eldest brother – Mary Sisson, a sweet resigned and yet cheerful lady, who needed all the Christian virtues to sustain her through the troubles of her shadowed life, and William Sisson, an excellent man of business with an intellect of some power, though troubled at times by the hereditary malady of his blood. Mary died while I was still a little boy. William lived on into the autumn of 1867. His friendship for me lasted for a quarter of a century; when he died, I found that he had confided to me a trust of consequence and delicacy, the more remarkable because its execution depended solely on my sense of honour.

The second brother, Richard Sisson, was undoubtedly insane. He died eventually in a madhouse. But during several years, when I used to meet him from time to time, the attacks of his disorder only necessitated occasional retirement to a private asylum in the neighbourhood. He used to go and come mysteriously, and was a gentle, dreamy easy-going fellow.

The second sister, Anne Sisson, terrified us children, for we not unfrequently saw her in the paroxysms of what looked like spasmodic epilepsy. I fancy that in her case the family disease assumed the form of dipsomania. Yet even she was a thorough lady in her intervals of health, and took great interest in natural history. She possessed a cabinet of minerals, stalactites and fossils, collected on the fells of Cumberland, which fascinated my imagination, partly by the beauty of the sparkling crystals, but more, I think, by the extraordinary enthusiasm with which she spoke about them and the tales she told about the places they came from. One frail finger of stalactite, white, and glistening like a fragment of Pentelican marble, had been brought between his teeth by her brother through a winter snowstorm, on a twenty miles' ride across the moors.

Elizabeth, the youngest sister, had lost her reason in early womanhood under peculiarly romantic circumstances. She was engaged to be married to a young squire of the neighbourhood. Their wedding day arrived, and she was dressed in her bridal clothes, ready to go to church. The bridegroom was expected on horseback. Instead of him, news came that he had been thrown from his horse and killed upon the spot, while riding to join the wedding party. From this shock she never recovered. When her malady assumed an acute form, it manifested the approaching crisis by her re-enacting the scene of that fatal morning. She sat up before a looking-glass, arranged her imaginary bridal wreath and kept asking why her lover did not come. Dickens can, I suppose, never have heard the story of Elizabeth Sisson. But when I read *Great Expectations*, I was not a little astonished to find its main point repeated in the eccentricities of Miss Haversham [sic].

Mr William Sisson died in November 1867. I was then at Cannes, too ill to take a journey. A copy of his will was sent me, by which it appeared that he had left the whole of his estate to three trustees during his sister's life, W. M. Gray Esq., Douglas Hebson Esq. and myself, with full powers of sale and disposable for his sister's benefit, and on her death the residue to myself unconditionally. The estate was almost entirely in land. It must at one time have been considerable.

His sister was not very old, and might live for many years. She occupied a house of her own in Victoria Square, number 2. I had recently bought a house in the same square, number 7. Her insanity rendered her totally helpless. She had a lady companion, a devoted female attendant, a manservant, a brougham, and two servants for the house. But her brother naturally thought that her property ought to be managed by trustees, and that it would be desirable to name as one of these trustees an old friend of the family, resident within a few doors of her abode. Certain memoranda relating to his estate showed that he thought it might be necessary, under possible eventualities, for the trustees to use his own capital as well as the income for his sister's portion for her maintenance. Being *non compos mentis*, but not legally declared so, her capital could not be touched. She had no power to make a will and her property would go upon her death to a relative, Colonel Salkeld.

With the will arrived a sealed packet from Mr Gray whom I have named above, and who was a solicitor in London. Together with a letter of explanation, it contained a copy of a short epistle addressed to me by Mr Sisson at the time he made his will. He set forth his reasons for selecting me as co-trustee for his sister and as residuary legatee after her decease. The terms used were highly honourable to myself. Then he proceeded to say that he hoped I would retain for my own use a farm on Derwentwater, called Thornyplatt, worth about £3000, and that I should expend the rest of the capital accruing from his residuary estate in certain charities, which he left to my judgement, only indicating the possibility of establishing a dispensary at Penrith or a village hospital or endowing Bible women for the countryside, or providing for the education of poor boys from the villages where his farms lay.

Miss Elizabeth Sisson lived on until April 1877. During this period of ten years I acted as her guardian and the controller of her household. The charge proved lighter than I had imagined it might be. At that time England did not suffer from agricultural depression. Rents came regularly in; and I placed my ward's expenditure upon a footing which left a fairly liberal margin for extraordinary disbursements. The income sufficed for the outgoing, and allowed us to keep the farms in decent order. I learned something of management by this discharge of duty, which proved eventually useful to myself. Regarding myself as steward for my dead friend, I dealt scrupulously with all the details of his property, and exercised an economy in his affairs which was alien to my nature. By acting thus, I acquired a sense of the relation between capital and expenditure, a feeling about money, an instinct as to the control of an estate, which nothing but the stern responsibility of honour could have taught me. A worse man of business than myself was never born. And if I have acquired the smallest capacity in that sphere, it is mainly owing to the peculiar conditions under which I accepted the abnormal duties forced upon me by the will of Mr Sisson.

Two grimly tragic incidents occurred during this ten years' guardianship of Miss Elizabeth Sisson. She had an old manservant from the North, called George. He used to drive her daily in her brougham, with the lady companion, Miss Kitteridge. The man was solemn, dumb, mechanical. One evening he left the house alone, and committed suicide by throwing himself from the suspension bridge above the Avon. After this catastrophe, I thought it best to job the brougham and horse, and put them under the charge of a man called Gerrish. Things went well for some months. The daily procession of my mad ward and her lady companion was dull enough, and sad enough, but decorous. It might have gone on for decades had not Gerrish taken the same course as George. The second coachman of Miss Sisson committed suicide by throwing himself from the suspension bridge above the Avon. Then I felt that madness might be a communicable malady, and that my poor ward's carriage was infected. I put it down. Henceforth she took her daily airing in hired vehicles.

Miss Elizabeth Sisson died in April 1877. Her own fortune passed to Colonel Salkeld. The family estate was sold. After the payment of legacies and the discharge of other obligations, I found myself, as Mr Sisson's residuary legatee, in possession of about £19,000. Of this I took for myself about £3000, that being the product of the farm on Derwentwater (Thornyplatt), he wished me to possess. The rest I placed out on good trustees' securities. At the present moment, 28 March 1889, the capital amounts to a trifle under £19,000, with which I have still to deal in the discharge of his private trust. Counsel's opinion, taken in 1884, warned me to be cautious how I used the property for charitable bequests. The suspicion of evasion of the Mortmain Act[18] clung to it; and the will might yet be subject to inquiry. I have therefore resolved to prorogue the final settlement of affairs until the Statute of Limitations renders my position as legatee irreversible. Meanwhile I have made provision by a codicil to my will for the separation of this portion of my estate from the rest. And every year I have spent a very small portion of the income on such private charities as fell within the scope of the testator's intentions. My personal accounts show how these monies have been expended.

Some of my father's relatives were settled in Bristol, Clifton and the neighbourhood. Having spoken of my mother's kindred, I will now narrate what seems to me at all noteworthy regarding my paternal kith. They were excellent folk, distinguished by the virtues of the backbone of the English nation – the great middle class. They also shared its faults – faults inseparable from a Nonconformist ancestry of several generations, complicated by ineradicable family pride. How this pride had formed itself, I am incapable of saying. They knew little about what was really interesting in their genealogy. A tradition, however, survived of ancient gentry sacrificed to a religious and political creed; they were proud of being members of a family which had relinquished the world, and dedicated all its energies during two centuries to the maintenance of an ideal. How narrow the ideal was, and how inconsistent with the progress of modern thought it had become, they did not stop to consider. If the *bourgeois* is a good element in society, then my paternal relatives were the salt of the earth. If impermeability to ideas, adherence to antiquated ways of thinking, conventional and commonplace notions about life, are detrimental to society, then these same persons have to be regarded as a stubborn sect of Jew among the Gentiles.

My father was a *rara avis*. They looked upon him with suspicion, modified by respect and admiration. Intellectually, he had joined the ranks of progress, and belonged to the age of widening thought. Morally, he held with them, and exemplified in his own life what was best and noblest in the family tradition. To keep himself unspotted by the world, to admit no transaction with base motives, to live purely and act uprightly, to follow honour, to postpone mundane and selfish interests to duty, to deal mercifully sympatheti-cally tenderly justly with his brother men, to be unsparing in condemnation of rebellious evil, painstaking and long-suffering with struggling good, these were the principles which ruled his conduct. He transfigured in himself the inheritance he derived from six genera-tions of Puritan ancestors, and he retained something of their rigi-dity. But he also felt the influence of the age in which he lived. He was open at all pores to culture, to art, to archaeology, to science, to literature. In a large and liberal sense he yielded his spirit up to beauty and imbibed the well-spring of modern philosophy. Judged by the narrow standard of his kindred, he was unsound on doctrine, dangerously alive with the revolutionary forces of the century. They not unnaturally regarded him as a bird of different feather from themselves; and while they looked up to him as the mainstay of their fortunes, the most eminent example of the vigour of their race, they felt a certain aloofness for this eagle born in the hen coop.

A son cannot speak adequately about his father. There is a certain impiety in formulating sentences about the author of our being and the moulder of our character. Still, though I cannot express the truth of what I feel, it is possible for me to state the mature opinion that my father typified an exceptionally interesting moment of English evolution. He had abandoned the narrow standpoint of Nonconformist or Evangelical orthodoxy. But he retained what was ethically valuable in the religious tradition. He opened his mind to every influence of knowledge and of culture. He relinquished nothing which affected character and principle. In this way he formed a link between the past and future, attaining to an almost perfect harmony of conservative and liberal ideas. I, the product of a younger period, regard his attitude with reverent admiration. I have been unable to preserve the equilibrium which he maintained, and which appears to me the flower of human virtue. He helped to liberate my spirit; and starting from the point which he reached, I have been carried further, not so wisely, not to a result so mellow, so morally and aesthetically beautiful. We dare not regret the inevitable. We are impotent to strive with fate. What I am, is what I had to be. But these reflections do not prevent me from recording the conviction that my father was a man of plastically noble character – plastic in the sense that Hegel attributed to that word – all functions of his nature meeting in a well-strung symphony which made the powerful yet kindly tempered personality he had.

His constitution favoured him perhaps. He always said that he was of a cold temperament, not indifferent to women, but not easily seduced by their attractions. Facts, which need not now be dragged from their oblivion, confirm this statement conclusively, and proved him always wise and honourable in circumstances of great delicacy. The serious obligation of his life, the duty of working for his family, helped him. And it must not be forgotten that his self-emancipation from the narrower conditions of his earlier environment absorbed a large part of his energy. This is no deduction from his merit. It only serves to show how natural bias and circumstance contributed to make him the fine specimen of English manhood in the second half of the nineteenth century which he became.

How I, the son of such a father, came to be what I am, is a problem I must leave to Francis Galton[19] and the students of heredity. Of my propensities, of my sensibilities, of my audacities he had no share. They were inborn in me, and I shall have to tell the truth about them.

Two of his near relatives had helped to form my father's character. These were his own father and his great-uncle, Dr John Addington, a courtly and stately old gentleman, who lived at Ashley Court in the northern side of Bristol. It was mainly by Dr Addington's advice that my father settled in that city. Dr Addington belonged to the small school of advanced thinkers who formed themselves in England of the type of the French *philosophes* and Hume and Hartley. He boasted of having been present at the Bastille dinner.[20] He was a friend of Ramahun Roy [sic].[21] He corresponded with the leading liberals in politics, religion and philosophy. His carriage, conversation and deportment combined aristocratic hauteur with the sarcastic wit and frankness of expression which characterized professed free thinkers at the beginning of the nineteenth century. This was remarkable in the case of a man, whose father was a non-juror[22] and Nonconformist minister, who claimed kinship with Lord Sidmouth,[23] and who had acquired a moderate fortune by the practice of medicine in London. He had no children, and after his decease this branch of the Addington family was represented by my father. From the point of view of genealogy and heraldry, the inheritance is interesting. Dr Addington, through his mother, represented the ancient family of Reymes of Overstrand County Norfolk. The arms of Addington ('per pale ermin and ermins, a chevron counter-changed') quartered with D'Abernon ('azure, a chevron or') together with the shield of Reymes ('sable, a chevron ermine between three lions rampant argent') were added to our coat. But this was all. My father derived no pecuniary benefit from his great-uncle, who not unwisely, being childless, used his fortune in his lifetime. Intellectually and socially, my father owed, I think, a great deal to the enlarged opinions and liberal breeding of this old Englishman, himself a *rara avis* in his family.

The gradual emergence from narrow intellectual conditions in a Puritan pedigree is always interesting. We see the process going forward in the case of Quakers and of Dissenters who have acquired importance at the present time. The annals of my own family furnish an excellent example. When I broke up our house in Clifton Hill in 1881, I deliberately burned the correspondence of five generations – the letters of my grandfather and of his immediate ancestors through four descents. I had two good reasons at the time for doing this. One was that I did not know where to deposit these bulky documents, some of which contained matters too personal for publication, or for transference to any public library. The other was that the perusal of them left a deeply painful impression on my mind. The intense preoccupation with so-called spiritual interests, the suffocating atmosphere of a narrow sect resembling that of a close parlour, the grim stern dealing with young souls not properly convinced of sin, the unnatural admixture of this other-worldliness with mundane marrying and giving in marriage and professional affairs, caught me by the throat and throttled me. I could not bear to think of my own kith and kin, the men and women who had made me, from whom 'eternity's sunrise',[24] the flooding radiance of nature's light, seemed ruthlessly excluded. So I committed an act of vandalism, whereof I am now half repentant and half proud. No doubt these documents, carefully sifted by successive members of the family from other papers of less moment in their eyes, epitomized the spiritual archives of a race who scorned their ancient and decaying gentry, and who boasted – I remember the phrase in one of these letters – that they had been 'reknowned for their piety through two centuries'. This, by the way, was written by the head of the family about 1830 to one of its younger members, who innocently asked for information about such insignificant trifles as Sir Richard Fitz-Simon, KG temp.: Edward III and the quartering of Mainwaring. He was told that seats and crowns in the heavenly Jerusalem had far more value and were far more difficult to win than coronets or garters bestowed by kings, or than arms inscribed after the Heralds' books by Clarencieux [sic],[25] an undoubted truth. The man who penned those sentences of scornful rebuke displayed no ignoble pride. Yet he was proud and stubborn to the backbone in his unworldliness; and if I have any grit in me, I owe it to this proud humility of my forefathers.

This brings me to speak of my grandfather, John Symonds of Oxford, who was the first to react against the hereditary narrowness of the family creed. Remaining a Dissenter, he became in mature life what may best be described as a Christian Stoic. He was a good Latin scholar and wrote voluminous diaries and meditations in the style of Seneca. Not an elastic or optimistic nature – rather on the contrary rigid and circumscribed, depressed by a melancholy temperament and by the gloom of Calvinism, which assumed in him the form of philosophical fatalism. This comparative disengagement from sectarian dogma, combined with the study of the Classics and of English thought down from Bacon through Locke to Hume and Adam Smith, formed a type of character well calculated to start my father upon his own path of emancipation. A severe uncompromising sense of duty, a grim incapability of any transactions with the world, marked my grandfather out as the lineal and loyal descendant of his Puritan ancestors. These moral qualities were transmitted to my father. In my father they became transfigured and spiritualized. The advanced ground reached by my father was the soil in which I grew up. These three generations of men – my grandfather, my father and myself – correspond to the succession of Aeschylus, Sophocles and Euripides, to the transition from early pointed Gothic to Decorated to Flamboyant architecture. *Medio tutissimus ibis.* 'You will go most safely by the middle course.'[26] The middle term of such a series is always superior to the first and vastly superior to the third. How immeasurably superior my father was to me, as a man, as a character, as a social being, as a mind, I feel, but I cannot express.

My grandfather left Oxford and came to live with his daughter Mrs James Nash at Cassington Villa, Clifton. He soon proposed to teach me Latin. I began to learn this language before I was five years old, and can remember declining some Latin nouns for my father on my fifth birthday. It was rather a long walk for a little boy from Berkeley Square to Cassington Villa, which stood in its own garden not far from Buckingham Chapel.

The grammar used for instructing me in Latin was, so far as I remember, one by Arnold.[27] When we came to the doctrine of the potential and subjunctive moods, I could not comprehend the rules and refused to learn them by rote. Considering that I was an extremely docile and timid child, this argued an extraordinary amount of intellectual repugnance.

My grandfather declared that he would not teach me any more. I was incorrigible, stupid or obstinate. I had to write an apological letter, which I remember doing with mighty solemnity and sense of importance, propped up on cushions at a big high table. On these conditions he took me back as a dull but repentant pupil.

The difficulty of grasping abstract statements made learning very irksome for me. Some branches of knowledge I wholly failed to acquire. Among these was arithmetic. I could not do the sums, because the rules, which were never properly explained, oppressed me with a nightmare sense of unreality. Even when I got hold enough upon them to apply them, I was sceptical about the results. The whole process seemed to me like a piece of jugglery, which offended my intelligence. Euclid, on the other hand, offered no obstacles. Geometry gave me pleasure by its definite objectivity, clear chains of reasoning and direct appeal to the senses. I could remember the figures, and work a theorem or problem out with ease. I always learned best through the eyes; and I am convinced that a tutor who discovered this bias in me for the concrete could have taught me anything in mathematics.

As time went on, I used to take country walks with my grandfather and cousins. What he told me then – the names of plants and the Latin words for things we saw – I have never forgotten.

During our excursions on the downs, nature began to influence my imagination in a peculiar way. When the light of the evening was falling, or when we found ourselves in some secluded corner with a prospect toward the Bristol Channel and the Welsh Hills, I passed from the sense of a tangible presence into a dream. This was a very definite phase of experience, approaching hypnotism in its character. I partly dreaded the subjugation of my conscious will, and partly looked forward to it with a thrill of exquisite anticipation. I learned to recognize the symptoms of this oncoming mood. But I could not induce it by an act of volition. It needed some specific touch of the external world upon my sensibility.

I am not sure whether this was the rudimentary stage of another form of self-absorption, which afterwards for many years recurred at intervals, giving more of serious disturbance than of pleasure when it came. That was a kind of trance. Suddenly, at church, or in company, or when I was reading, and always when my muscles were at rest, I felt the approach of the mood. Irresistibly it took possession of my mind and will, lasted what seemed like an eternity and disappeared in a series of rapid sensations which resembled the awakening from anaesthetic influence. One reason why I disliked this kind of trance was that I could not describe it to myself. I cannot even now find words to render it intelligible, though it is probable that many readers of these pages will recognize the state in question. It consisted in a gradual but swiftly progressive oblitera-tion of space, time, sensation and the multitudinous factors of experience which seemed to qualify what we are pleased to call ourself. In proportion as these conditions of ordinary consciousness were subtracted, the sense of an underlying or essential consciousness acquired intensity. At last nothing remained but a pure, absolute, abstract self. The universe became without form and void of content. But self persisted, formidable in its vivid keenness, asking or rather feeling the most poignant doubt about reality, ready as it seemed to find existence break as breaks a bubble round about it. And what then? The apprehension of a coming dissolution, the grim conviction that this state was the last state of the conscious self, the sense that I had followed the last thread of being to the verge of the abyss and had arrived at demonstration of eternal *maya* or illusion, stirred or seemed to stir me up again. The return of ordinary conditions of sentient existence began by my first recovering the power of touch, and then by the gradual though rapid influx of familiar impressions and diurnal interests. At last I felt myself once more a human being; and though the riddle of what is meant by life remained unsolved, I was thankful for this return from the abyss – this deliverance from so awful an initiation into the mysteries of scepticism.

This trance returned with diminishing frequency until I reached the age of twenty-eight. Though I have felt its approaches often, I have not experienced it fully now for many years. It served to impress upon my growing nature the phantasmal unreality of all the circumstances which contribute to a merely phenomenal consciousness. Often I have asked myself with anguish, on awakening from that formless state of denuded keenly sentient being, which is the unreality: the trance of fiery vacant apprehensive sceptical self from which I issue, or these surrounding phenomena and habits which veil that inner self and build a self of flesh-and-blood conventionality? Again: are men the factors of some dream, the dream-like unsubstantiality of which they comprehend at such eventful moments? What would happen if the final stage of the trance were reached – if after the abduction of phenomenal conditions beyond recovery, the denuded sense of self should pass away in a paroxysm of doubt? Would it be absorption into the real life beyond phenomena? Could another garment of sensitive experience clothe again that germ of self, which recognized the unsubstantiality of all that seem to make it human?

It is obvious that I am straining the resources of language at my disposal in the effort to adumbrate the exact nature of this trance. I find it impossible, however, to render an adequate account of the initiation. Nor can I properly describe the permanent effect produced upon my mind by the contrast between this exceptional condition of my consciousness and the daily experiences – physical, moral, intellectual, emotional, practical – with which I compared it. Like other psychical states, it lies beyond the province of language.

When I first read Pindar, his exclamation ἐπάμεϱοι τί δέ τις; τί δ᾽ οὔ τις; σκιᾶς ὄναϱ ἄνθϱωπος ('Things of a day! What is a man? What is a man not? A dream of a shadow is a man')[28] – this awoke in me reverberating echoes. It was for me no casual poet's question, no figure of rhetoric let fall to point the moral of man's fleeting day on earth. The lyric cry pierced to the very core and marrow of my soul.

When I was eight years old, my father sent me to a tutor, the Rev. William Knight. This gentleman kept a school. His house in Buckingham Villas (now part of the Pembroke Road) was at least a mile from Berkeley Square. I used to perform the journey, going and coming, four times in a working day. The institution was probably not worse than the majority of private schools. How bad it was, I dare not say. Mr Knight had little to do with the teaching. One of his ushers was a whoremonger, and the other a paederast. The boys – several of them sons of Somersetshire gentlemen, others, like me, day-scholars – did pretty much as they liked. Bullying of a peculiarly offensive sort took place there. But I am bound to say that I was neither bullied nor contaminated in my morals. I think that Mr Knight, owing special obligations to my father, insisted on my being treated with more consideration than the other pupils.

It was rather a *via dolorosa* from Berkeley Square to Buckingham Villas. The road led first through a street of poor people, among whom I became interested in a family of mulattoes, the children of a Negro sailor and a Bristol woman. A narrow alley led to the Roman Catholic church, then half finished; and this alley was always adorned on both sides with obscene or blasphemous *graffiti*. Emerging at the top, I passed through some dismal decaying terraces and villas, and then took a straight line along decent dwelling houses with a great field on the right hand until I eventually arrived at the school. The whole line of march recurs to my mind's eye but I am characteristically oblivious to the names of places.

Just before I reached Buckingham Villas, there was a tall house on the right, cresting the rising slope and looking down upon the large field I have mentioned. I think it was also called Buckingham something. There was a grating in the basement floor of this house, which gave light to a cellar of some sort. I fancied that a magician lived in the semi-subterranean apartment. I used to see him squatting by a fire on the floor, raking up embers and stirring ingredients in a cauldron. He became a positive reality to my imagination. But I never attempted to converse with him and did not feel sure whether he was a wizard or an alchemist. The alternative puzzled me.

About this figment of my fancy I spoke freely at home and proposed to take my sisters to watch the magician at work. My aunt, however, looked seriously on the matter, and requested me not to tell lies. The same thing happened when I arrived one evening in a state of considerable excitement at home and declared that I had been attacked by robbers on the way. The artlessness of my narration must have proved its worthlessness. I was soundly scolded. Yet neither the magician nor the robbers are less real to my memory than most of the people who surrounded me at that time. It was right to treat me harshly about such waking dreams. I learned in this way to distinguish what we call true from what we call false.

To my father I owe a debt of gratitude for his sympathetic treatment of quite a different occurrence. I sold my Latin dictionary to a comrade called Emerson for sixpence. When I was asked at home where I had lost it, I said that I did not know. Stings of conscience made me speedily confess the truth, and I did so with no little trepidation to my father in his library. He spoke gently and wisely on the topic, pointing out that lies were not only wrong but ignoble. What he then said touched my sense of honour, and struck my intelligence. I was thenceforward scrupulous about telling the exact truth.

The occurrences I have related seem to me important in the development of my character. They saved me from becoming a visionary, to which I was too prone by temperament. They forced me to draw a sharp line of distinction between what happened in my dreaming self and what impinged upon my senses from outside. They revealed the all-importance of veracity – the duty and the practical utility of standing on a common ground of fact with average men and women in affairs of life. In other words I became capable of discriminating between fancies and things, and I learned to abhor and scorn mendacity.

Chapter Two

Containing material which none but students of psychology and ethics need peruse

The plan of these memoirs, which are intended to describe the evolution of a somewhat abnormally constituted individual, obliges me to interpolate a section here which might otherwise have been omitted with satisfaction to myself. When the whole interest of a life centres, not in action, but in mental development and moral experience, truth becomes imperatively necessary with regard to points of apparent insignificance.

No one, however, can regard the first stirrings of the sexual instinct as a trifling phenomenon in any life. It is only prejudice and false shame which leads people to conceal the facts and phases of the *vita sexualis,* so essentially important is a formation of character and determination of mental qualities.

The earliest idea I gained of sex was caught from a coarse remark made by our head nurse Sarah Jones. We were out walking with the nursery-maid and my sisters, passing through a turnstile which led from George Street through the gravel path round Brandon Hill. The sudden revelation that there is something specific in the private parts, distinguishing them from other portions of the body, made a peculiar and uneasy impression on my sensibility – so strong that an image of the landscape, as it was that morning, remains imprinted on my memory: Bristol below, with its church towers and ships, the freshness of the west wind blowing from the channel, the wavering soft English sunlight.

About the same time, I heard much whispered conversation in our nursery concerning a man who stood and exposed his person before the maids at a spot fronting our back window. I could not understand the indignation mingled with excitement and curiosity expressed by the women.

Among my earliest recollections I must record certain visions, half-dream, half-reverie, which were certainly erotic in their nature, and which recurred frequently just before sleeping. I used to fancy myself crouched upon the floor amid a company of naked adult men: sailors, such as I had seen about the streets of Bristol. The contact of their bodies afforded me a vivid and mysterious pleasure. Singular as it may appear that a mere child could have formed such fancies, and unable as I am to account for their origin, I am positive regarding the truth of this fact. The reverie was so often repeated, so habitual, that there is no doubt about its psychical importance.

A handsome lad of a full-blown healthy type once masturbated in my presence during the period of childhood. He wanted me to try the game. But though the sight disturbed me not uncomfortably, I shrank with horror from his touch and managed to escape from the room. The attractions of a dimly divine almost mystic sensuality persisted in my nature, side by side with a marked repugnance to lust in action, throughout my childhood and boyhood down to an advanced stage of manhood.

At the same time, I was unfortunate enough to be thrown into the society of a coarse girl, who liked to expose herself and make me touch her sexual organs. It neither attracted nor repelled me, nor did they rouse my curiosity, only they displeased my sense of smell. Once when I found a male cousin of mine preparing to copulate with her, I felt a strange and powerful disgust.

A dirty-minded schoolfellow, when I was about nine years old, initiated me into the mysteries of sexual duality, coition, impregnation, childbirth. This interested my intelligence, but did not affect my imagination. My reveries still reverted to the naked sailors, whose physical contact seemed so desirable. And in all these early experiences, the sex which drew me with attraction was the male.

Our earliest memories of words, poems, works of art, have great value in the study of psychical development. They indicate decisive points in the growth of personality. The mere sharp recollection we retain of certain images is a sign of their potency. Now the first English poem which affected me deeply – as it has, no doubt, impressed thousands of boys – was Shakespeare's 'Venus and Adonis'. I read it certainly before we left 7 Berkeley Square and, I think, before I was ten years old. It gave form, ideality and beauty to my previous erotic visions. Those adult males, the shaggy and brawny sailors, without entirely disappearing, began to be super-seded in my fancy by an adolescent Adonis. The emotion they symbolized blent with a new kind of feeling. In some confused way I identified myself with Adonis; but at the same time I yearned after him as an adorable object of passionate love. Venus only served to intensify the situation. I did not pity her. I did not want her. I did not think that, had I been in the position of Adonis, I should have used his opportunities to better purpose. No: she only expressed my own relation to the desirable male. She brought into relief the overwhelming attraction of masculine adolescence and its proud inaccessibility. Her hot wooing taught me what it was to woo with sexual ardour. I dreamed of falling back like her upon the grass, and folding the quick-panting lad in my embrace.

I cannot of course tell what would have happened if Shakespeare had emphasized the fascination of the female instead of dwelling on the fascination of the male. Probably the poem would have made no more impression on me than did the 'Rape of Lucrece' to which I remained indifferent. As it was, I took 'Venus and Adonis' in the way Shakespeare undoubtedly meant it to be taken. And doing so, it stimulated while it etherealized my inborn craving after persons of my own sex.

Character might be described as the product of inborn proclivities and external circumstance. If we regard temperament as one factor and circumstance as another, we must also bear in mind that temper-ament takes and rejects, assimilates and discards, the elements of nutrition afforded by circumstance according to an instinct of selec-tion. Boys of more normal sexuality might have preferred the 'Rape of Lucrece' to 'Venus and Adonis'. Or, in the latter, they might have felt the attraction of the female – condemning Adonis for a simpleton, and wishing themselves for ten minutes in his place.

I am glad to close this section, in which, after long reflection, I have set down what I know to be absolutely certain facts about the development of sex in me before the age of eleven.

Note to the foregoing section

When I wrote these recollections of my earliest sexual impressions, I was not aware how important they were for the proper under-standing of *vita sexualis*, and how impossible it would have been to omit them from a truthful autobiography. I had not then studied the works of Moreau, Tarnowski, Krafft-Ebing,[1] who attempt to refer all cases of sexual inversion to a neurotic disorder inherited or acquired. I had not read the extraordinary writings of Ulrichs,[2] who maintains that the persons he calls *Urnings* form a sex apart — having literally a feminine soul included within a male body.

It does not appear to me that either Ulrichs or the school of neuropathical physicians have solved the problem offered by individuals of my type. The 'neuropathic grandmother'[3] is too common an occurrence in modern families to account for what is after all a somewhat rare aberration of sexual proclivities; and the hypothesis of a female soul shut up within a male body savours of bygone scholastic speculation.

The problem being then still one awaiting solution, all facts which throw light upon it, especially upon the origination of abnormal sexual feelings, their spontaneity and probable innate character, are scientifically useful.

It is certain that the medical school of theorists would claim me as a subject of neurotic disease. My mother's family on the paternal side (Sykes) was tainted with pulmonary phthisis, and on the maternal side (Abdy) with extreme nervous excitability, eccentricity, even madness. Of four male children conceived by my mother, two (twins) were still-born into the world, the third died of acute hydrocephalus: I, the last and the survivor, suffered from night terrors, extreme shyness, nervous affections, somnambulism; I shunned the society of masculine boys, disliked physical exercises of a violent kind, preferred solitude and study to games, because subject at the age of puberty to excessive involuntary losses of semen, stammered for a period in my speech; in short I exhibited many of the symptoms which Krafft-Ebing and his school recognize as hereditary neuroticism predisposing its subject to sexual inversion.

Still I do not think that the whole tenor of my life up to the age of fifty, which I have now reached, justifies the opinion that I have been the victim of conceptional neurotic malady. It is notorious that in literature I have done a very large amount of work, not only brilliant, but solid and laborious, which has placed me in the front rank of English authors. My literary achievement is no doubt due in part at least to a high degree of nervous sensibility; and compared with the average of men, I may be pronounced to have exhibited an abnormal strain of nervous energy. This nervousness has been a condition of my performance. But is it either logical or prudent to diagnose so marked a specimen of the artistic temperament as morbid? I leave that question to psychologists, only remarking that it seems to me dangerous to classify poets, men of letters, painters, almost all of whom exhibit some nervous abnormalities, with the subjects of hereditary disease. Here we approach too near to the paradox that genius is a species of madness.

Since this paragraph was written, we have had Lombroso's *Man of Genius*[4] and Nesbit's [sic] *Insanity of Genius*[5] upholding the hypothesis I attempted to combat.

With regard to Ulrichs, in his peculiar phraseology, I should certainly be tabulated as a *Mittel Urning*, holding a mean between the *Mannling* and the *Weibling*; that is to say, one whose emotions are directed to the male sex during the period of adolescence and early manhood; who is not marked either by an effeminate passion for robust adults or by a predilection for young boys; in other words, one whose comradely instincts are tinged with a distinct sexual partiality. But in this sufficiently accurate description of my attitude, I do not recognize anything which justifies the theory of a female soul. Morally and intellectually, in character and taste and habits, I am more masculine than many men I know who adore women. I have no feminine feeling for the males who rouse my desire. The anomaly of my position is that I admire the physical beauty of men more than women, derive more pleasure from their contact and society, and am stirred to sexual sensations exclusively by persons of the male sex.

Finally, it appears to me that the abnormality in question is not to be explained either by Ulrichs's theory, or by the presumptions of the pathological psychologists. Its solution must be sought far deeper in the mystery of sex, and in the variety of type exhibited by nature. For this reason, a detailed study of one subject, such as I mean to attempt, may be valuable.

Chapter Three

First period of boyhood, 1851–4,
Clifton Hill House

Up to this point I have recorded memories of my life before the age of ten, admitting only those which can be referred by some clear local indication to that period. I now pass from childhood to the first period of boyhood. The transition is defined by the change of residence from 7 Berkeley Square to Clifton Hill House.

This stage, which extended from June 1851 until May 1854, was one of greatly increased happiness. My health improved. We were nearer the country; and our new house satisfied my sense of what is beautiful. I had a pony and began to ride. This I enjoyed, though I did not become a good horseman, mainly, I think, because I was allowed to go out riding alone before I had been trained by a groom.

My youngest sister Charlotte and I became great friends, and we both profited by the companionship of her governess Mlle Sophie Girard, of whom I shall have more to say. We three formed a little coterie within the household.

Hitherto, so far as people were concerned, my inner life had been almost a blank.

It is a great misfortune for a boy to lose his mother so early as I did; and my father was so busy in his profession that he had very little time to bestow on me. Yet even in my childhood his strong and noble character, his sense of honour and duty, and his untiring energy impressed me. The drives I took with him were not thrown away. In the evenings also, when he had a spare hour, he used to read to us, chosing ballads, portions of Scott's poems, passages from Hood's 'Miss Kilmansegg',[1] stories from Hans Andersen, adapted to our intelligence. These readings stimulated my literary instincts.

So far as my father was concerned, I grew up in an atmosphere of moral tension, and came to regard work as the imperative duty imposed on human beings.

My aunt, who came to take our mother's place, exercised an opposite influence. It is difficult to describe her character with any exactitude or fairness. She was essentially kind, but neither just nor tender – variable in temper, nervous and timid in her dealings with my father. He demanded strenuous physical energy and unwavering rectitude from those who formed his household. These she was unable to give, being constitutionally of quite a different complexion – subject to sleeplessness, dyspepsia and headaches, and, what was worse in this respect, indifferent to truth in trifles. She therefore adopted a system of shifts, excuses and transactions, which to a child's keen instinct bore the aspect of unveracity. She had a great sense of humour; but she exercised this rather reluctantly, turning people to ridicule behind their backs and uttering offhand sarcasms which stung a child's sensitiveness like scorpions. By fits and starts, she showed real generosity and bursts of affection. You could always rely upon her liberal impulses on serious occasions. But justice had no place in her vocabulary, and her changes of mood were bewildering. Her religion was sincere. Yet it did not penetrate her daily life, and was mixed up with man-worship – at this epoch with, to my judgement, a wholly unaccountable enthusiasm for the Rev. William Knight and the Church Missionary Society. When she was not prostrated with headaches, or worried with uncongenial social duties, her cheerfulness made her an amusing companion. To sum up: her chief faults were the want of steadiness; the want of veracity, and the want of equity. Her position as head of our family without being either mother or wife was a very difficult one. I remained constant in my gratitude to her for what she meant to do and what she did through a long series of trying years.

It was a great day for all of us when my father announced on one June morning that he had bought Clifton Hill House, and we drove up in his carriage to visit our future home.

This house had been built by a Bristol merchant named Paul Fisher. It carries on its garden front the date 1747, together with the coat of Fisher impaling what other arms I knew not. Paul Fisher himself sleeps in Clifton churchyard, and the vestibule to what is now the parish church contains his defrauded and neglected monument.

At the time when this substantial piece of early Georgian architecture was erected, Clifton still remained a country village. Paul Fisher's habitation had no rivals in antiquity but the Church House and the Manor House, none in stateliness except the fine suburban villa of the Goldney family.

Bristol stands at the junction of the rivers Frome and Avon, which from this point flow together through a winding defile of high limestone cliffs to the Severn. Sea waters from the channel washed its walls, and tided merchant vessels to the quays of antique commerce. They brought with them the sugar and the spices, the tobacco and rare timber of Virginia and the Indies, to be stored in the warehouses of the city wharves. When Paul Fisher gazed from the windows of his new-built mansion over the expanse of verdure, he saw the streets and squares of the red-roofed town threaded with glittering waterways along which lay ocean-going ships, their tall masts vined with the spires and towers of clustered churches. St Mary de Redclyffe's broken spire, the square tower of the cathedral (that old abbey church of the Augustinian monks, enriched by barons of Berkeley Castle), the sharp shaft of St Nicholas, the slender column of St Stephen, surveyed from the altitude of Clifton Hill, were all embedded in groves of limes and elms and masts with pennons waving from their tops.

Clifton Hill House, at the present day, turns a grim grey frontage to the road. It is a ponderous square mansion, built for perpetuity, with walls three feet in thickness, faced with smooth Bath stone. But, passing to the southern side, one still enjoys the wonderful prospect that I described. Time has done much to spoil the landscape. Mean dwellings have clustered round the base of Brandon Hill, and crept along the slopes of Clifton. The city has extended on the further side toward Bedminster. Factory chimneys, with their filth and smoke, have saddened the simple beauty of the town and dulled the brightness of its air. But the grand features of nature remain. The rolling line of hills from Lansdowne over Bath, through Dundry with its solitary church tower, to Ashton guarding the gorge of Avon, presents a free and noble space for cloud shadows, a splendid scene for the display of sunrise. The water from the Severn still daily floods the riverbeds at Frome and Avon; and the ships still come to roost, like ocean birds, beside the ancient churches. Moreover, the trees which Paul Fisher planted in his pleasance have grown to a great height; so that a sea of many-coloured foliage waves beneath the windows of his dwelling house.

On that eventful June morning, I entered the solemn front door, traversed the echoing hall, vaulted and floored with solid stone, and emerged upon the garden at the further end. An Italian double flight of balustraded steps, largely designed, gives access to the gravelled terrace which separates the house from the lawn. For us it was like passing from the prose of fact into the poetry of fairyland.

The garden, laid out by Paul Fisher in 1747, had not been altered in any important particular, except that a large piece of it was cut away at the bottom to build a row of houses called Bellevue Terrace. Four great tulip trees, covered with golden blossoms, met our eyes at four points of vantage in the scheme. Between them, on either hand, rose two gigantic copper beeches, richly contrasted with the bright green of the tulip trees. Eight majestic elms, four on each side, guarded the terrace. They dated from an earlier period than the foundation of the dwelling house. The grove which clustered round the central grass plot was further diversified by ilexes and mulberry trees, wych elms and pear trees, a fragile ilanthus and a feathery acacia, with cypresses from the black boughs of which the clambering roses fell in showers. Sycamores, beeches and walnuts formed a leafy background to these choicer growths, and marked the ugly frontage of Bellevue.

Two ponds, quaintly enclosed with wire railings, interrupted at proper intervals the slope of soft green turf. Each had a fountain in its midst, the one shaped like a classic urn, the other a cupid seated on a dolphin and blowing a conch. When the gardener made the water rise for us from these fountains, it flashed in the sunlight, tinkled on the leaves and cups of floating lilies, disturbed the dragonflies and goldfish from their sleepy ways. Birds were singing, as they only sing in old town gardens, a chorus of blackbirds, thrushes and finches. Rooks cawed from the elms above. The whole scene was ennobled by a feeling of respect, of merciful abstention from superfluous meddling. When Paul Fisher planned his pleasure ground, he meant it, according to the taste of that period, to be artificial and yet to vie with nature. Now nature had asserted her own sway, retaining through that century of wayward growth something which still owed its charm to artifice.

Although I am speaking of my home, and must of necessity be partial, I do not think I violate the truth when I say that this garden possessed a special grace and air of breeding, which lent distinction to the dignified but rather stolid house above. It was old enough to have felt 'the unimaginable touch of time'[2] and yet not old or neglected enough to have fallen into decay. Left alone, it had gained a character of wildness; and yet kind touches had been given which preserved it from squalor. Wealthy folk had always inhabited the mansion and their taste reflected the peculiar beauty of the place. Afterwards, at New College and St John's, among the Oxford college gardens, I recognized the same charm. But the distinctive feature of the Clifton Hill garden was that the ground fell rapidly away from the terrace and the house – so that the windows above enjoyed a vast prospect, across its undulating roof of verdure, to the towered city, the glimpses of the Avon, the seagoing ships, and, far away beyond all that, to the hills of Bath and the long stretch of Dundry. It was a remarkable home for a dreamy town-bred boy of ten to be transported into.

On that eventful morning, the air hung heavy with a scent of hidden musk. The broad flowerbeds upon the terrace and along the walls were a tangle of old-fashioned herbs in bloom – mulberry-coloured scabrius, love-in-idleness, love-in-a-mist, love-lies-a-bleeding, corncockles, devil-in-the-bush, hollyhocks, carnations, creeping-jenny, damask and cabbage and York-and-Lancaster roses. The mingled perfume of musk and rose pervades my memory when I think of that day; and when I come by accident upon the scent of musk in distant places, I am again transported to the fairyland of boyhood. The throat-notes of thrush and blackbird, the music of tinkling fountains, the drowsy rhythm of hammers struck on timber in the city dockyards, blend in my recollection with pure strong slumberous summer sunlight and rich odours.

There was much in the mansion itself which satisfied my craving for architectural solidity and stateliness. The pediment of stone above our front door in Berkeley Square had, as I have already mentioned, consoled my childish senses. The style of that detail was here expanded through the whole substantial edifice. The rusticated work upon this spacious massive basements, the balustraded stair-cases descending to the terrace, the huge balls of Bath stone placed at proper intervals upon the lower line of office buildings, the well-proportioned if too lofty rooms, the dignified waste of useful space in the long passages: all these characteristics of the Georgian manner gave satisfaction to my instincts of what is liberal in art, though of course they could not feed my fancy. I did not then reflect how gloomy that square house might be, how prosaic the inspiration of its builder was, how like prisons the upper rooms with their high windows are and how melancholy the vast prospect over city, sky and stretching hills would afterwards appear to me in moods of weariness.

Then there were stables with haylofts and a paved yard, where my father generally kept eight horses; a summerhouse, upon the walls of which vines clambered and nectarines ripened; a kitchen garden full of strawberries and currant bushes, apricots and plums and peaches. The top of the house itself formed a capital playing ground for us children. A rambling attic, which we called the loft, stretched away into mysterious recesses and dark corners. In some of these obscure chambers cisterns were hidden, which supplied the house with rainwater; from the narrow windows of others we could climb out upon the roof, the sloping gables of which were covered with solid lead and fenced about with broad slabs of rough clean chiselled stone. From this height the eye swept spaces of the starry heavens by night; by day, town, tower, and hill, wood, field and river lay bathed in light and flecked shadows of the clouds.

The transition from Berkeley Square to Clifton Hill House contributed greatly, I am sure, to make me what I am. I cannot, of course, say what I should have become had we remained in our old home. But I am certain that the new one formed my character and taste at a period when youth is most susceptible. My latent aesthetic sensibilities were immediately and powerfully stimulated.

Some years after the time of which I am writing, I brought a Balliol friend to stay with me at Clifton. On taking leave at the end of his visit, he remarked, 'I understand you now, and know what it is that made you what you are.' He was right, I believe. Places exercise commanding influence in the development of certain natures. Mine is one of them; and Clifton, with the house we lived in, had a magic of its own.

My tutor, the Rev. William Knight, gave up his school and came to live at no great distance from our house. He occupied a dreary abode in Wetherell Place, the outer walls rough-cast and painted a dull lilac, standing in a stuffy plot of shrubbery between a blank wall to the front and a tall row of houses to the back. How any reasonable human being could in Clifton – the very essence of which place was poetry in some form or another – whether of the ancient town beside it, or of the free nature on its northern borders – have selected to abide in Wetherell Place, that region of shabby-genteel

71

prose and stifling dullness, I am not prepared to say. Probably there were economical reasons, and social inducements, together with conveniences of contiguity to the Blind Asylum and St Michael's Church, which determined Mr Knight in his choice. But the choice sufficiently indicated the nature of the man, who was dyspeptic, melancholic, constitutionally indolent, hopelessly unpractical and clogged with pecuniary and domestic cares. He realized the notion of a disappointed man; one who thought he had the right, and in some respects had really the right to expect from life more than he extracted from it; but who was baffled by debilities of will and character deeply seated in his temperament.

At the time of which I speak, Mr Knight was already ageing. He had lost his wife and had several children to provide for. There were two invalid daughters, hunchbacked Hester and gentle Margaret, who passed her life upon a couch. The eldest son, William, was a secretary to the Missionary Society and came at intervals to collect funds at Bristol for the Tinnevelly Station.³ How I hated and mistrusted the cooked accounts and sordid pietisms of that vaunted Mission! The Greek in me instinctively rebelled against the methods used for drawing money from our purses to provide some scores of rupee-Christians for the faith – the faith of what? A narrow, hidebound, starched, commercial, middle-class, Anglo-Saxon Evangelicalism. The Rev. William Knight Jr did much to evoke my hostility against English missionaries into existence. Even as a boy, and long before I could reason, I was profoundly sceptical. The second son, Robert, was at college in Cambridge, preparing himself for orders. Of him I shall speak when I describe my entrance into Harrow. There was a third son, Charles, who went to sea in boyhood, and was now beginning his career as marine and landscape painter. I always liked this man the best of the whole family, with the exception of gentle and uncomplaining Margaret, stretched on her invalid's bed. A third daughter I ought not to omit. She was called Agnes: a good girl, I believe, but hard, ill-favoured, and sharing the personal ungraciousness which distinguished all the Knights – Margaret, the invalid, alone excepted.

It was necessary to describe the Knight family, since they played a considerable part in my life for several years to come.

Mr Knight could not be called an ideal tutor. He was sluggish and had no sympathy for boys. Yet he was a sound scholar of the old type, and essentially a gentleman. He let me browse, much as I liked, about the pastures of innocuous Greek and Latin literature. He taught me to write Latin verses with facility. If I did not acquire elegance, that was the defect of my own faculty for style. I think he might have grounded me better in grammar than he did; and it would have been an incalculable advantage to me if he had been able to direct my keen, though latent, enthusiasm for books. In this respect, I owe him one and one only debt of gratitude. We were reading the sixth book of the *Aeneid*. He noticed what a deep hold the description of Elysium took on my imagination and lent me Warburton's *Divine Legation of Moses*.[4] A chapter in that book about the Mysteries opened dim and shadowy vistas for my dreaming thoughts. I cannot remember any other instance of my tutor's touching the real spring of thirst for knowledge in my nature. For the rest, he took care that I should understand the *Odes* of Horace and be capable of reproducing their various metres. This gave me a certain advantage when I came to Harrow.

Mr Knight had generally one or two pupils living in his house, boys who were being prepared for the university. I had not much to do with them. But I remember one well. I think his name was Metcalfe. He had just left Harrow – why, I do not know – and something of the place still clung about him. I liked the big long lad, and sat upon his knees, and felt that it was good to sit there. Once he kissed me; but I sprang away from him with an undefined impulse of pride mingled with resentment and the tumultuous stirring of some perilous sense. He must have been a good youth, for he did not follow up his obvious advantage. He only laughed and said, 'When you go to Harrow, you will be "sent up for first copy, and you will be some fellow's . . .".' He stopped before the word escaped his lips. But in a year or two I learned what his respect for my innocence had left unuttered. The prophecy was not fulfilled, except as regards my facile successes with bad Latin verses.

With Mr Knight I read a large part of the *Iliad*. When we came to the last books, I found a passage which made me weep bitterly. It was the description of Hermes, going to meet Priam, disguised as a mortal:[5]

κούρῳ αἰσυμνητῆρι ἐοικώς,
πρῶτον ὑπηνήτῃ τοῦ περ χαριεστάτη ἥβη.

['Like a young prince with the first down upon his lip, the time when youth is the most charming.'] The Greek in me awoke to that simple, and yet so splendid, vision of young manhood. 'In the first budding of the down on lip and chin, when youth is at her loveliest.' The phrase had all Greek sculpture in it; and all my dim forebodings of the charm of males were here idealized. The over-powering magic of masculine adolescence drew my tears forth. I had none to spare for Priam prostrate at the feet of his son's murderer; none for Andromache[6] bidding a last farewell to Hector of the waving plumes. These personages touched my heart and thrilled a tragic chord. But the disguised Hermes, in his prime and bloom of beauty, unlocked some deeper fountains of eternal longing in my soul.

Somewhat later, I found another line which impressed me powerfully and unsealed hidden wells of different emotion. It was in the Hippolytus of Euripides:[7]

$$\text{ἡ γλῶσσ' ὀμώμοχ', ἡ δὲ φρὴν ἀνώμοτος.}$$

['My tongue it was that swore, my heart remains unpledged.'] The sense of casuistry and criticism leapt into being at that touch. I foresaw, in that moment, how pros and cons of moral conduct would have to be debated, how every thesis seeks antithesis and resolution in the mental sphere.

These were but vague awakenings of my essential self. For the most part, I remained inactive, impotent, somnambulistic, touching life at the edged point, very slowly defining the silhouette of my eventual personality.

Walking to and fro between Clifton Hill and Wetherell Place, I used to tell myself long classic stories, and to improvise nonsense verses on interminable themes. The vehicle I used was chiefly blank verse or trochaics. I delighted my sense of rhythm with the current of murmured sound. The subject I chose for these peripatetic rhapsodies was the episode of young Apollo in his sojourn among mortals, as the hind of King Admetus.[8] What befell him there I expanded into nebulous epics of suffering and love and sorrow-dimmed deity involved with human sympathies. I declaimed the verses *sotto voce* as I walked. But now I can recall no incidents in the long poem, which, like a river, flowed daily, and might for ever have flowed on. The kernel of my inspiration was that radiant figure of the young Apollo, doomed to pass his time with shepherds, serving them, and loving them. A luminous haze of yearning emotion surrounded the god. His divine beauty penetrated my soul and marrow. I stretched out my arms to him in worship. It was I alone who knew him to be Olympian; and I loved him because he was a hind who went about the stables, milking cows. All this while, I felt that the god of my adoration drank life and love among the sheep-cotes of Admetus, clasped with that sturdy shepherd folk, more naturally than on the peaks of Parnassus, surrounded by the nine Muses.

As in the case of Adonis, I was in fact reading myself into this fable of Apollo; and quite unconsciously, as I perceive now, my daydreams of the sailors and myself among them had assumed an objective and idealized form. Indeed, this preoccupation with the legend of the discrowned Phoebus casts vivid light upon my dumbly growing nature. It is singular that a boy should have selected any legend so dim and subtle for treatment in the way I have described. But, what is far more curious, it seems that I was led by an unerring instinct to choose a myth foreshadowing my peculiar temperament and distant future. I have lived to realize that obscure vision of my boyhood. The sequel of this autobiography will show that I have brought my cultured self into the sheep-cotes, have lost it or disguised it there, and have found with hinds and peasants pleasure and profit which Parnassus and the Muses could not yield me.

I took no pleasure in athletic sports of any kind. To ramble over the downs and through the woods was enough for me. I hated the exertion, rivalry and noise of games. Want of muscular vigour and timidity combined to make me solitary. Yet I could run well and jump standing the height of my own shoulders. I liked riding also, but was neither a bold nor expert horseman. What I most enjoyed was leading a band of four boys, my cousins, in wild scrambles over Durdham Downs and on the rocks that overhang the Avon. We played at defending and attacking castles, which were located upon points of vantage in the gully near the sea walls and the steep descent of cliff beneath St Vincent's Rock. No harm came of these adventures, although we defied each other to deeds of daring in places where a fall would have been perilous exceedingly. Tired out and panting with this kind of exercise, I used to fling myself upon some grassy ledge among the lady's-bed-straw and blue harebells, watching the ships come floating down the Avon or the jackdaws chattering in their ivy-curtained crannies.

For everything which I took up, whether study or amusement, I showed a languid dilettante interest, pursuing it without energy or perseverance. Thus I played with an electrical machine and microscope, collected flowers and dried them, caught butterflies and pinned them upon corks; but I was far too dreamy and impatient to acquire any solid knowledge of natural science. I crammed my memory with the names of infusorial animal-cules, seaweeds, wild flowers – a great many of which still lie in the lumber room of my brain. I got to know the aspects of such things, and enjoyed the places where I went to find my specimens. But of animal or vegetable physiology I learned nothing. One reason was, perhaps, that I had no one to teach me and no attractive textbooks. The real secret of my inefficiency lay, however, in want of will and liking for accurate study. I was a weakling in mind and body, only half awake.

Early in the winter of one year I fell ill of chronic diarrhoea. To this I had been subject at intervals from my earliest infancy; and now I poisoned myself by drinking some cheap effervescing mixtures. My father sent me to stay with friends at Torquay. They lived in a little cottage with a front garden full of sweet-smelling violets, fuchsias, and shrub veronicas in bloom. I date a considerable mental progress from this visit. There I learned the beauty of the sea – low tides and pools upon the shore of Torbay. Dr Tetley used to drive me about the country in his carriage; and a diminutive naturalist was very kind to me. He took me with him out upon the reefs to gather seaweeds. I made a huge collection of such things. Even now I can remember the solemnity with which my friend exclaimed, when I hauled some spidery black weed out of a pool, 'I do believe that you have captured *Gigantea taedii!*' All through the remainder of the winter and spring, after I returned to Clifton, hampers sent by a Torbay fisherman used to arrive stuffed with the wrack of the shore. Charlotte, Sophie Girard and I divided the shiny mass into three equal portions, floated our booty in three separate tubs, and fished with eager fingers for *Delesseria sanguinea*, *Padina pavonia*, or a fine specimen of *Plocamium coccineum*.

It was on my return from this visit to Torquay that I first set eyes on Sophie Girard. She had arrived in my absence to be my sister's governess. They came back from a walk while I was standing in the hall between the dining-room and drawing-room doors. Her bright face rosy with the freshness of the open air, her laughing eyes and abundance of glossy yellow hair made a very pleasant impression on me. I felt at once that she would be a great addition to our home circle; and this in truth she was, far more than I could then imagine. She taught me German; the little I know of that language I owe entirely to her. She had a gift for teaching and was the first person from whom I consciously learned anything whatsoever.

About this time I began to walk in my sleep. It seemed to me that a corpse lay beside me in the bed. To escape from it, I got up and roamed about the house; but there were corpses standing in the doorways as I hurried through the long dark corridors. One night I wandered into the loft, and was walking straight into an open cistern which collected the rainwater from the roof, when I felt the hands of a great angel with outspread wings laid upon my shoulders. For a moment I woke up, and saw the moonlight glinting on the water through some cranny. Then I fell asleep again, and returned unconsciously to bed. Next morning my shins and thighs were badly bruised, and the footman who slept in the loft had a mysterious tale to tell about a white being who had moved about the furniture and boxes. It appeared that the stupid fellow had allowed himself actually to be shoved by me, bed and all, from the door through which I passed into the remote corner where the cistern lay. It was a pity that he had not had the courage to look up, or the impulse to take me into his bed! Something might then have happened which would not, I think, have been otherwise than good for my peculiar nature. After this occurrence my father had me tied into bed by one of my ankles every night. When the corpse came to expel me, I floundered on the floor until I woke and crept back shivering between the sheets. This spartan discipline effectually cured me of sleepwalking.

A recurrent dream of quite a new sort now visited my slumber. It was the beautiful face of a young man, with large blue eyes and waving yellow hair which emitted a halo of misty light. He bent down, gazing earnestly and tenderly, until his lips touched my forehead. Then I woke and beheld the aureole fading away into the darkness.

Much might be written about the self-revealing influence of dreams and the growth of the inner man in sleep. This vision of ideal beauty under the form of a male genius symbolized spontaneous yearnings deeply seated in my nature, and prepared me to receive many impressions of art and literature.

A photograph of the Praxitelean Cupid:

> ... that most perfect of antiques
> They call the Genius of the Vatican,
> Which seems too beauteous to endure itself
> In this mixed world —[9]

taught me to feel the secret of Greek sculpture. I used to pore for hours together over the divine loveliness, while my father read poetry aloud to us in the evenings. He did not quite approve, and asked me why I would not choose some other statue, a nymph or Hebe.[10] Following the impressions made by Shakespeare's Adonis and the Homeric Hermes, blending with the dream I have described and harmonizing with my myth Phoebus in the sheep-cote, this photograph strengthened the ideal I was gradually forming of adolescent beauty. It prepared me to receive the *Apoxyomenos*[11] and Marlowe's Leander, the young men of Plato and much else besides. I was certainly a rather singular boy. But I suppose, if other people wrote down the history of their mental growth with the same frankness and patience, I should not stand alone. What I really wanted at this period was some honest youth or comrade, a sailor or a groom or a labourer, who would have introduced me into the masculine existence for which I craved in a dim shrinking way. My equals repelled me. The Cretan customs of heroic *paiderastia* had much that was good in them. The love of a robust and manly lad, even if it had not been wholly pure, must have been beneficial to a boy like me. As it was, I lived into emotion through the brooding imagination; and nothing is more dangerous or unhealthy than this.

I was very fond of picturebooks and drew a great deal from Raphael, Flaxman and Retzsch.[12] Our house was well stocked with engravings, photographs, copies of Italian pictures and illustrated works upon Greek sculpture. Lasinio's Campo Santo of Pisa, Sir William Hamilton's vases, the Museo Borbonico and the two large folios issued by the Dilettante Society,[13] were among my chief favourites. But I carried my habitual indolence and irresolution into these studies. I had no artistic originality, and would not take the trouble to learn to draw well. We went to an art school just then established in Bristol. The hexagons, cubes, patterns they gave me to copy filled me with repugnance.

It is probable that the abundance of art material at home was not an unmixed good. It certainly familiarized me with a large variety of masterpieces and taught me to discriminate styles. But when I came to study critically, my mind was stocked with a mass of immature associations and imperfect memories. The sharp impression made on me by Botticelli, Tintoretto, Signorelli, Mantegna, Bellini, Luini and Gaudenzio Ferrari during my earliest Italian journeys may be ascribed to the fact that their works were almost entirely unrepresented in my father's library. We had a piece of Signorelli by the way. It was MacPherson's photograph of the Fulminati at Orvieto.[14] It had come, by accident, I think, and nobody knew what it represented or who had painted it. I used to brood over the forcible spasmodic vigour of this tragic group – feeling it quite different, far more penetrative, than anything in Raphael or Michelangelo. Yet Duppa's large studies from the Last Judgement in the Sistine[15] were well known to me. Toschi's admirable engravings of Correggio's frescoes at Parma,[16] which were sent to us at intervals by Colnaghi[17] as they appeared, taught me to appreciate the melodic suavity of design. I always connected them with the airs from Mozart's masses which my sisters used to play.

My sensibility to natural beauty meanwhile expanded. The immersion in the mystery of landscape, which I have already described, yielded to more conscious pleasure and a quicker sympathy. Yet I grew but slowly, and disengaged myself with difficulty from the narcotism of my mental faculties.

When the family was gone to bed, I spent hours alone in my bedroom at the north-east angle of the house, watching the clouds and mists of autumn drifting and recomposing their flying forms around the moon, high up above the city lamps.

I woke at dawn to see the sunrise flood the valley, touch the steeples of the town, shimmer upon the water where ships lay and glance along the stirless treetops of the garden, green and dewy depths below me.

After my recovery from the illness alluded to above, an amateur artist, Mr Stanhouse Vigor, painted the portrait of me in oils which now hangs in the dining room of Sidbury Manor.[18] I used to sit for this picture in the studio, which was a north room of a house in the Royal York Crescent. The likeness was reckoned very good. It shows me to have been a slight boy with abundance of brown hair, soft brown eyes, delicate hands and a dreamy expression.

I am sure that I was not personally vain. My aunt twitted me so unmercifully with my mealy complexion, snub nose, broad mouth and naked gums that I almost shrank from sight and felt grateful to people who did not treat me with merited contempt. 'Oh Johnnie, how mealy you are!' 'You look as yellow as a lemon this morning!' 'There you go with your mouth stretching from ear to ear!' These were some of her amenities, not unkindly meant, and only expressive of a real concern about my weakened constitution, which developed in me a morbid and unamiable self-consciousness. I had no power of reacting vigorously, and did not set my back up or assert myself. But I nourished a secret resentment and felt obstinate aloofness.

Physical weakness depressed me. I had more nervous vitality than muscular robustness, a small share of bodily pluck, and no combativeness. Naturally shy and timid through sensitiveness, though by no means morally a coward, I sought to be left alone, convinced that I could interest nobody.

But I developed some disagreeable qualities akin to vanity. My aunt often told us that our name was what she called 'so common', though the difference between Symonds and Sykes from a social point of view did not seem to me apparent. The sound of both became odious to my ears. I have never overcome my dislike of hearing my own name roared out by a flunkey, and have neglected many useful opportunities in life through this foolish pride.

She also reminded us, and I think rightly, that the ease in which we lived, the number of servants who waited on us, the carriages and horses, the large house and its profuse objects of interest and beauty, the dinner parties we gave and the crowds of distinguished people who visited our home, were all contingent on my father's professional success. Doctors, she added, have no rank in society. This was very true, and it argued something ungenerous in my nature that I did not accept it cheerfully.

I soon perceived that my father's character, ability and many-sided culture separated him from the ordinary run of medical men. He was sought after on his own rare merits by men and women of birth, position, political and social importance. The friend of John Sterling, Frederick Maurice, Myers of Keswick, Lord Lansdowne, Hallam, Jowett, Lord Monteagle, Principal Forbes, Lord Aberdare, Lady Dufferin, Dean Eliot, Sir Edward Strachey, Dr Carpenter, Dr Prichard, Sir Montagu McMurdo[19] and scores of others I could mention, was an exceptional physician; and his only son enjoyed exceptional advantages in the society of such people.

This did not, however, compensate to my own cross-grained consciousness for the patent facts of my personal drawbacks. I was a physically insignificant boy, with an ill-sounding name and nothing to rely on in the circumstances of my family. Instead of expanding in the social environment around me, I felt myself at a disadvantage, and early gained the notion that I must work for my own place in the world – in fact that I should have no place till I had made one

John Addington Symonds in 1864,
soon after his marriage

Catherine North

Right: John Addington Symonds
with his daughter Margaret,
Clifton, 1872

Below: Janet Symonds

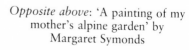

Opposite above: 'A painting of my
mother's alpine garden' by
Margaret Symonds

Opposite below: Boys with sculpture – a
photograph from an album compiled by
Margaret Symonds in 1894

Catherine Symonds – a late photograph by I. Broadbent

for myself. The result was that, instead of being flattered, I almost resented the attentions paid me as my father's son, and was too stupid to perceive how honourable as well as valuable they might be if I received them with a modest frankness. I regarded them as acts of charitable condescension. Thus I passed into an attitude of haughty shyness, which had nothing respectable in it except a sort of self-reliant, world-defiant pride, a resolution to effectuate myself and to win what I wanted by my exertions.

The inborn repugnance to sordid things, which I have already described as one of my main characteristics, now expressed itself in a morbid sense of my physical ugliness, common patronymic, undistinguished status and mental ineffectiveness. I did not envy the possessors of beauty, strength, birth, rank or genius. But I vowed to raise myself, somehow or other, to eminence of some sort. How this was to be done, when there were so many difficulties in the way, I did not see. Without exactly despairing, I felt permanently discouraged.

My ambition took no vulgar form. I felt no desire for wealth, no mere wish to cut a figure in society. But I thirsted with intolerable thirst for eminence, for recognition as a personality. At the same time I had no self-confidence, no belief in my intellectual powers. I was only buoyed up by an undefined instinct that there was stuff in me. Meanwhile, all I could do was to bide my time, and see how things would go, possessing my soul in silence and wrapping a cloak of reserve about my internal hopes and aims.

The state which I have just described began to define itself during the first period of boyhood. But it grew and strengthened with the following years. It was highly characteristic of my temperament that, powerfully as I felt these cravings, they did not take a very distinct form and did not stimulate me to any marked activity.

The depressing conviction of my own unattractiveness and inefficiency saved me perhaps from some evil. If I had been a little vainer, I might have become presumptuous or vulgarly ambitious. I might perhaps too have fallen into moral difficulties; for I was ready to love and be loved. As it was, this conviction kept me aloof from companions and I wonder whether this seclusion from vice, involving a seclusion from sympathy, was salutary.

I have painted myself at this period in an unamiable light, but truthfully I think. And I must proceed with the not very flattering analysis.

The result of my habitual reserve was that I now dissembled my deepest feelings, and only revealed those sentiments which I knew would pass muster. Without meaning to do so, I came to act a part, and no one knew what was going on inside me. A boy wants a mother at such periods of uneasy fermentation. I was ready enough in writing to communicate such portions of my experience as I chose to exhibit – impenetrably reserved in the depth of myself, rhetorically candid on the surface. My father, not unnaturally, misunderstood this complication. He afterwards told me that he sent me with undoubting confidence to Harrow, because he had no conception that I was either emotional or passionate. The unconscious dissimulation I habitually practised blinded him to the truth. Feeling that I was growing and must grow in solitude to an end I could not foresee, which no one could help me to shape, and which I was myself impotent to determine, I allowed an outer self of commonplace cheerfulness and easy-going pliability to settle like a crust upon my inner and real character.

Nothing is more difficult than to analyse such psychological conditions without attributing too much deliberation and consciousness to what was mainly a process of spontaneous development. Congenital qualities and external circumstance acted together to determine a mental duality – or shall I call it duplicity – of which I became aware when it had taken hold upon my nature.

On my twelfth birthday I went up as usual to kiss my father. He said gravely: 'Shake hands; you are grown too old for kissing.' I felt rather ashamed of having offered what my twelfth birthday rendered unseemly, and took a step upon the path toward isolation. But there was something virginal and savage in me which accepted the remark with approval. Henceforth I shrank from the exposure of emotion, except upon paper, in letters, and in studied language.

I have drawn a somewhat disagreeable picture of my early boyhood. It is very probable that I am to some extent importing into this period qualities which were really developed by my intense hatred for life at Harrow.

Still it must not be imagined that I was a moody discontented miserable boy. I had high spirits enough, and knew how to make myself agreeable in congenial society. I was talkative, easily interested, ready to find amusement in all sorts of petty things – so long as these were not school games and involved no sort of physical competition. The inner growth was so much more important to myself, and still remains so, that I have failed to communicate a proper notion of the whole. Indeed, no one can get outside himself and see what he appears. He only knows himself inside, and knows that aspect only in part.

One thing is certain. I acquired a passionate affection for my home and Clifton, which included my family – although I think I cared for them chiefly as forming parts of the delightful environment.

Chapter Four

Second period of boyhood, 1854–8, Harrow on the Hill

When I left home for Harrow in the spring of 1854 – it was the month of May – I had acquired a somewhat curious personality. Weakness and strength, stoicism and sensibility, frigidity and tenderness, ignorance of the world and stubborn resistance to external influences, were strangely blent in my raw nature. The main thing which maintained me was a sense of self, imperious, antagonistic, unmalleable. But what that self was, and why it kept aloof, I did not know.

My aunt and my sister Edith left me at the King's Head. They drove back to London. I walked down alone to my tutor's house. This was the house of the Rev. Robert Knight, son of my Clifton tutor and curate to the vicar of Harrow. He took, so far as I remember, three boys as lodgers; a son of Abel Smith the banker, a young Wingfield and myself. We slept in one room.

I felt that my heart would break as I scrunched the muddy gravel, beneath the boughs of budding trees, down to this house. But I said to my heart, I have to be made a man here. This was the one thought uppermost.

Sometimes, when I was alone in bed, I cried – thinking of Clifton. I remember one night when I felt sure that I had been at home, and stood in twilight at the end of the bedroom corridor, looking through elm branches into the grey south-western sky. I did not doubt that my spirit could somnambulistically travel from the place I hated to the place I loved.

But this made no impression on my daily conduct. I accepted life at Harrow as a discipline to be gone through. It was not what I wanted. But being prescribed, it had its utility. Thus from the commencement of my schooling I assumed an attitude of resistance and abeyance. Unutterably stupid this, perhaps. Yet it could not have been otherwise. Such was my nature.

I had never been thrown so entirely on my own resources before. The situation accentuated that double existence which I have described, and which was becoming habitual. Internally, as a creature of dreams, of self-concentrated wilfulness, of moral force sustained by obstinate but undeveloped individuality, I was in advance of my new comrades. Externally, compared with them, I was a baby – destitute of experience, incapable of asserting myself, physically feeble, timid, shrinking from contact.

The imperious, unmalleable, uncompromising egotism, which dwelt unformed within me, kept me up. I did not realize whither I was going. I felt that my course, though it collided with that of my schoolfellows, was bound to be different from theirs. To stand aloof, to preserve the inner self inviolate, to await its evolution, was my dominant instinct. I cannot imagine a more helpless and more stiff-necked, and more unloveable boy than I was.

To make the situation worse, I had no escapement from self, no really beautiful enlargement of nature at Harrow. I shrank from games of every sort, being constitutionally unfit for violent exercise and disliking competition. I had a perfect horror of cricket, football, raquets and I even disliked fencing. My muscular build was slight, I could not throw a ball or a stone like other boys. And, oddly enough, I could not learn to whistle like them. And yet I was by no means effeminate. My father, judging rightly or wrongly of my physical capacity, took measures for having me excused for playing either cricket or football. I was placed too high in the school for fagging. In this way I did not come into salutary contact with my schoolfellows. It would assuredly have been far better for me had I been cast more freely upon their society. My dislike for games has more to do with a dreamy and self-involved temperament than with absolute physical weakness. I could jump standing to a height just below my own chin, and could run with the swiftest. Fagging again would have brought me into practical relations with the elder boys, and have rubbed off some of my fastidious reserve.

Intellectually, in like manner, I did not prosper. I got a remove from one form into the next above it every term, and always at the head of the new detachent. But none of my form masters, who were Cober Adams, Rendall, Ben Drury, Harris and C. J. Vaughan, took hold upon my mind or woke me up. I was a very imperfect scholar when I left Harrow in 1858; and though I competed for the prizes – Latin and Greek verse; English essay and poem – I invariably failed. Such mark as I made was due to general ability and punctuality in work.

The spring for which my whole nature craved did not come for me at Harrow. My tutor Rendall – to whose house, called Monkey's, I went at the end of my first year – used to write in his reports that I was 'deficient of vigour both of body and mind'. I do not think he was mistaken. Want of physical and cerebral energy showed itself in a series of depressing ailments. I slept uneasily and dreamed painfully. Repulsive weaknesses – boils, styes in the eyes, tedious colds which lasted the whole winter – lowered my stamina and painfully augmented my sense of personal squalor. I grew continually more and more shy, lost my power of utterance, and cast a miserable figure in form. I contracted the habit of stammering. This became so serious that Vaughan put me off having to read and construe Greek. The monitors had to recite poems on Speech Day which were previously rehearsed before the school. On one occasion I chose Raleigh's 'Lie' for my piece. At the rehearsal I got through the first stanza, well or ill. Then my mind became a blank; and after a couple of minutes' deadly silence, I had to sit down discomfited.

My external self, in these many ways, was being perpetually snubbed and crushed and mortified. Yet the inner self hardened after a dumb blind fashion. I kept repeating, Wait, Wait! I will, I shall, I must! What I was to wait for, what I was destined to become, I did not ask. But I never really doubted my capacity to become something. In a vague way, I compared myself to the ugly duckling of Andersen's tale.

Life at Harrow was not only uncongenial to my tastes and temperament. It was clearly unwholesome. Living little in the open air, poring stupidly and mechanically over books, shut up for hours in badly ventilated schoolrooms or my own close study, I dwindled physically. A liberal use of nerve tonics, quinine and strychnine, prescribed by my father, may have been a palliative; but these drugs did not reach the root of the evil and they developed other evils which I afterward discovered.

It is no wonder that I came to be regarded as an uncomradely unclubbable boy by my companions. Yet I won their moral respect. The following little incident will show what I mean. One day the mathematical master accused me before the form of cribbing or copying from my neighbour's papers. I simply declared that I had not cribbed. He punished me with 500 lines. I accepted the punishment in silence. Thereupon the other boys cried loudly, 'Shame! Symonds,' they shouted, 'cannot crib'; and those who were sitting near me said I was a fool to bear it.

In like manner, though I was neither intellectually brilliant nor athletic, I acquired a considerable influence in my house, of which I was the head for nearly two years. I maintained discipline, and on one occasion I remember caning two big hulking fellows in the Shells[1] for bullying. When I left Harrow the boys at Monkey's subscribed to present me with a testimonial. It was Muir's [sic] history of Greek literature,[2] handsomely bound, which my successor Currey handed to me with a speech of kindly congratulation.

Rendall, I think, made a great mistake in not consulting me with regard to the management of the house. According to the Rugby system, which Vaughan applied with certain modifications at Harrow, important duties resolved upon the sixth form, and monitors were theoretically held responsible for the behaviour of their juniors. Yet I cannot remember any act of personal friendliness or sympathy on Rendall's part towards myself. He never asked me to breakfast or to walk with him, never invited me to talk with him in the evenings, never consulted me about the conduct of the lower boys or explained his own wishes with regard to discipline. I dare say he did not feel the want of my assistance for he was very well served by his house tutor, John Smith. But he missed the opportunity of discharging his duties toward the ostensible head of his house with kindness, and through me of making his authority felt.

These remarks will serve as prelude to an incident which illustrates my isolation and at the same time serves to define the specific moral fibre of my character. The sixth form were competing for a scholarship given by the headmaster. Henry Yates Thompson[3] was head of the school. Alfred Pretor[4] and I sat as junior members on the bench of monitors. As luck would have it, I came out far away first in the examinations, and Pretor second. We both of us won this distinction rather by our regularity in all-round work than by brilliant quality in any one department. Thompson was naturally mortified. But instead of stomaching the disappointment, he lost his temper. Rushing from the sixth-form room, after the lists had been read out, he seized Pretor and myself by the collar of our coats and half hurled, half kicked us down the steep steps which lead from Great School to the gravel yard below. This happened before the eyes of a whole crowd of boys, senior and junior. The insult was brutal, and it seemed to me unpardonable. That the head of the school should thus maltreat two monitors merely because they had beaten him fairly in an examination was bad enough. But that he should have done so trusting to their physical inferiority and unpopularity was worse. What became of the belauded monitorial system, how could we maintain our supposed authority, how could we support respect due to our office, if we sat down meekly after this outrage? Picking myself out of the mud, I said to Pretor, 'We shall go at once to Vaughan, and ask for redress.' Pretor refused to do so. I exerted my superior moral force and dragged him to the School-house door. We were shown, with battered top hats and draggled swallow-tails – such was then the Harrow costume – into Vaughan's study. I told him what had happened, said that I relied upon his sense of justice, and added that unless I obtained an ample apology from Thompson, my position at Harrow would become intolerable; I should request my father to withdraw me from the school, and I knew that he would place the cause of my removal before the public. Vaughan of course acceded to my demand. That afternoon Thompson read out an apology before the whole sixth. That happened in November 1857.

It required a certain amount of moral courage to act so promptly as I did in this affair. Boys dislike nothing more than what they call sneaking. But I saw that in the present case there was no question of being called a sneak. The only other alternative open to me would have been to summon the monitors and seek redress from them. Unfortunately, I could not put the necessary machinery into motion; and if I had been able to call an assembly of my peers, the body of that time was not likely to have done me justice. I was forced therefore either to swallow the humiliation in silence or to invoke the only power superior to the head of the school. The former course was not to be thought of for a moment. The latter had this propriety, that Thompson's insult was a wholly unprecedented violation of the principle on which school discipline rested. Nobody but the headmaster was fit to deal with it. I might indeed have gone first to Rendall and asked his advice. This I should probably have done, if he had made a friend of me. That was, however, not the case. And after all, to put the matter into Rendall's hands would have been a half-measure.

As a matter of fact, the soundness of my reasoning obtained immediate recognition. Instead of losing, I gained respect; and I must add that Thompson digested the pill he had to swallow, like a man. On leaving Harrow he presented me with a book – the *Ballad of Lenore* illustrated by Maclise.

A sign that Harrow did not suit me any way was the sentiment approaching to aversion which I felt for the flat clay soil and pasture landscape of the country round it. During long summer days, the slumbrous monotony of grasslands and hedgerows, buzzing flies and sultry heat oppressed me. I could not react against the genius of the place, and kept contrasting it with Clifton's rocks and woods and downy turf.

Sordid details, inseparable from a boy's school life, in a cheaply built modern house, revolted my taste: the bare and dirty rough-cast corridors, the ill-drained latrines, the stuffy studies with wired windows, the cheerless refectory. But these things, I reflected, were only part of life's open road, along which one had to trudge for one's affairs – not worse, not more significant to the in-dwelling soul of man, than the *via dolorosa* from Berkeley Square to Buckingham Villas had been.

The uncongeniality of Harrow life and landscape made my holidays at Clifton very charming by contrast. There were long walks and talks with Charlotte and Sophie Girard, rides on the downs and toward the Bristol Channel, drives with my father through the Somersetshire lanes, discussions about poems and pictures, ramblings in the city streets, prowlings around the shelves of musty bookshops, musings in the Cathedral of St Mary Redclyffe, dreamy saunterings in the alleys of our garden, lonely hours upon the house-top with that wide and varied scene outspread beneath me, dinner parties and the company of cultured men and women.

All this, as I have said, contrasted only too sweetly with Harrow and the realities of school existence. In justice to myself, I think I ought to say that, although I always returned to Harrow unwillingly, I did so with the sense that Clifton was a Capua, and Harrow the camp,[5] where I had to brace myself to discipline.

Meanwhile, I formed the habit of idealizing Clifton with results which the history of my aftergrowth will make apparent. More and more it became for me the haunt of powerful emotions, the stage on which my inner self would have to play its part.

It would be absurd to pretend that I formed no friendships at Harrow. In order to complete the picture of my life there, I must devote some paragraphs to sketching them.

The Rev. John Smith takes the first place. To his generous sympathy, manly and wise, at a period when I sorely needed sympathetic handling, I ascribe the only pure good of my Harrow training. Doubtless, not I alone, but hundreds of boys who came within the influence of that true Christian gentleman, whether they are now alive or sleeping in their graves upon all quarters of the habitable globe, would deliver the same testimony. It is possible, however, that I enjoyed a double portion of his kindly interest; for he had recently settled at Harrow, as form master and house tutor to Monkey, at the time when I was cast adrift upon school life. He took notice of me, and must have felt my special needs. Without making any demonstrations of friendship, he so arranged that a peculiarly delightful comradeship should spring up between us. We took long walks together through the fields. It was our custom on these walks to repeat alternate passages from Shelley, Tennyson and Keats, which we had previously learned by heart. In this way I absorbed a stupendous amount of good English verse. The house where his dear old mother dwelt at Pinner was frequently the goal of our excursions. Here we rested, after spouting 'The Skylark' or 'The Palace of Art', 'The Two Voices' and the 'Ode to a Nightingale', during an early-morning or late-evening passage over dewy fields and high-built stiles. There was always a cold veal-and-ham pie to be eaten with voracious appetite, strawberry jam to follow, and an excellent brew of tea with thick country cream. Gradually I learned much about the history of this pure-hearted friend – his father's death by suicide – his own dread of hereditary madness – the deep humility of his strong patient nature – the calm and mellow touch of his religious philosophy upon feverish things of human life.

Gustavus Bosanquet[6] comes next. He joined the school in the same term as I did; and though I left him behind in our progress through the forms, we remained firm friends until the last. His parents, or rather his mother, who was a Miss Bevan, had trained him in narrow Evangelical principles. These did not sit quite easily upon the boy. His exuberant affectionateness, indomitable humour and generous devotion to a few friends raised him in the moral sphere high above the ranks of mere intelligence. Down to this day, I owe him a deep debt of gratitude for the love he gave me, for the admiration which he felt for me, for the loyalty with which he sustained me in my hours of self-abasement, and for the homely cheerfulness of his familiar conversation. We chummed together, cooked sausages together, played childish pranks and called each other by ridiculous nicknames, living a little life of comradeship secluded from the daily round of lessons and school business. Gustavus had his feet more firmly fixed upon the common ground of experience than I had. He saw the comic side of things, and this was very helpful to me. With him I was able to laugh and joke about incidents which angered and depressed my solitary nature. In return I gave him something from my ideality. Our fraternal love was very precious during my school life; and if I were asked who was my bosom friend at Harrow, I should reply, 'Gustavus Bosanquet.'

Randall Vickers was a boy at Monkey's with whom Bosanquet and I had much to do. He tickled Bosanquet's sense of humour by his devout moon-stricken manners. Bosanquet was round and sturdy, with a large pale face and a great nose which he flapped on both sides of his ample cheeks. I christened him the Buzzard because of his awkward unwieldy flopping flight. He called me Monny, an affectionate diminutive of Simonides,[7] my patronymic in the isles of ancient Hellas – not without burlesque satire on my lofty aspirations. Vickers, the lean lanky stripling, sallow-complexioned, black-haired, with sleek demure veiled eyes and cat-like movements, formed a contrast to us both. He had no humour, no intelligence, no struggles, no moral or mental energy of any kind. A living mask of humanity I should say, as I now look back upon him. But he possessed what neither Bosanquet nor I could boast of – the insect-like devotion to a creed. This was Ritualism, then in its green infancy. Half-laughing at Vickers and ourselves, we followed him to nones and complines,[9] donned surplices and tossed censers, arrayed altars in our studies, spent spare cash on bits of execrable painted glass to dull our dingy windows, and illuminated crucifixes with gold dust and vermilion.

Three of my comrades in the sixth form must be placed upon this list of friends, though they stood distinctly apart from the others. One of these was Alfred Pretor, a fair scholar, but a vain light-headed and corrupt lad, without intellectual or moral foundation. As he was superficially bright and attractive, I got into the way of passing a good deal of my time with him. We were drawn together by the common interest of schoolwork. Charles Dalrymple of New-hailes, a well-born well-connected Scotchman, Scotch to the backbone, was another. Cat-like and precise, delicate in his tastes, thin in mental quality, but gifted with a certain fastidious distinction, he chimed in with some of my supposed qualities and occupied a fair amount of leisure. Robert Jamieson, a raw youth from Glasgow, with the face of a convict but gifted with a powerful personality – strong in the brain, indolent in the will, wanting in real intelligence of life, essentially perverse and cross-grained – was the third of these friends. Juxtaposition brought us four together – so dissimilar in our temperaments, destined to such different lines in life, fated so soon to be divided by a cruel stroke of fortune. Pretor became a tutor at Cambridge, Dalrymple a leading Scotch Member of Parliament, Jamieson I know not what, I an exile at Davos.

In the company of these five boys – Bosanquet, Vickers, Pretor, Dalrymple, Jamieson – I was confirmed. Confirmation ought, if it means anything, to exercise a decisive influence over the religious life of the individual – to mark a new epoch in his spiritual progress. To some extent it did so with me. The preparation for the sacrament worked like a plough-share on the sub-soil of my piety. It turned up nothing valuable, but it stimulated my aesthetical and emotional ardour. I now inclined to the farcical ritualism of Vickers, handling pseudo-sacred vessels in a nightgown surplice before a pseudo-altar. I laid myself open to enthusiasms of the shrine and sanctuary, which afterwards coalesced with a wholly human passion for a chorister. In a dim way I felt God more. But I did not learn to fling the arms of soul in faith upon the cross of Christ. That was not in me. And it would be unfair to expect from any sacrament of the Church that it should work a miracle on catachumens.

At this period of my misused boyhood, I dreamed a great deal of my time away and wrote a vast amount of idiotic verses. During the night-time I was visited by terrible and splendid visions, far superior to my poetry. In the long slow evolution of my self, it appears that the state of dreamful sub-conscious energy was always superior to the state of active intelligent volition. In a sense different from Charles Lamb's, I was a dream child, incapable of emerging into actuality, containing potential germs of personality which it required decades to develop.

In this respect I was probably by no means singular. The situation might be summed up in one sentence: I was a slow-growing lad.

The memory of my experience at Harrow – of my non-emergence, of my intense hidden life, of my inferiority in achievement to people like Thompson, Jamieson, Pretor, and others who could easily be mentioned – not to speak of the superb athletic beings round me, whose lives were completely joyous to themselves and satisfying to aesthetic contemplation – has made me infinitely tender toward young men in whom I recognized the same qualities of tardy laborious growth.

I have left for a separate chapter the consideration of a matter deeply important to my inner self at Harrow.

Chapter Five

Painful circumstances connected with the last year of my life at Harrow

One thing at Harrow very soon arrested my attention. It was the moral state of the school. Every boy of good looks had a female name, and was recognized either as a public prostitute or as some bigger fellow's 'bitch'. Bitch was the word in common usage to indicate a boy who yielded his person to a lover. The talk in the dormitories and the studies was incredibly obscene. Here and there one could not avoid seeing acts of onanism, mutual masturbation, the sports of naked boys in bed together. There was no refinement, no sentiment, no passion; nothing but animal lust in these occurrences. They filled me with disgust and loathing. My school-fellows realized what I had read in Swift about the Yahoos.

I particularly disliked two boys: a clever Irish lad called W. J. Currey and a brutal clown called Clayton. Of Clayton I need speak no more. He was too stupid and perverse and clumsy to deserve description. Currey, on the other hand, was a better scholar than myself, and possessed a variety of facile talents. He spent much of his time on music and drawing, played games, and loafed. Yet though he never seemed to work, he always took a good place in his form. Unfortunately he was dirty in his dress and person, filthy in his talk, and shamelessly priapic in his conduct. We went through the school side by side. At the end of our time together, I discovered really fine intellectual and emotional qualities beneath his Satyric exterior. I imagine that he may have permanently injured his constitution by his youthful vagaries; for Currey's career in afterlife has not been as distinguished as might have been expected.

A third boy, named Barber, annoyed and amused me. He was like a good-natured longimanous ape, gibbering on his perch and playing ostentatiously with a prodigiously developed phallus. A fourth, Cookson, was a red-faced strumpet, with flabby cheeks and sensual mouth – the *notissima fossa*[1] [the most infamous trench] of our house.

I have seen nothing more repulsive in my life – except once at the Alhambra in Leicester Square, when I saw a jealous man tear the earrings out of the ruptured lobes of a prostitute's ears, and all the men in the saloon rose raging at him for his brutality – I have seen nothing more disgusting in my life, I say, than the inhuman manner in which this poor creature Cookson came afterwards to be treated by his former lovers. What he did to deserve his punishment I never heard, not being initiated into their mysteries. But, after a certain period – after they had rolled upon the floor with him and had exposed his person in public – they took to trampling on him. Whenever he appeared in that mean dining room, about those dirty passages, upon the sordid court through which we entered from the road into our barracks, Currey and Clayton and Barber and the rest of the brood squirted saliva and what they called gobs upon their bitch, cuffed and kicked him at their mercy, shied books at him, and drove him with obscene curses whimpering to his den.

These four were all at Rendall's. A fifth fellow, E. Dering, in Steele's house, both fascinated and repelled me. He resembled a handsome Greek brigand in face. I remember noticing a likeness to his features in the photograph of one of the decapitated Marathon cut-throats. His body was powerful, muscular, lissom as a tiger. The fierce and cruel lust of this magnificent animal excited my imagination. Dering used to come into our house after a plump fair-haired boy, called Ainslie, whom we dubbed Bum Bathsheba because of his opulent posterior parts.

So much had to be said in general about the moral atmosphere into which I was plunged at the age of thirteen. It will appear in the sequel that Harrow exercised a powerful influence over certain phases of my development. But I must not omit to mention that, while I was at school, I remained free in fact and act from this contamination. During my first half year the 'beasts', as they were playfully called, tried to seduce me. But it was soon decided that I was 'not game'.

The distinction in my character between an inner and real self and an outer and artificial self, to which I have already alluded, emphasized itself during this period. So separate were the two selves, so deep was my dipsychia,[2] that my most intimate friends there, of whom I shall soon speak, have each and all emphatically told me that they thought I had passed through school without being affected by, almost without being aware of, its peculiar vices. And yet those vices furnished a perpetual subject for contemplation and casuistical reflection to my inner self.

The earliest phase of my sexual consciousness was here objectified before my eyes; and I detested in practice what had once attracted me in fancy. Personally, I thought that I had transcended crude sensuality through the aesthetic idealization of erotic instincts. I did not know how fallacious that method of expelling nature is. The animalisms of boyish lust sickened me by their brutality, offended my taste by their vulgarity. I imagined them to be a phase of immature development, from which my comrades would emerge when they grew to manhood. Nevertheless they steeped my imagination in filth. I was only saved from cynicism by the gradual unfolding in myself of an ideal passion which corresponded to Platonic love. This ideal was not derived from Greek literature; for I had not yet read the works of Plato and Theocritus. It sprang up spontaneously, proving that my thought was lodged in ancient Hellas.

While my school-fellows, therefore, regarded me as an insensitive student, immersed in what they called 'swatting' and incapable of active good or evil, I was theorizing, testing and sublimating the appetites which they unthinkingly indulged.

An incident occurred which made a deep impression on my mind. Dering sent a note in school time to a handsome lad, O'Brien, who went by the name of Leila. It informed him that Dering had a good bed ready, and asked him to come there in the interval between third and fourth school – that is from 4 to 5 p.m. This note fell into the hands of the form master, who gave it up to Vaughan. The whole school was summoned to the Speech Room. Here Vaughan met us alone, without any of the other masters. He read the letter aloud, strongly condemned the use of female names for boys, and pronounced sentence on the culprits. Dering was to be 'switched' and O'Brien had lines set him – how many I do not recollect.

The conclusion which I drew from this very inadequate form of punishment was that our masters did not realize what the matter meant, and how widespread was the evil in the school. In my own mind I felt sure that these vices were pernicious to our society; and

I regarded them as sins which ought to have been harshly dealt with. Accordingly this episode added to my mental and moral confusion.

In the month of January 1858 Alfred Pretor wrote me a note in which he informed me that Vaughan had begun a love affair with him. I soon found that the boy was not lying, because he showed me a series of passionate letters written to him by our headmaster.

When I recovered from the first astonishment into which Pretor's extraordinary revelation plunged me, I submitted the fact to casuistical analysis. It proved convincingly that I was wrong in imagining that this species of vice formed only a phase of boyish immaturity. I was disgusted to find it in a man holding the highest position of responsibility, consecrated by the Church, entrusted with the welfare of six hundred youths – a man who had recently prepared me for confirmation, from whose hands, kneeling by the side of Alfred Pretor, I received the sacrament, and whom I had been accustomed to regard as the pattern of my conduct. Disgust, however, was mitigated by a dumb persistent sympathy. My own inclinations, the form which my erotic idealism had assumed, prevented me from utterly condemning Vaughan. I did indeed condemn Vaughan's taste; for I regarded Pretor as a physically and emotionally inferior being. But the love drama which I now watched daily, perusing the enthusiastic letters submitted to my curiosity by Pretor's vanity, roused a keen inquisitive interest in my mind. A sense of humour supervened – 'What a topsy-turvy world is this that I am living in!' After all, I think that indignation against our headmaster prevailed. I knew what serious harm the school was suffering from these customs, so ill-adjusted to the spirit of the times we lived in. I felt acutely the moral perplexities which the observation of them bred in me. And here was he, not merely trifling with them, as in the case of Dering and O'Brien, but recklessly indulging his own forbidden impulse.

Boys are singular beings in this that they easily accept a situation, however abnormal it may be. I vaguely wondered whether I ought not to tell my father. But the knowledge had already begun to sophisticate my moral sense. I felt also bound to respect the seal of secrecy. At any rate I ought first to use my influence with Pretor. This I did, and begged him to break off the connection. But I soon found it impossible to persuade him. Then I wondered whether I should confront Vaughan, and ask him bluntly what the whole thing meant. I used to take essays and verses at intervals to Vaughan in the study, which was the scene of his clandestine pleasures. It was a fairly sized square room, dark, on the ground floor, looking upon the street. On those occasions my young brains underwent an indescribable fermentation. I remember once that, while we sat together reading Greek iambics, he began softly to stroke my right leg from the knee to the thigh. This insignificant caress, of which I should have thought nothing two months earlier, and which probably meant nothing, seemed then disagreeably suggestive. I never liked the man; he did not possess the intellectual qualities I admired. Now I began positively to dislike him.

Nothing could have been worse for a boy of my temperament than this unhealthy state of things. It poisoned and paralysed my moral nature, confused my judgement, perplexed my thoughts about religion. Had it not been for a strong physical repulsion, I should certainly have taken to bad courses. As it was, I began to coquette with vice. I fell in love with a handsome powerful boy called Huysche, and I remember stealing his hymnbook from his seat in chapel; but I never spoke to him. I also fell in love with Eliot Yorke, who used to come to my room; but I kept at a respectful distance from him. There must have happened some change in my manner or appearance; for a very depraved lad, whom I had known for three years, on one occasion finding me alone in my room, suddenly dared to throw his arms round me, kissed me, and thrust his hand into my trousers. At that moment I nearly gave way to sensuality. I was narcotized by the fellow's contact and the forecast of coming pleasure. But in this, as in all other cases, the inclination for vulgar lust was wanting. That saved me from self-abasement and traffic with the unclean thing.

A fatigued cynicism took possession of me. My health, which had never been good, suffered. I neglected my work. At the same time, my self-consciousness became enormously developed. I felt a terrible new sense of power. For the first time I seemed able to survey myself and the world, to grasp the facts of human nature from a point of view outside my inner and outer egotism. It is certain that, though I grew unhealthily and perversely during this period, I grew fast and to some purpose. I acquired then a certain disengagement from things which are not essential, a certain habit of doubting appearances and disdaining trifles. This attitude of mind has, I believe, been useful to me. But the price paid in disillusionment and moral befoulment outweighed the gain of mental grit.

The progress of a lad of seventeen has to be reckoned not by years but by months.

We were reading Plato's *Apology* in the sixth form. I bought Cary's crib,[3] and took it with me to London on an *exeat*[4] in March. My hostess, a Mrs Bain, who lived in Regent's Park, treated me to a comedy one evening at the Haymarket. I forget what the play was – except that there was a funny character in it, who set the house in a roar by his enunciation of this sentence: 'Smythers please, not Smithers; Smithers is a different party, and moves in quite a different sphere.' When we returned from the play, I went to bed and began to read my Cary's Plato. It so happened that I stumbled on the *Phaedrus*. I read on and on, till I reached the end. Then I began the *Symposium*; and the sun was shining on the shrubs outside the ground-floor room in which I slept, before I shut the book up.

I have related these insignificant details because that night was one of the most important nights of my life; and when anything of great gravity has happened to me, I have always retained a firm recollection of trifling facts which formed its context.

Here in the *Phaedrus* and the *Symposium* – in the myth of the Soul and the speeches of Pausanias Agathon and Diotima – I discovered the true *liber amoris* at last, the revelation I had been waiting for, the consecration of a long-cherished idealism. It was just as though the voice of my own soul spoke to me through Plato, as though in some antenatal experience I had lived the life of philosophical Greek lover.

Harrow vanished into unreality. I had touched solid ground. I had obtained the sanction of the love which had been ruling me from childhood. Here was the poetry, the philosophy of my own enthusiasm for male beauty, expressed with all the magic of unrivalled style. And, what was more, I now became aware that the Greek race – the actual historical Greeks of antiquity – treated this love seriously, invested it with moral charm, endowed it with sublimity.

For the first time I saw the possibility of resolving in a practical harmony the discords of my instincts. I perceived that masculine love had its virtue as well as its vice, and stood in this respect upon the same ground as normal sexual appetite. I understood, or thought I understood, the relation which those dreams of childhood and the brutalities of vulgar lust at Harrow bore to my higher aspiration after noble passion.

The study of Plato proved decisive for my future. Coming at the moment when it did, it delivered me to a large extent from the torpid cynicism caused by the Vaughan episode. At the same time it confirmed my congenital inclination toward persons of the male sex, and filled my head with an impossible dream, which controlled my thoughts for many years.

What I have just written will perhaps surprise those who may happen to read these pages after I am dead. My friend Professor Jowett, with whom I revised his translation of the *Symposium* at Davos in 1888, wrote to me not long ago expressing his astonishment at my regarding the study of Plato as dangerous to certain characters in youth. The following copy of a letter I addressed to him in reply will not inappropriately close this chapter.

<u>PRIVATE</u>

Am Hof,
Davos Platz,
Switzerland.
1 February 1889

My dear Master – I am glad to hear from the last letter you wrote me that you have abandoned the idea of an essay on Greek love. Little good could come of such a treatise in your book.

It surprises me to find you, with your knowledge of Greek history, speaking of this in Plato as 'mainly a figure of speech'. – It surprises me as much as I seem to surprise you when I repeat that the study of Plato is injurious to a certain number of predisposed young men.

Many forms of passion between males are matters of fact in English schools, colleges, cities, rural districts. Such passion is innate in some persons no less than the ordinary sexual appetite is innate in the majority. With the nobler of such predetermined temperaments the passion seeks a spiritual or ideal transfiguration. When, therefore, individuals of the indicated species come into contact with the reveries of Plato (clothed in graceful diction, immersed in the peculiar emotion, presented with considerable dramatic force, gilt with a mystical philosophy, throbbing with the realism of actual Greek life) the effect upon them has the force of a revelation. They discover that what they had been blindly groping after was once an admitted possibility – not in a mean hole or corner – but that the race whose literature forms the basis of their higher culture lived in that way, aspired in that way. For such students of Plato there is no question of 'figures of speech', but of concrete facts, facts in the social experience of Athens, from which men derived courage, drew intellectual illumination, took their first step in the path which led to great achievements and the arduous pursuit of truth.

Greek history confirms, by a multitude of legends and of actual episodes, what Plato puts forth as a splendid vision, and subordinates to the higher philosophic life.

It is futile by any evasion of the central difficulty, by any dexterity in the use of words, to escape from the stubborn fact that natures so exceptionally predisposed find in Plato the encouragement of their furtively cherished dreams. The *Lysis*, the *Charmides*, the *Phaedrus*, the *Symposium* – how many varied and imaginative pictures these dialogues contain of what is only a sweet poison to such minds!

Meanwhile the temptations of the actual world surround them: friends of like temper, boys who respond to kindness, reckless creatures abroad upon the common ways of life. Eros Pandemos is everywhere. Plato lends the light, the gleam, that never was on sea or shore.

Thus Plato delays the damnation of these souls by ensnaring the noblest part of them – their intellectual imagination. And strong as custom may be, strong as piety, strong as the sense of duty, these restraints have always been found frail against the impulse of powerful inborn natural passion and the allurements of inspired art.

The contest in the soul is terrible, and victory, if gained, is only won at the cost of a struggle which thwarts and embitters.

We do not know how many English youths have been injured in this way. More, I firmly believe, than is suspected. Educators, when they diagnose the disease, denounce it. That is easy enough, because law and social taste are with them, and because the person incriminated feels too terribly the weight of law and custom. He has nothing to urge in self-defence – except his inborn instinct, and the fact that those very men who condemn him have placed the most electrical literature of the world in his hands, pregnant with the stuff that damns him. Convention rules us so strangely that the educators do all this only because it always has been done – in a blind dull confidence – fancying that the lads in question are as impervious as they themselves are to the magnetism of the books they bid them study and digest.

Put yourself in the place of someone to whom the aspect of Greek life (which you ignore) is personally and intensely interesting, who reads his Plato as you would wish him to read his Bible – i.e. with a vivid conviction that what he reads is the life record of a masterful creative man-determining race, and the monument of a world-important epoch.

Can you pretend that a sympathetically constituted nature of the sort in question will desire nothing from the panegyric of paiderastic

101

love in the *Phaedrus*, from the personal grace of *Charmides*, from the mingled realism and rapture of the *Symposium*? What you call a figure of speech, is heaven in hell to him – maddening, because it is stimulating to the imagination; wholly out of accord with the world he has to live in; too deeply in accord with his own impossible desires.

Greek love was for Plato no 'figure of speech', but a present poignant reality. Greek love is for modern students of Plato no 'figure of speech' and no anachronism, but a present poignant reality. The facts of Greek history and the facts of contemporary life demonstrate these propositions only too conclusively.

I will not trouble you again upon this topic. I could not, however, allow the following passage in your letter – 'I do not understand how, what is in the main a figure of speech should have so great power over them' – to go unnoticed without throwing what light I can upon what you do not understand.

I feel strongly on the subject; and where there is strong feeling, there is usually the risk of overstatement. But I do not think I have exaggerated, and I hope I have not spoken rudely. It is indeed impossible to exaggerate the anomaly of making Plato a textbook for students, and a household book for readers, in a nation which repudiates Greek love, while the baser forms of Greek love have grown to serious proportions in the seminaries of youth and in great centres of social life belonging to that nation.

Ever most sincerely yours
J. A. Symonds

March came to an end, and brought this eventful term to its conclusion. In April, at the very beginning of the month, I went to Clifton for the Easter holidays. They lasted three weeks. It was an early spring that year – mild, clear and beautiful; with swift and unchecked unfolding of all fair things in nature.

The change from Harrow to my home always tranquillized and refreshed me. It renewed that sense of dignity, repose and beauty in existence which was absolutely necessary to my spiritual being.

This time I felt the change more strangely than was usual. Clifton did not offer the same simple satisfaction as before. I was jaded, restless, disappointed, perplexed. The recent quickening of my intellect by casuistry, the knowledge of the secret which I carried, the revelation I had found in Plato, removed me almost suddenly away from boyhood. I was on the verge of attaining to a man's self-consciousness.

On the first Sunday morning after my arrival, I attended service in Bristol Cathedral. It was a radiant forenoon and the light streamed in from those large southern windows. My ritualistic pranks with Vickers at Harrow had this much of reality in them, that they indicated a natural susceptibility to the aesthetic side of religion – I felt a real affection and natural reverence for grey Gothic churches. The painted glass and heraldries in this cathedral, crusaders crosslegged on their tombs, carved woodwork and high-built organ lofts, the monuments to folk long dead, and, over all, the quiring voices and reverberations of sweet sacred music, touched me to the quick at a thousand sensitive points. There was no real piety, however, in my mood. My soul was lodged in Hellas; and the Christian in me stirred only, like a torpid snake, sunned by the genial warmth of art.

On this, the morning of all mornings in my life, my eyes fell on a chorister who sat nearly opposite the stall which I had taken. His voice charmed me by its sharp ethereal melancholy. In timbre and quality it had something of a wood instrument; and because of my love for it, I have ever since been sensitive to the notes of hautbois and clarinet. As I gazed and listened through the psalms and service and litany, I felt that a new factor had been introduced into my life. The voice dominated. But the boy who owned that voice seemed the only beautiful, the only flawless being I had ever seen.

From the church I walked home, enveloped in a dream. All that afternoon and evening I dreamed of Willie Dyer. I have forgotten how I discovered his name. At earliest daybreak I leaned from my bedroom window, sending my soul out to him, greeting the cathedral tower beneath me. This went on for two or three days. Ah, those April mornings – that hush of thin-leaved trees and dewy lawns, those notes of blackbirds, the stillness of the sleeping town, the poetry of flooding light, the steady thrill of flooding love!

There had been nothing like to this emotion in my past experience. It precipitated the turbid mixture of my blood and brains. I saw ahead of me the goal to which I had been tending. The close blind alley into which I had blundered at Harrow, and from which there was no escape, seemed now to expand into infinities of free and liberal experience.

I was so intoxicated with the moment that I demanded nothing from the future. I did not inquire how – my present mood of feeling squared with the philosophy of love I had imbibed from Plato.

Looking at the boy in church, hearing him sing, dreaming of him at home, were not enough. For the first time in my life, I knew that I must take possession of the dream and clasp it. The experience of the last few months had brought me so far forward that I was capable of acting. My will demanded that the boy and I should be united. What I meant to do had to be done by and for myself alone. There was no question of making any member of my family or his an intermediary.

I wrote to Willie Dyer and asked him for his portrait. I gave my address 'A.B., Clifton Post Office'. He responded with a photograph. Next I begged him to meet me. He replied that I might find him in the cathedral cloisters at 10 a.m. upon the 10th of April. Why the boy corresponded to my wishes in this way, I do not know. I only know that he was simple and guileless; and I adored him so that his father and his friends had subsequently nothing to complain of in my treatment of him. Looking back across so many years, it seems to me strange, however, that we should have been permitted to meet together for the first time in this way.

We met then on the morning of 10 April 1858. Swallows were reeling in sunlight round the tower. The clock struck. I took Willie's slender hand into my own and gazed into his large brown eyes fringed with heavy lashes. A quite indescribable effluence of peace and satisfaction, blent with yearning, flowed from his physical presence and inundated my whole being with some healing and refreshing influence.

From that morning I date the birth of my real self. Thirty-two years have elapsed since then; and still I can hardly hold the pen when I attempt to write about it.

Much sentimental nonsense has been talked about first love. Yet I am speaking the bare truth when I say my affection for this boy exhausted my instinctive faculty of loving. I have never felt the same unreason and unreasoning emotion for any other human being.

I could not marry him; modern society provided no bond of comradeship whereby we might have been united. So my first love flowed to waste. I was unable to deal justly with him; the mortification of the anomalous position he and I were placed in did much to degrade my character.

These things, however, were not felt at once. From 10 April in that year 1858, for many months to come, I used either to see Willie or wrote to him daily. He returned my affection with a simple loyal love. Our intimacy, though clandestine – though we two boys, the elder by three years and the younger, met together and exchanged our hearts without the sanction of family or friends – was wholly respectful and absolutely free from evil. More than a year elapsed before I dared to do more than touch his hand. Twice only in my life did I kiss him on the lips. The first time I did so I almost fainted from the intense rapture of the contact. We were together alone, I well remember, in a clearing of Leigh Woods – where the red quarries break down from tufted yews and dwarf peaches and wych elms plumed upon the cliff to the riverside. The afternoon sunlight fell upon glassy ivy, bluebells and late flowering anemones. We were lying side by side. The plash of paddle wheels and the chant of sailors working a seagoing vessel down the Avon, rose up to us between the two long kisses which I took.

Leigh Woods used to be our favourite resort. In those days there was no suspension bridge. We crossed the ferry, and clambered up the sides of Nightingale Valley until we found some coign advantage where we rested. Not a soul disturbed our solitude. The wild rabbits were not more innocent of guile than we were.

I still possess a white anemone gathered on the spot of that first kiss. It marks the place in my Theocritus, where this phrase occurs:

$$\tilde{\eta} \; \dot{\varrho}\alpha \; \tau \acute{o}\tau' \; \tilde{\eta}\sigma\alpha\nu$$
$$\chi\varrho\acute{\upsilon}\sigma\epsilon\iota\upsilon \; \pi\acute{\alpha}\lambda\alpha\iota \; \acute{\alpha}\nu\delta\varrho\epsilon\varsigma, \; \acute{o}\tau' \; \acute{\alpha}\nu\tau\epsilon\phi\acute{\iota}\lambda\eta\sigma' \; \acute{o} \; \phi\iota\lambda\eta\theta\epsilon\acute{\iota}\varsigma.$$

['Men *were* of the Golden Age long ago, when the beloved boy returned one's love.'][5] Gratitude mingled with my love for Willie. He had delivered my soul from the Egyptian house of Harrow bondage. He enabled me to realize an ideal of a passionate and yet pure love between friend and friend. All the 'rich foreshadowings of the world'[6] which filled my boyhood with the vision of a comrade, seemed at the time to be made actual in him. He restored me to a healthy state of nerves by the sweet magnetism of his presence. In him too I found the final satisfaction of that dim aesthetic ecstasy which I called religion. Music and the grandeur of Gothic aisles, the mystery of winter evenings in cathedral choirs, when the tumultuous vibrations of the organ shook the giant windows and made the candles in their sconces tremble, took from him a poetry that pierced into my heart and marrow.

My love enisled me in an enchanted garden, round which the breakers of the world of fact fretted without disturbing the delightfulness of dreaming. I no longer cared for work. I ceased to be ambitious. It was enough to live. My love seemed to me more real than aught in life beside. I came even into sympathy with Harrow – not indeed into harmony with what had poisoned and perplexed me there – but with the comely aspects of the place, the swiftness of young cricketers, the bodies of divers curving for their plunge, the mirth of laughing boys, the rich empurpled distance of the champaign when the sun sank over those immeasurable fields. These things I hitherto foolishly, arrogantly, neglected. My senses had been blind to them. Now love unsealed the eyes of my soul.

I kept my love secret, and hugged the treasure jealously. It was the final flower of my long cherished inner self. Secrecy added charm to its romance. Thus it came about that I practised much deceit, and had a lover's lies often on my lips at home. But I said to myself that Harpocrates and Eros[7] are one deity. Unhappily there was a grain of evil conscience in the mixture of love's medicine. My thoughts were lodged in Hellas; but centuries rolled between my soul's home in Athens and the English places I was born again to live in. Only too well enough I knew, alas! that if I avowed my emotion to my father or his friends, I should meet – not merely with no sympathy or understanding or credence – but that I should arouse horror, pain, aversion.

At this period of my youth, I devoured Greek literature and fed upon the reproductions of Greek plastic art with which my father's library was stored. Plato took the first place in my studies. I dwelt upon the opening pages of the *Charmides* and *Lysis*. I compared these with the *Clouds* of Aristophanes and the erotic dialogues of Lucian and Plutarch. I explored Theognis[8] and the *Anthology*;[9] learned Theocritus by heart; tasted the fragments of Anacreon and Ibycus and Pindar.[10] I do not reflect upon the incongruity of this impulse which threw me toward medievalism. The Confessions of St Augustine lay side by side upon my table with a copy of the *Phaedrus*. I fancied that I was realizing the antique amorous enthusiasm, while kneeling in a cathedral stall, listening to antiphones, gazing on a beautiful face.

The confusion of ideas was grotesque enough; and gradually it introduced a discord into my life. Yet it marked a period of vigorous development. If the modern man is destined to absorb and to appropriate the diverse strains which make him what he is, some fresh fermentation cannot be avoided. He emerges from it with a mind determined this way or that, and retains a vital perception of things that differ, grounded in his personal experience.

My mental and moral evolution proceeded now upon a path which had no contact with the prescribed systems of education. I lived in and for myself. Masters and schools and methods of acquiring knowledge lay outside me, to be used or neglected as I judged best. I passed my last term at Harrow, between that April and the ensuing August, in supreme indifference. I left the place without regret, and looked forward to the university without ambition. Life was neither here nor there for me. The lord of my life was love, by whom I had been inducted into a world of wonders and who had opened my eyes and fortified my understanding.

Chapter Six

Adolescence, life at Oxford, and the painful incidents of my first year there

My first feeling upon coming up to Balliol in the autumn of 1858 was one of relief. The greater freedom of university as compared with school life, both as regards the employment of time and the choice of studies, suited my temperament. I was not one of those boys who after hugely enjoying their career at Eton or Harrow, leave their hearts to some extent behind them. Nor again was I abandoning that prestige and flattering sense of self-importance which a popular head of the school resigns when he enters the ranks of freshmen in a first-rate college. I on the contrary had everything to gain and nothing to lose by the change.

Cambridge absorbed the majority of Harrovians who went up to the universities. Consequently I was but poorly furnished with school-friends. Four may be mentioned with whom I had in different ways to do. These were Robert Jamieson, Randall Vickers, Edwin Arkwright and a handsome cricketer named Munro. I began at the same time to make friends with freshmen – Urquhart, Duncan (afterwards Lord Camperdown), Stephens (a nephew of the Lord Chancellor Hatherley), Malcolm (now a partner in Coutts bank), Cecil Bosanquet (the brother of Gustavus), Cholmeley Puller and Wright (two scholars at Balliol), Lyulph Stanley, and others whom I find recorded in my diaries at that date. During my first term I also became acquainted with Edwin Palmer (now Archdeacon of Oxford), Robinson Ellis (the eminent Latin scholar) and Prof. John Conington. These elder men introduced me to their several sets. I came thus early in my career to know people of distinction like Goldwin Smith, Charles Parker, Charles Pearson, Arthur P. Stanley,

Albert Dicey, T. H. Green, Mark Pattison, Francis Otter, A. O. Rutson.[1]

There were two sides to my life. One was healthy and stimulative, the other unwholesome and relaxing. Urquhart, a Scotchman of perfervid type, developed a violent personal affection for me. He had High Church proclivities and ran after choristers. Vickers was a man of somewhat similar stamp. In their company I frequented antechapels and wasted my time over feverish sentimentalism. But when I perceived that Urquhart was making a dead set at me, I broke off the connection. Whatever I felt about comradeship I was not prepared to be made love to; and Munro did me the good service of pointing out how easily I might be compromised by Urquhart's attention. There was no harm in the man. On the contrary, I have every reason to believe that he grew up a good clergyman and excellent husband. But he had acquired the unpopularity which attached to awkward excitable enthusiasts in a mixed society of young men.

The association with Conington was almost wholly good. It is true that I sat up till midnight with him nearly every evening, drinking cup after cup of strong tea in his private lodgings above Cooper's shop near University. This excited and fatigued my nerves. But the conversation was in itself a liberal education for a youth of pronounced literary tastes. Now and again it turned on matters of the affections. Conington was scrupulously moral and cautious. Yet he sympathized with romantic attachments for boys. In this winter he gave me *Jonica*; and I learned the love story of its author William Johnson (now Cory) the Eton master, and the pretty faced Charlie Wood (now Lord Halifax)[2] of Ch. Ch. who had been his pupil. That volume of verse, trifling as it may appear to casual readers, went straight to my heart and inflamed my imagination. It joined on in a singular manner to my recent experiences at Harrow, and helped to form a dream world of unhealthy fancies about love. I went so far as to write a letter to William Johnson, exposing the state of my own feelings and asking his advice. The answer, addressed to O.D.Y. at the Union, duly came. It was a long epistle on paiderastia in modern times, defending it and laying down the principle that affection between people of the same sex is no less natural and rational than the ordinary passionate relations. Underneath Johnson's frank exposition of this unconventional morality there lay a wistful yearning sadness – the note of disappointment and forced abstention. I have never found this note absent in lovers of my sort and Johnson's, unless the men have cast prudence to the winds and staked their all on cynicism.

My studies advanced so badly that I was plucked for Smalls in the spring of 1859. A man called DuBoulay of Exeter[3] made me conjugate the Greek verbs εἰμί, to be, and εἶμι, to go, tense by tense. This was perhaps rather severe on any candidate for his *testamur* in Responsions.[4] The examination, however, was meant to search our knowledge of the rudiments; and nobody can deny that an accurate knowledge of the Greek auxiliary verbs is a rudimentary requisite of scholarship. I failed to fulfil the conditions, and deserved to be plucked. The test selected by Mr DuBoulay discovered the weakest point in my panoply, and paralysed a mind which, however quick and sympathetic, was never very self-controlled or ready at a pinch. To confuse me with the multiplication table would have been equally easy. I did not greatly mind this rebuff. I had been gathering fritillaries in Magdalen meadows all the afternoon, and enjoying the sunset from the top of Magdalen Tower. The memory of that pleasant May day is fresher now than my recollection of the disagreeable news that I was plucked. But I greatly disliked having to go down to Clifton and tell my father that I had been 'ploughed in Smalls for Greek grammar'. Fortunately, before the end of June, I had been elected together with Charles Elton[5] to an open Exhibition at Balliol and won the Newdigate prize for English verse. At least I think it was in this summer that I got the Newdigate. It may have been in 1860, when I also took a first-class in Moderations.[6] At all events my father's wounded feelings were soon soothed by quite sufficient academical successes; and my own sense of duty in study was sharpened by the salutary snub inflicted on my not too stubborn vanity. A dim consciousness of latent ability sustained me, and rendered me equanimous though somewhat harder. I was still the ugly duckling – *voilà tout*.

In the summer term of this year, 1859, I was talking one hot afternoon with Conington about *Jonica* and what I then called *Arcadian* love. Heaven forgive the innocent euphemism! I took it from an oracle from Herodotus which had attracted my attention by its simple strength and beauty: Ἀρκαδίην μ' αἰτεῖς; μέγα μ' αἰτεῖς· οὔ τοι δώσω. ['You ask me for Arkadia; a great request you make of me. I will not grant it.'][7] This and another oracle which I only remember in the Latin version – *Spartam nactus es, hanc orna*: ['You have received Sparta; look after her']⁸ – remained in my head like maxims, and were always applied to my outward lot in the domain of the emotions. Well: some turn in the argument – for we were discussing the casuistry of unrecognized passion between male persons – forced me to blurt out what I had so long concealed about Vaughan's story. Conington was deeply moved. He shrank into himself, and told me that such things ought not to be lightly spoken of. I replied that I could support what I had said by evidence, and that I was certain of my facts. This happened at the end of term, when we were both going to join a reading party at Whitby. Green, Rutson, Puller, myself and Conington formed the party and we had engaged a lodging house, kept by a woman called Storm, whom Conington christened λαῖλαψ [violent storm, hurricane]. By the way, I may mention that the village churchyard at Whitby is full of graves erected to captains and sailors of the name of Storm, many of whom had perished as whalers and fishers on the northern sea. The church itself was an old-fashioned edifice built on the cliff's brow, with galleries in which the choir sat and droned out hymns and anthems to the accompaniment of a string and brass band. It affected my imagination with the feeling of generations of shipwrecked seamen, as though it had been itself a hulk stranded up there and redolent of marine reminiscences. This church was the place in which I passed many poignant hours of mental tension and moral scrutiny in the company of Conington, Green, Rutson, Puller, boxed up together in a narrow wooden pew.

For here, at Whitby, when we had settled down to our academic studies – Conington to his notes on Virgil, Rutson to his modern history, Green to his German philosophy, Puller and I to our Greek and Latin poets and copies of verses – the question about Vaughan was reopened. I remember a forenoon conversation on the cliff, during which I convinced Conington that I had spoken the truth. He recommended me to go at once with Pretor's letter and my Harrow diaries to Clifton. My father ought to know the fact, whatever happened.

I took two solitary journeys that summer from Whitby to Clifton and back upon this business. I remember reading *Alton Locke*⁹ on one of them, and seeing a grand evening sky behind the towers of Lincoln Cathedral, the pathos and the calm of which sank into my troubled soul with soothing. It was a singular position for a youth of eighteen. I had become the accuser of my old headmaster, a man for whom I felt no love, and who had shown me no special kindness, but who was after all the awe-inspiring ruler of the petty state of Harrow. My accusation rested solely upon the private testimony of an intimate friend, whose confidence I violated by the communication of his letter to a third party. To complicate matters, I felt a deeply rooted sympathy with Vaughan. If he had sinned, it had been by yielding to passions which already mastered me. But this fact instead of making me indulgent, determined me to tell the bitter truth. At that period I was not cynical. I desired to overcome the malady of my own nature. My blood boiled and my nerves stiffened when I thought what mischief life at Harrow was doing daily to young lads under the autocracy of a hypocrite.

So I went through with the business of exposure, painfully but steadily. It took as little to convince my father as it had taken to convince Conington. The evidence was plain and irrefragable.

What eventually happened was this. My father wrote to Vaughan, intimating that he possessed proofs of his correspondence with Alfred Pretor. He promised not to make a public exposure, provided Vaughan resign the headmastership of Harrow immediately and sought no further advancement in the Church. Otherwise the facts would have to be divulged. On the receipt of my father's ultimatum, Vaughan came down to Clifton where he inspected Pretor's letter. He accepted the terms dictated to him. Mrs Vaughan followed after a few days and flung herself at my father's knees. 'Would Dr Symonds not withhold the execution of his sentence? Her husband was subject to this weakness, but it had not interfered with his usefulness in the direction of the school at Harrow.' My father remained obdurate though he told me he suffered keenly at the sight of this unhappy woman – a Stanley – prostrate on the ground before him. He judged it would be wrong to hush up such a matter of such grave importance to a great public school. In this view of his duty, he was supported by Conington, and also by the friends whom Vaughan employed in the transaction – his brother-in-law Arthur P. Stanley and Hugh Pearson, afterwards Canon of Windsor.

Vaughan then had to withdraw from Harrow; and he did this with consummate skill. No one knew the reason of his sudden abdication except Conington, my father, myself, and a few undergraduates at Cambridge and Oxford, of whom I shall have to speak.

At the banquet given in his honour when he left Harrow to

the care of Montagu Butler[10] (now Master of Trinity, Cambridge) Vaughan said that fifteen years of headmastership was as much as a man's strength could stand and quite enough for the welfare of the school he governed. The public acclaimed this act of resignation with enthusiasm. The government offered him two bishoprics in succession – those, I think, of Worcester and Rochester. He declined the former though it was well known that he was ambitious for a seat as bishop in the House of Lords. He accepted the latter. But my father telegraphed, on hearing of the news, that he must cancel the act of acceptance. Accordingly, Vaughan again retired, somewhat ambiguously, from the post of honour which the ministers of the Crown wished to force upon him. Both Stanley and Pearson, his advocates and friends, were of opinion that the English Church might suffer by Vaughan's advancement to the episcopacy. Therefore they approved of my father's Rhadamanthine justice. The withdrawal of Dr Vaughan into private life, and his refusal of two sees, were, however, so mysterious and so dramatic that the suspicions of worldly people awoke and we had some difficulty for several years to suppress the real history of the case.

The main conduct of this affair lay in my father's hands. He consulted Conington at every important turn, while Vaughan, as I have said, was advised by his brother-in-law Arthur P. Stanley and by his old friend Hugh Pearson. Alfred Pretor naturally did not remain in ignorance of what was going on. He informed Charles Dalrymple and Robert Jamieson, both of whom highly disapproved of the course which I had taken. In their eyes nothing could justify the disclosure of Pretor's letter upon which the whole case rested. They did not take into account the danger which Vaughan incurred so long as he remained at Harrow, although they were aware that Pretor was in the habit of confiding the story with incredible levity and imprudence to anyone he thought it would impress. They were in fact irreconcilable upon the point of honour. All three broke off communications with me, and I have had nothing to do with them since that summer of 1859.[11]

It was inevitable that this view taken of my action by my three most intimate Harrow friends – each of whom I visited in their homes the year before – should cause me grave disquietude. My father, Conington, Stanley and Pearson approved what I had done emphatically. But the approval of these elder men and the thanks expressed by Vaughan's advisors for what they considered my discharge of a public duty and a private service were not sufficient to relieve me from painful heart-searching. Conscience, it is true, supported me. I felt that the course I had followed was right. But I could not shake off the sense that I appeared disloyal to my friends. I still think that I ought to have informed them of the step I meant to take – in fact that there were other ways of dealing with the problem. Until I told Conington at Oxford what I knew, I had not planned a formal disclosure. Having told him, it was evident that the matter could not rest there. It virtually passed out of my hands. His advice that I should deliver it over to my father was sound. They both held that the importance of the affair for Harrow, for English society and the Established Church annihilated all considerations of confidence between two boys *in statu pupillari* [of student status]. They were undoubtedly right; and I do not know how I could have acted otherwise than I did in the summer of 1859, after I had made my first impulsive communication to Conington. Nevertheless, I suffered deeply both in spirits and in health from the long exhausting correspondence with Pretor and Jamieson and Dalrymple, crossing and confusing the correspondence carried on by my father with Conington and Vaughan and Stanley. My brain and moral consciousness – the one worn with worrying thought, the other racked by casuistical doubts – never quite recovered from the weariness of those unprofitable weeks.

One thing which rendered the charge of broken confidence ridiculous, was the comparative levity with which Pretor himself and his other confidants had whispered Vaughan's story about. Several irresponsible lads were acquainted with it; and precautions had to be taken lest they should still further divulge the secret.

Hugh Pearson, with whom I became intimately befriended, told me a singular anecdote which illustrates the delicacy of the situation. The Bishop of Oxford, Samuel Wilberforce, came to him one day at Sonning on the Thames and said, 'I am certain that Vaughan had some grave reason for leaving Harrow and refusing two mitres. An ugly story must lie behind. You had better make a friend of me. If I discover the truth I shall be an enemy.'

Pearson replied, 'Even if I knew something, it would be my duty to withhold it. But you have no right to suppose that I do.'

'Very well,' said the Bishop, 'I shall find out. And I have warned you.'

Some while afterwards he came again, and told Pearson that he had learned the whole secret. 'How and where?' asked Pearson.

'At a dinner party from a lady next whom I was sitting,' answered the Bishop.

'And what have you done?'

'Oh, I've told the Archbishop of Canterbury and the Prime Minister.'[12]

It is singular that a secret possessed by several people should not have transpired while curiosity was still alive. So many years have now elapsed that its disclosure would neither startle nor shock. Vaughan still lives;[13] and I have not heard that Pretor is dead. My father, Conington, Stanley and Pearson have passed away. What became of Jamieson I do not know. Charles Dalrymple is an active Conservative Scotch Member of Parliament. The documents relating to the affair were enclosed in a sealed packet by my father. This I have never opened. It lies among my private papers endorsed for destruction by my executors.*

It was not to be expected that Stanley should feel cordially toward me. He asked me to his rooms at Ch. Ch. and afterwards to the deanery at Westminster. I used to go there because my father wished that appearances should be kept up and, in case of public exposure, that my recognition by the Dean should be a matter of notoriety. But I always felt extremely uncomfortable in his society, and could neither act nor talk with freedom.

Vaughan I never saw again. This was owing partly to accident and partly to my steady avoidance of Speech Day at Harrow. When his nephew T. H. Green married my sister, I had to inform Green, in order that a possible collision might be obviated. It is curious, I think, that we have never met at the Athenaeum. But I go there very little even when I am in London.

Pearson, as I said, became my friend. I owed much to his companionship. He was a man of the most cordial character – sweet, gentle, wise and sociable and charming. To an extensive knowledge of good literature he added genial humour and considerable insight into character. A sound churchman, of liberal and tolerant views, he made Sonning a model parish by his human sympathy and tolerance.

---

*Note appended in margin: 'We took this as a proof that J.A.S. could not have intended his autobiography to be published *in extenso*. H.F.B., 40 Margherita Ligerne, 28 February 1903.'

It was a severe strain upon my nervous and moral strength – this probing of Vaughan's case, this separation from old friends on a question of casuistry, this forced envisagement of my own emotional attitude. I do not think that I have ever quite recovered tone and equilibrium after the tension of those weeks; in the course of which I learned much about human nature and the world's opinion, without sacrificing a point of my volition or reconciling the discords of my individuality in any compromise.

The chief good which emerged from so much evil for me was that I grew to be an intimate friend of my father. No veil remained between us. He understood my character; I felt his in sympathy and relied upon his wisdom. We joined hearts, not only as son and parent, but also as men of diverse temperaments and ages aspiring to the higher life in common.

When my father learned the truth about my romantic affection for Willie Dyer, he thought it right to recommend a cautious withdrawal from the intimacy. The arguments he used were conclusive. Considering the very delicate position in which I stood with regard to Vaughan, the possibility of Vaughan's story becoming public, and the doubtful nature of my own emotion, prudence pointed to a gradual diminution or cooling-off of friendship.

At that important moment of my life, I could not understand, and I've never been able to understand, why people belonging to different strata in society – if they love each other – could not enter into comradeship. But my father made me see that, under the existing conditions of English manners, an ardent friendship between me (a young man, gently born, bred at Harrow, advancing to the highest academical honours at Balliol) and Willie (a Bristol chorister, the son of a Dissenting tailor), would injure not my prospects only but his reputation. The instincts of my blood, the conventionalities under which I had been trained, the sympathy I felt for sisters and for brothers-in-law, the ties which bound me to the class of gentlefolk, brought me to look upon myself as an aberrant being, who was being tutored by my father's higher sense of what is right in conduct. Furthermore, I recognized that in my own affection for Willie there was something similar to the passion which had ruined Vaughan. I foresaw the possibility, if I persisted in my love for him, of being brought into open rupture with my family, and would involve my friend thereby in what would hamper his career by casting the stigma of illicit passion on our intercourse.

116

Under this pressure of arguments from without, of sense of weakness within, and of conventional traditions which had made me what I was, I yielded. I gave up Willie Dyer as my avowed heart's friend and comrade. I submitted to the desirability of not acknowledging the boy I loved in public. But I was not strong enough to break the bonds which linked us or to extirpate the living love I felt for him. I carried on our intimacy in clandestine ways and fed my temperament on sweet emotion in secret. This deceit, and the encouragement of what I then recognized as an immoral impulse, brought me cruel wrong.

*Here I feel inclined to lay my pen down in weariness. Why should I go on to tell the story of my life? The back of my life was broken when I yielded to convention, and became untrue in soul to Willie.

But what is human life other than successive states of untruth and conforming to custom? We are, all of us, composite beings, made up, heaven knows how, out of the compromises we have effected between our impulses and instincts and the social laws which gird us round.

Had Willie been a boy of my own rank, our friendship need not have been broken; or had English institutions favoured equality like those I admire in Switzerland, he might have been admitted to my father's home. As it was, I continued for some years to keep up an awkward and uncomfortable intercourse with him, corresponding by letters, meeting him in churches where he played the organ and going with him now and then to concerts. I paid the organist of Bristol Cathedral fifty guineas as premium for Willie's musical education, and thus was responsible for starting him in a career he wished to follow.

In the autumn of 1859 there came a young man from Rugby to Oxford who was destined to exercise a good deal of influence over my life. His name was C. G. H. Shorting. After trying for the Balliol scholarship without success, he obtained one at Corpus. We soon became intimate and I discovered that he shared my Arcadian tastes. He was rather good-looking, with a mass of curly shining yellow hair. For scholarship in the technical sense of the word he showed considerable ability; but he had little or no gifts for the severer

*Instructions to omit this passage from original ms.

117

studies of the university. There was something attractive about him, in spite of a difficult temper and an obstinate perverse will. The men of my set – Conington, Edwin Palmer, C. C. Puller, A. O. Rutson, Francis Otter, Robinson Ellis – took a fancy to him. We became intimate friends, until his conduct with regard to boys, especially the choristers at Magdalen, brought him into serious trouble. Reading through the diaries which I then kept, I see that my whole nature was harassed by the quarrels, reconcilements, jealousies, suspicions, which diversified our singular sort of comradeship.

There is little of importance to relate about the ordinary life of an Oxford undergraduate. The predominant purpose of these memoirs is to supply veracious data for the psychical history of one individual. To digress upon the broader fields of reminiscence and experience, would be to violate the intellectual order of the theme proposed. I am condemned by my plan to a close and irksome egotism. But it is also my business to supply, by short jottings and indirect notations of fact, some notion of the circumambient atmosphere in which that individual grew and came to his maturity.

Omitting photographic details and larger surveys over Oxford life, I have, therefore, to describe in outline the way in which I spent my remaining years at Balliol.

In the summer term of 1860, if I mistake not, I won the Newdigate Prize for an English poem on 'the Escorial'. When I came to recite my poem in the rostrum, Matthew Arnold, then our Professor of Poetry, informed me very kindly, and in the spirit of sound criticism, that he had voted for me – not because of my stylistic qualities, but because I intellectually grasped the subject, and used its motives better and more rationally than my competitors. This sincere expression of a distinctive judgement was very helpful to me. It gave me insight into my own faculty and preserved me from self-delusion as to its extent. I do believe that I then possessed, and have never lost, the candour which precludes a false estimate of mental powers.

In the same term, unless I am confusing dates, not having a calendar at hand, I obtained a first class in Moderations; and so was immediately started upon my work for the final schools in Litterae Humaniores – philosophy, logic, history.

Conington formed a second reading party. He and Green and Rutson and Puller and myself went to live in a farmhouse upon the lake of Coniston, facing the shore which Ruskin has since made classical. Shorting came to see me there, and brought his peculiar atmosphere of boy-love into my neighbourhood. This signified little; for the deep seas of my soul, so sorely troubled by Vaughan's affairs last year, were now subsiding.

Green coached me privately in Plato. I do not think I got much from him. His own views were turbid at that period. He had just begun to grapple with Hegel; and he never possessed, even to his last days, a complete grasp of his own philosophical ideas. In the summer of 1860, being in a phase of mental storm and stress, he was not a very lucid leader of the blind.

A trifling incident occurred at Coniston, which I shall relate because it is more powerfully imprinted on my memory than all the other details of those weeks. I had been talking to Shorting upon a grey stone wall, tufted with *Cystopteris* and *Ruta muraria* – the ordinary fern-grown sort of wall which divides fields in the Lake District. When twilight fell, he went off to his lodging and his loves. I returned to the little room in the farmhouse where I pursued my studies. There I sat and read. Conington and Green were conversing in the paved kitchen, used by us as a dining room; and perhaps they were not conscious of my presence. There was only a door between the two chambers.

Conington said: 'Barnes will not get his first.' (They called me Barnes then, and I liked the name, because they chose it.)

'No,' said Green, 'I do not think he has any chance of doing so.'

They then proceeded to speak about my aesthetical and literary qualities, and the languor of my temperament. I scraped my feet upon the floor, and stirred the table I was sitting at. Their conversation dropped. But the sting of it remained in me; and though I cared little enough for first-classes, in comparison with lads' love, I then and there resolved that I would win the best first of my year.

This kind of grit in me has to be notified. Nothing roused it so much as a seeming slight, exciting my rebellious manhood. It was the same spur as when Rendall wrote home of me 'wanting in vigour both of body and mind', and Conington once more in the course of a long Clifton walk remarked upon my 'languor', and Jowett told me I had 'no iron to rely upon', and Fred Myers[14] said I had 'worked myself out in premature culture', and an MP at Mr North's indulgently complimented me on 'writing for the magazines'. All these excellent people meant little by what they said and assuredly forgot soon what fell so lightly from their lips. But they stimulated my latent force by rousing antagonism. I knew that my right hand was useless – firmly clenched in the grip of an unconquerable love, the love of comrades. But they stung me into using my left hand for work, in order to contradict their prognostications.

The autumn of this year, 1860, before I returned to Balliol, was spent in a Belgian tour with Charles Cave, my sister Edith, his wife, and my sister Charlotte – and upon the top of that a rapid scamper with my father through Berlin, Prague, Vienna, Salzburg, Munich. We saw churches, picture galleries, castles, palaces, hospitals, all day, and travelled all night. The diary of these travels I possess; and it shows how hard I worked at art and nature.

I do not think that I have yet said that my sister Maribella (the second) was married in my last year at Harrow to Sir Edward Strachey of Sutton Court, Somersetshire, Bt; and my sister Edith (the eldest) in my first year at Oxford to Charles Daniel Cave Esq., now of Sidbury Manor, Cleve Hill, and the Old Bank, Bristol. With my father and my aunt Miss Sykes, my third sister Charlotte and I remained the only members of the Clifton Hill House family.

The winter of 1860–61 brought me into relations with Jowett and other acquaintances of a distinguished sort at Oxford. I also began to visit at Lord Lansdowne's country seat of Bowood, where I met Dean Milman, Mrs Higford Burr,[15] and the lions of the period. Throughout these distractions of society and study, the tread of love – love for boys, love of comrades, absorbing personal preoccupations of the passions – was carried with ever increasing intensity. I expanded in mere intellect. But the real man developed secretly through an emotional experience which was morbidly acute, because it had no proper outlet. Shorting too, the troublous friend, who had chosen the broad way of self-indulgence, plagued me by his influence – by the sympathy I felt for him, my horror of his course, the love I nourished in my bosom for a man I could not respect.

In the summer of 1861 my father took me on an all-delightful tour to Chamonni, where we explored the glaciers of Mont Blanc under old Auguste Balmat's guidance and thence to Lombardy. For the first time I crossed the Simplon and the Gothard, and saw the city of Milan and the Italian Lakes.

Meanwhile, work for the final schools was going diligently forward. The ms. books which contain my diary of study show an average of six hours a day spent in reading – how many hours expended on 'Seelensehnsucht' [the soul's longing and vain struggling to escape from love] is not recorded. During the spring of

1862, I was alone with W. R. W. Stephens[16] at Malvern. Then I went up to Oxford, and got a first-class in Litterae Humaniores – the best first of my year, as I was told, and as I had promised myself at Coniston. But I was physically exhausted. The strain of so much headwork, so much society, so much travel, and such perpetual conflict with emotion, left me weak.

I shall soon resume the record of my external existence. But here I must interpolate an episode which is more important for my soul's life than any list of prizes, honours, journeys or the like.

The quest of ideal beauty, incarnated in breathing male beings, or eternalized in everduring works of art, was leading me to a precipice, from which no exit seemed possible except in suicide or what I then considered sin.

Chapter Seven

An important episode in my Oxford life: Alfred Brooke

Working thus and living in a very varied society at Oxford, I maintained the dual life – emotional and intellectual – esoteric and external – which had been habitual.

It was a period of great activity. At Balliol I devoted my time mainly to writing essays and making the necessary studies for them. But I worked even harder at Clifton. All the morning was given up to the books I had to prepare for examination. In the afternoon I walked or rode alone, consuming my heart with vain longing and writing the lyrics which are called 'Dead Love'. I usually read again from 5 till 6.30; dined almost always in company, at my father's house or abroad with friends; sat up talking till a late hour with my father in his library, and then snatched a short unrefreshing sleep. I dreamed very vividly, and suffered from seminal losses.

Mental growth was rapid in this round of occupations. I devoured literature of all sorts with activity; and when I was tired of history, philosophy, and the classics, I composed in verse and prose for my own amusement, or else read poetry and studied pictures.

In the midst of this home life I fell violently in love with a cathedral chorister called Alfred Brooke. The passion I conceived for him differed considerably from my affection for Willie Dyer. It was more intense, unreasonable, poignant – at one and the same time more sensual and more ideal. I still think that this boy had the most beautiful face I ever saw and the most fascinating voice I ever heard.

The days and nights were horrible sometimes. It was a sustained conflict between desire and conscience, in which the will exercised a steady empire over action, while dreams and visions inflamed the fancy and irritated the whole nervous constitution – a maddening mixture of Thucydides and Livy, Aristotle and Mill, with burning

122

memories, feverish reveries, brain-thrilling songs, the tempting of the inner voice: 'Stretch forth thy hand and pluck and eat!' And all this had to be controlled and covered up under my masked manner of self-presentment to my father and his friends. Truly I wrote out of my own heart's experience when I thus described the Genius of Greek Love poring upon a magic beryl. . . .

> How his lips quivered as with eyes of fear
> And fascination o'er the filmy sphere
> He pored, and read his own deep thoughts thereon –
> Fables and symboled shapes of joys forgone
> And longings strangled! All the sterile years,
> The vain expense of salt soul-draining tears,
> The keen divisions of quick thoughts, the void
> Of outstretched arms, the subtle suicide,
> The pale recurrences of palsying dreams,
> The broodings and the ecstasies, the schemes
> That never can be counted, the despair
> Of hope or health or comfort anywhere,
> The yea and nay twinned in a single breast,
> The feverish pillow and the blank unrest
> Of solitary midnight – all were there,
> Limned on the sphere as by a painter's care.
> Then could I see how to his side there came
> Twin forms, the one with eyes of eager shame,
> The other with quenched orbs, children of Hell,
> Named Vain Desire and Everlasting Farewell.
>   I looked and loved him, for he is the Lord
> Who on his knees hath nursed me, who hath stored
> My soul with tenderness and slumbering fire,
> Who with his earnest eyes hath quelled desire
> Or fanned it flaming, who hath set my feet
> Upon the barren path, where bitter-sweet
> Grow the love-apples ruddy to the core,
> Whereof who tasteth slumbers nevermore,
> But knows the secret of forbidden things,
> And thirsts with thirst unslaked by any springs.

The state of my mind during this preponderance of an ever-recurrent, ever-repressed longing for Alfred Brooke will be shown by the following prose dithyramb I find among my papers. It was written down, I think, in the year 1865 when the tyranny had been overlived but still vibrated in memory.

Quemadmodum desiderat cervus ad fontes aquarum[1] ['Just as the hart longs for the water springs . . .']

I

Of Alfred Brooke: of the face that ceases not to haunt me – the body, voluptuous and stalwart, that deprives me of my natural rest.

Light hair; bright purple-blue eyes; pale delicately flushed complexion; firm bold level gaze; square white forehead; large red humid mouth; vibrating voice; athletic throat and well-formed breast; broad hard hands; poise of trunk upon massive hips; thick and sinewy thighs; prominent and lusty testicles; brawny calves; strong well-planted feet.

Womanly whiteness and fullness in spite of all this; softness mingled with audacity; lasciviousness beneath the virile bosom; love-languor in the large bold steady eyes; invitation in the ringing voice; readiness to grant favours; knowledge and appreciation of sensual delight.

I roll on my bed in the night watches; I clench my fists and beat my brow. The flesh rises within me, and the soul is faint through longing. I thirst for him as the hart panteth after water brooks. I cry after him from whom I turn aside. I scorn myself when I remember what he offered and I refused.

II

Before my study window he passed one morning.* I raised my head from the desk where Plato lay. He looked from the pavement, nodded and smiled. Even now I can see him with the frank and open face, the face of invitation, the body that exhaled delight, the glance that said 'I wait for you.'

I let the lad pass, held my breath tight, and caught at the window-curtain. He was gone. Down into the street I rushed; dared not cry out nor follow; flung myself upon the grass and dead leaves of the garden; groaned aloud for him, and wrestled.

I knew that he was waiting to assuage my soul's thirst. Yet I refrained.

III

To my bedroom at another time he came.* His voice was husky, and his lips seemed drowthy for kisses.

---

*'This incident happened on Monday, Oct. 7, 1861. I find two sonnets written immediately after Alfred had passed by, in my diary under that date. They have since been printed in *Vagabunduli Libellus* under the title of "Renunciation", pp. 136, 137. Only *she* has been substituted for *he:*' – J. A. S.

*In ms. 'To offer himself he came' crossed out. – Editor.

I was in my dressing-gown. My bed stood in a corner of the room.

I spoke to him reservedly – sent him away without one kiss. He met my father on the staircase.

I lay awake all that night, kissing the bed on which he sat, watering the coverlid with tears, praying and cursing in one breath.

In the morning my father said: 'Son, you have a fever.' That day I left home, and returned not for many weeks.

IV

Shall I speak of a third time? – Late in the evening of a dull October day the hunger to see Alfred came upon me. I walked to his house, three miles away. I found him with his father and his brothers; he was in his shirt-sleeves, copying attorney's parchments. Down to the hall-door he came, athletic, radiant, the sweetest and the strangest sight to see.

I took him with me. Out into the night we went, the Clifton night, the night of moist west winds and flaring gas lamps. We stood at gusty corners, looked at each other's faces by the quivering light. The magnetism of his hand was on my arm; the fascination of his voice and breathing drowsed me.

We drove together; up and down in the dark night we drove. He knew what I desired. I felt what he was willing to grant. Yet the shyness of my heart raised a barrier between us. Our words fell like straw flakes down a deep well.

At midnight I released him. Of my money he took good store. He walked away, careless, scornful, disappointed. There was that he loved better than gold, and I had not offered that. Yet he liked gold too, and what gold bought, wine, good cheer, pleasure.

He called me a simpleton no doubt. Yet he feared and respected me. Verily I think he loved me.

But I, when I was left without him, balked, ashamed, regretful, thrilling – and how shall I describe the tension of the aching brain and overwrought nerves, the blushing cheek and burning head, the parched throat, the self-scorning and deeply degraded soul, the thirst and stretching out of wistful arms, empty, never to be filled, the desire, despair, prostration, godlessness, the tyranny of the flesh, the aspiration of the spirit?

They called my ensuing illness the result of overwork and religious perplexity.

V

Shall I speak of a fourth time? – George Riseley and Alfred Brooke were sauntering in College Green. It was a May morning; their arms were interwoven.

George Riseley's arm lay on Alfred's neck, and Alfred's arm rested on George Riseley's waist. Lovingly, like comrades, they sauntered on the pavement.

Lime leaves trembled in the branches over them; the cathedral wall behind their sun-lit faces made a grey and shadowy background.

Then I knew what jealousy the heart can feel – the jealousy of things we may not share.

To have been a third between them, I would have sold my scholarship, my prizes, my first classes, my fellowship.

VI

Shall I speak of a last time? – I stood alone on the bare Durdham Down. By three boundary stones, at the edge of the gully which goes down to the Avon stream, I stood. Alfred passed, smiled, beckoned with his eyes, bade me leave the stones and be with him. But I moved not.

I saw him go: that white face offered to my mouth for kisses, the red lips paling with passion, the splendid eyes and throat, athletic and magnificent curve of broad square shoulders, and imperial poise of sinewy trunk upon well-knitted hips and thighs.

His dress concealed him not. With my soul's eyes I grasped his body in all its parts. He knew this; and therefore he smiled, beckoned, invited, promised, wooed. For he too was lascivious; my soul was not more lascivious than he; and he had many lovers.

Still I suffered him to pass. Wherefore? O Soul, thou canst tell. Thou knowest, O my soul, when with faithful and infallible eye thou didst search the secrets of his flesh, that even then thy cry was one of bitterest disappointment. The flesh could not content thee, nor assuage the hunger which it stirred. In the moment of longing and lust, in that gaze of devouring curiosity and desire, thou didst perceive that he could only yield thee shame and want and hunger reborn after short satiety.

Thereupon the three boundary stones became for me a symbol; as it were a triple Hermes; a Hermes of Uranian Eros, Priapus and Persephone, Uranian Eros, thwarting his next neighbour appetite. Persephone darkening both with fate and death and the anguish of rebelliousness.

That day, the day on which I set up those three memorial symbol stones upon the edge of the grey valley, was in some sort a day of victory. But the victory was even such a one in which the captain falls and the victorious hosts are smitten to the earth.

I cease not to be troubled by Alfred Brooke. In my visions he perturbs me. Oftentimes the beast within roars angrily for that its hunger was not satiated.

Who knows, who knows how long the victory shall last? Peradventure, Alfred Brooke, if not himself, yet in spirit, shall return and conquer – standard-bearer of legions stronger than the soul which triumphed at that moment – general of armies which shall overwhelm resistance?

It is indubitable that this passion for Alfred Brooke was a very real thing. It runs like a scarlet thread through the diaries of several years. It was the chief preoccupation of my mind during the period when I gained the Magdalen Fellowship and began to write regularly for the *Saturday Review*. Yet, looking backward from the vantage ground of middle life, I feel unable to explain the disastrous hold it took upon my nature. I cannot comprehend how I trifled with it in the way I did. Unjust to myself and him, I sought no proper opportunity of fusing this vehement craving in a natural comradeship. Experience teaches me that had I done so, I should perhaps have sinned, perhaps have involved myself in some scrape. But I should have emerged from the close unwholesome labyrinth of tyrannous desires and morbid thoughts in which I wandered. A respectable regard for my father, an ideal of purity in conduct, a dread of the world's opinion forced upon me by Vaughan's and Shorting's histories, combined to make me shrink from action. Still I could not suppress my inborn unconquerable yearnings. I went on accumulating fuel for my own damnation.

Sins of the body are less pernicious than sins of the imagination. Vicious act is not so baleful to the soul as vitiated fancy. Many a man who never stooped to any carnal deed has wallowed in the grossest sensuality of thought. Inside the sphere of their desires such men are agent and patient, double-sexed, immersed in epicene voluptuousness, for ever longing, for ever picturing delights, for ever unassuaged. In waking and sleeping dreams they run the whole round of desire, beginning with reveries that hardly raise a blush, advancing toward pruriency, dallying with the sensual ware, at last wading in chin-deep, deeper and deeper in, until no bottom is untried, and no part or portion of the deflowered soul is pure. A day comes when they would rather bear the remembrance of brothels than carry about with them the incubi and succubi of their own creation – incestuous broods, defiling the spirit which begat them, despotic, insatiable, that may no longer be denied.

I do not for a moment doubt that Alfred Brooke lived a far more natural life than I did. I am sure that whatever he may have felt and acted, he remained a healthier man. My conception of him, contaminated by my own unwholesome fancy, would have vanished like a vision at the first touch of physical and moral contact. But this I shrank from for a score of unpractically prudent reasons. And I believe that the picture I have drawn of him as the dream object of my permanent desire is a gross libel upon the flesh-and-blood being he was. . . .

I take farewell of the purely ideal being whom I have called Alfred Brooke. I cannot call him by another name; for a real boy growing into superb adolescence and the beauty of young manhood under my fascinated eyes evoked this figment of my fancy. This boy owned the name of Alfred Brooke. But the real Alfred Brooke was probably quite different from the creature who attracted me. Let no one imagine that the man who bore or peradventure still bears this name, corresponded in any essential particular to the dream around which my unhealthily repressed desires crystallized. Would to God that I had fraternized with him! Would to God that I had sought and he had suffered that carnal union, which the world calls sin, but which leads, as I know well, in frequent cases to brotherhood and mutual good services through life.* Then I should certainly not have penned these pages, which may, in spite of all I assert to the contrary, cast a shadow of unmerited blame upon him from my own dark and brooding self.

I had been taught that the sort of love I felt for Alfred Brooke was wicked. I had seen that it was regarded with reprobation by modern society. At the same time I knew it to be constitutional, and felt it to be ineradicable. What I attempted to do in these circumstances was to stifle it so far as outward action went. I could not repress it internally any more than I could stop the recurrence of dreams in sleep or annihilate my native instinct for the beauty of the world. Nothing remained but to relegate it to the sphere of the imagination. The result was what I have above described.

*Added to margin in original ms. – Editor.

Chapter Eight

End of my Oxford life, wanderings in Switzerland, Rosa Engel and Catherine North, Italy

Such was my state of mind and feeling toward the end of my Oxford career. An unhealthy, painful state enough. And yet I was continually striving to repress instinct, and to put aside the tyrannous appeals of sense.

I took a first-class in Litterae Humaniores during the summer of 1862. Immediately after this, my father, my sister Charlotte and I travelled through Munich and Innsbruck and the Finstermünz to Venice. For the first time I touched the city of the lagoons. We occupied the first floor of the Hotel d'Europa. The days spent there were enchantment. The magic of the place enthralled me; and it has never wholly lost that early fascination, although now I have lived into it. Returning by the Simplon, I fell ill at Visp in the Rhône Valley – some violent fever in which the brain was involved. My father treated me heroically; and I recovered slowly, but painfully, upon the journey home.

In the autumn I was elected to an open fellowship at Magdalen College. I had long wished to enter that establishment on the founda-tion – attracted by its medieval beauty, its solemn chapel and the choiring voices of the singing boys. These were not perhaps the best reasons for seeking a fellowship at Magdalen; but beyond the vulgar ambition to win a coveted prize, and to beat Lyulph Stanley, Chav-asse, Marshall,[1] and twenty more competitors of distinction, I had no better.

Here are some passages from my diary, written during the exam-ination. It took place in the Hall, which is only separated from the chapel by a wall; so that I could hear the ground reverberations of the organ and the lyric cry of the boys' voices, clamboring in antiphones or riding on the wings of fugues, while I was writing papers on philosophy and history:

25 October. Yesterday in the afternoon I found, while I was doing verse composition, that a little greenfinch had flown into the hall, and was unable to get out. The bird's feet were entangled with cobwebs from the ceiling, and it clung blindly to the wires of the oriel window on the dais which looks out upon the cloister quad. The poor thing was tame and exhausted. I took it in my hands and removed the cobwebs. Then I opened the window and let it fly out into the clear autumnal air, fresh with sunlight after rain. The finch sat dazed upon a battlement, then hopped to another, pecked a little moss, at last felt its freedom, chirrupped, and was away toward the woods. So would that someone might release me!

On Thursday I heard 'Let the bright Seraphim' sung divinely by Goolden (a chorister). Oh, how I long to enter here! Quam dilecta sunt templa Magdalenae! Numquam aliquid alius adeo desideravi.[2] [How lovely are the temples of Magdalen! Never have I desired anything so much.] Still I recognize that it might be a blessing in disguise to be rejected.

27 October. At 11 a.m. I was admitted Probationary Fellow of Magdalen, after taking the usual oaths to the House of Hanover, and kneeling before the President among the Fellows in the Hall.

It would have been indeed for me a blessing in disguise if I had been rejected at Magdalen. One name occurs frequently in my diary of those days – the name of C. G. H. Shorting. I had promised to coach him in philosophy; and when he found that I was elected Fellow of Magdalen, he hoped to use his opportunities as my pupil for gaining access to the college and carrying on flirtations with the choristers. After I entered into residence, occupying rooms in the cloister quad nearly opposite the state apartments, I perceived that it would not be loyal or convenient for me to introduce Shorting into Magdalen. He was regarded by the dons and the men with aversion and suspicion, having already intrigued tactlessly and pertinaciously with one of their choristers, Goolden. Accordingly, I told him that I felt obliged to coach him in his lodgings. But this provoked an angry letter of expostulation.

Meanwhile I began to make friends with the tutors and fellows of Magdalen, and endeavoured to get work in the college as a lecturer. I made the acquaintance of Richard Congreve,[3] which afterwards developed into a close intimacy. I received an invitation through the Hon. and Rev. W. Fremantle[4] to go as tutor to Lord Pembroke,[5] then a boy of fifteen, which I sagely refused. And so it happened at this juncture that Gustavus Bosanquet wrote to me from Cambridge, informing me that A. Pretor had been blabbing to him about Vaughan's troubles. This information I copied out and sent through Conington to Arthur Stanley.

Shorting, on his side, was planning mischief.

20 November. I went to an Italian lesson at C. D. Cobham's and stayed afterwards to talk. He told me that Shorting had been dining at University, and said that he was going to take his revenge on me; Cobham would soon know what it was. Urged with the baseness of such conduct, he replied that he did not expect his friends to 'cut him', and that 'he could do me great harm, though he could not suffer anything himself'. I felt that what Shorting said was only too true. He might damage me at Magdalen. Before going to bed, I saw Conington who reassured me, and I read in the green book of texts belonging to my mother these verses for the day: 'As one whom his mother comforteth, so will I comfort you,' and 'Blessed be God who comforteth us in all our tribulation.'

Small comfort was I to have for many days and weeks and months – nay years. But such comfort as I got came from God in solitude, and from the image of God, the love of friends.

I was in London, staying with A. O. Rutson at 7 Half Moon Street, when the storm broke on Monday 24 November. A letter from Cobham brought me news that Shorting had sent a document defamatory of myself, and containing extracts from my private correspondence and my poems, to six of the Magdalen fellows. His object was to prove that I had supported him in his pursuit of the chorister Goolden, that I shared his habits and was bent on the same path. All my letters of expostulation and reasoning with him he had destroyed, and had cut out and pieced together little hints and fragments which gave a plausible colour to his charges.

Fortunately for me, my conscience was absolutely clear. I knew that I had done nothing that was wrong, and that the whole tenor of my action with regard to Shorting – perfectly well known to Conington, F. Otter, Edwin Palmer, A. O. Rutson and a score of other friends – had been salutary and dissuasive. Yet I had to stand my trial, and Magdalen at that time was so antagonistic to the liberalism of Balliol and so averse to the system of open fellowships based upon it by the last commission, that things were not unlikely to go hard with me. At the same moment I was grieved by hearing that Lyulph Stanley, whom I beat at Magdalen, was elected Fellow of Balliol. I would sooner have gained the Balliol fellowship; but a modest estimate of my own capacity, in relation to certain competitors, especially G. A. Simcox,[6] had made me resolve to try for the first that came. And so I won Magdalen – not without aesthetic gratification.

> *30 November.* Green breakfasted with me, and said they had elected Stanley at Balliol. Simcox turned out a feeble delusion. They were sorry I had slipped through their fingers. Thus the unlucky resolve to stand for fellowships in order, Conington's exaggerated opinion of Simcox, the peculiarities of Magdalen society, my feeling of delicacy about coaching Shorting there, his unparalleled treachery, have all worked to one end. My name is soiled with an unbearable suspicion; my usefulness in the college is destroyed, and Oxford is made an impossibility. All has come by folly. Of guilt I feel none, and only wonder. The dons wish me to go down tomorrow and to prepare some defence.

I did go down, and received letters of support from some of the most distinguished men in Oxford and in England – numbers of them – which were placed in the President of Magdalen's hands, together with my own statement, which I wrote at Earley Court near Reading (the home of my friend Stephens) with a burning head, sore eyes, and heavy heart in indignation. After some time, on 18 December, a general meeting of the College of Magdalen acquitted me of the charges brought by Shorting. I have a copy by me of the note which was inserted in the President's book, and which Dr Fisher,[7] one of the oldest fellows, described as 'a complete acquittal, the terms not quite as I should wish'. In fact, two of the letters in my handwriting which Shorting sent in were 'strongly condemned'. My father regarded the verdict of the college as 'an act of meagre justice'; and certainly if Shorting had exploded the same hand grenade against me in the Balliol common room, it would have merely stirred the air. But Magdalen, as I have already said, was hostile to Jowett's pupils and suspicious of the clever young liberals whom their new statutes forced them to receive.[8]

Of Shorting, I need not say that I have heard and seen nothing since that time. He left Oxford in disgrace, and has lived a life of obscurity.

My diary shows that I bore up bravely through these troubles.

But the long month's strain – 'the month of weary vexation and deep regret', as I described it – told upon me only the more powerfully, I think, because the effects were not felt at once. I went up again to Magdalen, resided there in my former rooms, coached pupils in philosophy, and was well, though not over-cordially received by the fellows. I do not think I should ever have got on with the Magdalen fellows of that epoch; and now I was so sorely wounded in my soul, so sensitive and shy, that I could not dream of admitting one of them to my intimacy. I only stayed up at Oxford in order to please my father, who judged this prudent, and until I could decide on some practical course of action.

At the end of December 1862, W. R. W. Stephens[9] and I set off for a visit to Belgium in bitter winter weather. Our steamer broke down off Calais pier. A rowing boat put out, in a tremendously high sea, to take over the mails; and we insisted upon getting into it. The consequence was that we nearly lost our lives; for tide and wind drove us beyond the harbour piers, and the sailors had the utmost difficulty to row us round again. People were standing on the pier with life-preservers, ready to throw down when we should be dashed by the breakers up against the wooden stakes. For about two hours the labour lasted; of course we were drenched to the skin, and our luggage was soaked with sea water, which began to freeze upon us when we got on shore. We slept at Tournay, and woke up with severe chills and rheumatism, which did not quit us on the rest of that dismal journey. I was reading books on the Renaissance, having in contemplation the writing of an English essay on that subject for the Chancellor's Prize.

I began the next term with six pupils in philosophy. But after three weeks my health failed suddenly; and I have never been a strong man since. Shorting indeed had his revenge. He was of so strange a nature than even could he have foreseen all the trouble he was bringing on me, and the ruin of my health, I believe he would not have desisted from his dastardly action. Peace be with him all the same!

My illness declared itself one night in the form of a horrible dream; the motive of which was that I saw a weak old man being gradually bruised to death with clubs. The anguish of his eyes pierced my soul; and even now, after the lapse of twenty-seven years, I can see them. Next morning I rose with the certainty that something serious had happened to my brain. Nor was I mistaken. During the next three years I hardly used my head or eyes at all for intellectual work and it was fully ten years before they recovered anything like their natural vigour; as I shall have to relate, I had, in the interval, begun to be consumptive. I do not doubt that the larger part of this physical distress was the result of what I suffered at Magdalen, coming after the labour of reading for my degree and the obscure fever I had at Visp.

The weeks dragged wearily along through those months of ungenial late winter and delaying spring at Oxford. I was like a creature which had been racked, and felt pain in every nerve and sinew. Of bodily suffering I had enough and to spare in the aching eyes and dull pain-shotten brain — never forgetful, that pain-burdened brain, waking or sleeping, of its deep unaccountable malady. The slumber of health became a boon remembered.

Nature relentlessly denied it now. Night brought frightful visions; and waking was the act of slow uncoiling from the serpent coils of an oppressive incubus. But the mental suffering was worse. If my body throbbed with dull persistent aches like a beast that has been racked or vivisected, my spirit burned in flames of shame and indignation and rebellion against faith. Scorpion-like it turned round in a circle of fire and stabbed its vitals with the sting it carried. I bred no bitterness against mankind and I did not curse God. I wanted eagerly to love my brothers and to reconcile myself with God. But I was weak and outcast in a wilderness of inarticulate anguish; bruised and pounded and reduced to earth — benumbed by the grey of all these things, and nourishing a blind corporeal resistance, combined with the awful sense of time that must be spent and wasted on the effort to revive. Shorting's blow had fallen, more cruelly than the poor fellow whom I have loved too weakly and not well, perhaps intended.

The foregoing paragraph may read a little laboured and too high-flown in rhetoric. If it is laboured that comes from the impossible task of describing a sentient being still plagued at every point of consciousness. If it is high-flown that must be conceded to the difficulty of expressing by any means of style the labyrinth of a young soul, lost, and seeking light in darkness.

I had recourse to the one thing which has sustained me through the troubles of this life. I went to Malvern with my sister Charlotte, and wrote an essay on the Renaissance. Wearing blue spectacles and a green shade, because I could no longer distinguish the pupils of my eyes in their red sea of inflammation, I put my thoughts on paper. The manuscript was sent to Oxford and won the Chancellor's Prize. Poor academical success: only valuable because in those weeks of blindness I determined to resist, did something and laid unconsciously the foundations for future work.

I did not care about the prize. Such things have always seemed to me insignificant and out of all proportion to the suffering and the pleasure of life . . . .

Long before the crisis which Shorting made in my life, I felt the necessity of growing into a natural man. That is, I think, how the problem presented itself to my innocence. I thought that by honest endeavour I could divert my passions from the burning channel in which they flowed for Alfred Brooke, and lead them gently to follow a normal course toward women. I neglected the fact that poetry and power of expression and the visionary pomp of dreams awoke in me only beneath the touch of the male genius. I wanted to do right. To be as one of those I loved and honoured, the nobler men I knew around me. Therefore in all simplicity and sober diligence I addressed myself to the task of stimulating a romantic feeling for women.

Mrs Josephine Butler[10] exercised her unhealthy spiritual fascination (a mixture of religious fervour and flirtation) and her really brilliant physical influence upon me in vain. I was worried by the agitation into which she threw me mentally – appealing to my sentimental instincts under the dubious aspects of theological and personal emotion. My senses responded but dumbly to her feminine charm though I recognized their aesthetic value. In both ways she failed to win me, albeit she did her best to do so, risking what might have been perilous to herself, if I had been normally constituted.

Mme Goldschmidt (Jenny Lind), in my opinion a very far superior woman to Mrs Butler, did really take hold upon my nature. But here there was no question of sexual or sentimental influence. I admired her as a power in art. I respected her as a world-experienced personality, who had kept herself unspotted and unspoiled. I went to her for counsel and converse as though to a Diotima or Egeria.[11] She never knelt down before her God, as Mrs Butler was wont to do front to front with a looking glass, calling some young man in to view the process and become enamoured of her God through her attractiveness. Mme Goldschmidt told me that in those vast theatres she trod, among the shouting crowds, she always sang to God, and let the wreaths and plaudits fall. I admired her as a comrade, revered

135

her as a disciple, learned from her to expect greatness from women. It was Mme Goldschmidt who prepared me for my wife.

These two ladies, Mrs Josephine Butler and Mme Goldschmidt, affected my character at the time when I was resolved to warp the congenital bias of my sexual instinct. Unfortunately neither of them did more than to awake in me an aesthetic sense for feminine beauty and an admiration for female genius and force of character.

For the main purposes of life, it might have been better if I had got me to a brothel and tried all its inmates by turns. What I needed was the excitation of the sexual sense for women, and the awakening to their sexual desirableness, combined with the manifold sympathies, half brutal and half tender, which physical congress evokes.

In a dumb blundering way I knew that the egotistical enthusiasms of Mrs Butler and the grand art of Mme Goldschmidt were not respondent to my needs. I saw through the former, as one sees mere fact through coloured glass. The other evoked my sentiments of comradeship and loyal devotion. Both roused my intellectual curiosity about women. Neither of them touched my sex.

In April 1863, having nothing to do at Clifton, I cast eyes upon a young lady called Letitia. She was our near neighbour at Clifton. The diary, which I am following as a faithful guide in these reminiscences, describes a cool romantic episode connected with this maiden. Her parents would have liked me for a son-in-law. My father threw his weight into the scale against my lukewarm passion. This circumstance fanned the sluggish coals of my emotion. I dreamed for four weeks that I should like – might like – could probably come to like, to marry her. The accent of the diary is, nevertheless, quite different in all that concerns her from its pregnant uncouth confidence about Alfred Brooke. I, the good boy, was then undoubtedly endeavouring to fall in love with a girl, and very proud of myself when I thought I had achieved that object. Here is a self-revealing sentence: 'It is much to feel that a woman is my ideal.'

A real woman-lover could not have written that sentence. It shows the honest intention of an abnormal but highly moralized young man. I never wrote such words about Willie Dyer or Alfred Brooke. Passion, in their case, and love, leapt out in simple unreflective utterances.

Suddenly, on 4 May, Letitia disappears from the diary. I left Clifton for London and Oxford, apparently without a regret for her, and certainly without a single word recorded of any after-memory concerning her. Poor pale shadow of a coaxed-up emotion! The impulse to love Letitia, in my soul, was honest enough; but it was also selfish and untrue. I hope that I caused the girl no pain. I think I must have disappointed her parents. But although I may perchance have stirred her maiden fancies by my conversation and persistent dogging of her paths, I am blameless of having cast a single spark of a real man's passion into Letitia's heart.

My health continuing miserable, I left Clifton, at my father's bidding and much against my own will, for Switzerland on 25 June 1863. At that time, though I had enjoyed the valley of Chamonni and the glaciers of Mont Blanc, I did not care for Alpine scenery. The prospect of dragging my pain and weariness and aching eyes among a crowd of tourists through Swiss inns disgusted me.

In Cecil Bosanquet, brother of my Harrow friend Gustavus, I had a kind and amusing travelling companion. He knew I was ill, and must have seen that I had something weighing on my mind. But I did not confide to him my Magdalen troubles. I had done so to no one who was not brought into the affair by necessity, not even to W. R. W. Stephens, at whose house I composed my defence before the college. Cecil's freely given sympathy and funny ways were a great solace to me at the commencement of a tedious journey.

This summer in Switzerland turned out so decisive for my future that I shall dwell upon [some of] its incidents, drawing from the diary I still kept pretty regularly.

[One] day we walked up to Mürren from Lauterbrunnen, where I was destined to abide, with one brief interval, until 31 August: a memorable period for me.

In those days there was only one little wooden inn at Mürren, the Silberhorn, kept by Herr Sterchi and his family. Life was very primitive; few people staying in the house beside ourselves; troops of tourists coming up from Interlaken to lunch and going noisily away again. The George de Bunsens[12] were our companions for some while; and while they were still there, an English family arrived. I can remember looking out of Cecil's window, and spying their advent, one bright afternoon in early August. It annoyed us to think that the hotel would now be fuller.

They were Mr Frederick North, MP for Hastings, and his two daughters. Both the young ladies were devoted to sketching. The eldest was blonde, tall, stout, good-humoured, and a little satirical. The second was dark and thin and slight, nervous and full of fun and intellectual acumen. The one seemed manager and mother, the other dreamer and thinker. Neither was remarkable for beauty; but the earnest vivacity of the younger grew upon me, and I could soon have fallen in love with her. Her name was Catherine. Mr North is kind and easy-going. They seemed to have travelled in most parts of Europe.

Such is the entry in my precious priggish diary about the woman whom I was destined to marry. I carried the thought of Catherine North, like a sleeping seed, in my mind through the next ten months, sought her out in London then, and did what will be afterwards related. The Norths stayed only a week, I think, at Mürren; but that was time enough to form a tolerably just conception of them. Alpine inns are favourable places for hatching acquaintance and gaining insight into character.

My health revived daily; in spite of frequent drawbacks and persistent trouble in the brain, I grew stronger and lighter-hearted. And what was more hopeful, I began spontaneously to love a woman – not Catherine North as yet – but Rosa Engel.

Early in August: All the people of the inn at Mürren are charming. Herr Sterchi comes from Widerswyl near Interlaken, where he spends the winter. He was a cavalry soldier in the Swiss army, and is a tall, handsome man, polite in manners. On Sundays he goes out for a ride upon his black horse along the terraced path above the Staubbach. His wife is a neat little body, rather shy. They have several children, all young. The waiting in the inn is done principally by a good-natured girl hired as a servant. She has a chubby round face and wears a coloured kerchief over her head tied beneath the chin. Like most girls in Swiss mountain inns she seems to have a chronic toothache. I christened her 'the motherly maid', because she was good and unruffled in her temper. Then there is a little chambermaid with a mousy face, something like a very pretty Esquimaux girl, dark and black-eyed, but snub-nosed and pouting. She wears a fichu and the head-kerchief always. But the most attractive damsels are two whom I saw at once to be no hired servants. I told Cecil, what turned out to be fact, that they had come up here to learn housekeeping and take a summer holiday. They took turn and turn about to wait at table and to help in the kitchen; a week to each duty. One of them I named 'the pretty maid', the other 'the pseudo-pretty maid'. (I was carrying on, apparently, old reading-party habits.) From the former I gained this information respecting the house; and she won my heart. She is called Rosa Engel, and is not that a pretty name? She comes from Thun, where, as she told me with some pride, her father is the only owner of the name of Engel. She is the prettiest girl I ever saw, since I had eyes to see. About her every moment there is the charm of grace, agility, and lightness – in her eyes a sparkle – in her carriage a trustfulness like that of a tame wild creature – and all her limbs move to the music of such gladsome youth that my gaze always follows them.

After this there comes a detailed description of her Bernese costume and the heavy silver chains she wore. I did not then know that she was the daughter of the chief jeweller in Thun, a man renowned now for his old-world silver gear.

I grew to love her by mere looking, then began to talk, shyly at first, afterwards more freely on the balconies at night, when the housework was over for the day. We spoke in French.
9 August. Cecil was going home to England, and I to Zürich to meet T. H. Green. I asked Rosa to accept some wild roses I had gathered for her on the hills. She said she would keep and dry them in remembrance of my visit to Mürren. We wished each other goodbye; and as we shook hands, I stole a kiss. The feeling of her lips on mine is still fresh. It was the first time I had ever kissed a woman. Then she left us blushing, and went below and sat on the balcony singing with the other maids. These songs from the girls, on warm evenings, after the day's work is finished, in the midst of their simple lives, in front of the great crags and glaciers and stars, has a strange, soothing, irritating melancholy. They drive me in upon myself. Next morning we were up at five. I took another kiss from Fraülein Engel, as we left the house, and one too from the motherly maid.

Cecil left me at Olten on 10 August, and I found T. H. Green, after a long search through all the hotels of Zürich. Green and I next day walked up to Uetliberg and set ourselves down there in a little wooden tavern for a week. But a great longing came over me for Mürren. I remembered its unrivalled purity of air – those walks upon the Schilthorn, in the Sefinenthal, towards Trachsilauenin. I heard the aerial echoes of the Alpenhorn ascending from Lauterbrunnen or floating from the Wengern Alp, and gaining melody upon the way. I longed for the immediate presence of the giant mountains with their glaciers. And the simple folk kept calling to me. And Rosa Engel was the soul and centre of these things.

Green wanted us to go to Gais in Appenzell. But I over-persuaded him. I must return to Mürren, and he must come with me. We agreed on these terms. He was to take the route by Rapperschwyl, Einsiedeln, Schwyz. I hurried straight by Thun. There I visited Rosa's home, and made acquaintance with her mother, who seemed a little suspicious of me. She had probably some right to be so; for I doubt not that, in my simplicity, I let her infer that I was going back to Mürren for her daughter's sake.

I walked up to Mürren on 18 August in drenching rain. And it rained and snowed incessantly for three days after I arrived. Rosa, who knew that I had come again to see her, and who did not understand what all this meant, kept severely aloof, avoiding me on purpose.

Twice I have passed the window where she was sitting. Once I saw her writing; and I thought that she was watching me. I walked past, fondling the great white dog. She bent over her letter, and only the friend who was with her could see my anxious glances. The next time it was worse. She sat sewing, and I smiled as I passed. But she stared stonily, and then looked down. So I have never given her the greeting of her mother, which I hoped would be a way to reach her heart; although I told Madeleine, the maid, about the visit to Herr Engel's shop in Thun. I have never given her the book of German poems which I bought for her in Zürich – or the German verses which I wrote on my return to Mürren. These I set down on paper under the direction of her friend, Herr Sterchi's cousin, and gave them to the friend, hoping she would show them to Rosa.

The other girls in the house, it is certain, kept Rosa well informed about me; and they probably showed her my German poem, which was as outspoken a declaration of love as its bad grammar permitted. At any rate, she told me two years ago (in 1887) that she was perfectly well aware of my affection for her, but considered that no good could come of such a flirtation between an English gentleman and a Swiss girl. She liked me and felt drawn toward me. But prudence made her assume that attitude of cold reserve. It may also be supposed that the Sterchis, under whose charge she was, opened their eyes when I returned, and gave her wholesome counsel.

However this may have been, Green's appearance on 21 August made a change. Perhaps he inspired confidence. Perhaps, now that I was not quite alone, she could not resist the pleasure of a little courting.

22 August. Green came yesterday; and at nine this morning the sun shone out. We walked together in the deep snow, which lay thick upon those late summer flowers. They, poor things, revived immediately beneath the genial warmth and lifted their pretty heads from wells of melting snow wreaths. The whole world seemed to feel returning spring. Birds floated in dense squadrons overhead, whirling and wheeling on the edges of the clouds, which kept rising and dispersing in the eager air above our valley. Far away the mists rolled, like sad thoughts that dissolve in tears.

Later in the day we sat upon those rocks, the crests of precipices fifteen hundred feet in height, whence the eye plunges so giddily to the Lutschinen torrent, and where it is so pleasant to rest among the tufted stone-pinks (*Stein-Nelken*) in the cool of afternoon.

Well: while I was seated on the rocks, I noticed that Frau Sterchi and Rosa had left the inn, and were sorting linen in the chalet opposite. They had placed a table and chairs before the house door, under the projecting eaves. So I left the rocks and Green upon them, meditating the pages of his Baur. Very shyly, I determined to walk by the chalet, and see what happened. As soon as Rosa caught sight of me, her eyes went down, veiled in their soft dark lashes. But soon she lifted them again, and gave me a smile of recognition. I left the path and crossed the palings of the chalet garden. She held her hand out. I took it, and conveyed her mother's greetings, and spoke about my visit to her house in Thun. Frau Sterchi, busied with her linen, perplexed and curious, and shy, not understanding what we said in French, cast anxious glances. The point is gained, however, the ice broken; and like the Alpine flowers beneath the melting snow, my thoughts and hopes of love revive.

How much of real feeling was there in all this? To what extent was I living out an idyll and amusing my imagination – with that incorrigible habit of 'poetizing the facts of existence', which Flaubert sneers at in women? How far was affection for Rosa teaching me to love the Alps; or was she only the central figure in a landscape which took hold upon my aesthetic sensibilities through the revival of health and strength in a congenial milieu? It is difficult to answer these questions. I only know for certain that the image of Rosa remained for a long while after I left Mürren, imprinted on my memory, and that I have never been drawn so spontaneously toward any other woman. Yet I doubt whether I was governed by the genuine sexual desire. Only physical possession could have tested this factor in the emotion she inspired. And that of course I never had.

25 August. I discover that Rosa is only fifteen, the same age as Juliet, Virginia, Gretchen. She is a woman in the eyes of love, but the grace and bloom of childhood linger round her still.

Last night she ran out with Madeleine upon the balcony – to see the stars, she said. I followed, and found them leaning over the parapet and listening to Nathalie who was singing by the kitchen door. I knelt upon the seat at Rosa's side, and make her ask Nathalie to sing the song of '*Röslein, Röslein, Röslein rot, Röslein auf der Heide*'. The melody was often broken by the laughter of the girls. – Oh, the fair moon, the silver stars, the dim tresses of the cataracts! The tall mountains stood grey, discrowned of their snows. The depth of the valley was grey, and very grey the bald bare rocks of the black Monk. The moonlight seemed made for us alone and for the music. It fell on Rosa's face, and I could follow the working of her fingers by its light. I softly touched her arm, and once I dared to play with her hands and the rings she wore. I made her put on mine.

So the diary goes on its way, minutely detailing the tiny incidents of this slight idyll. I picked bunches of fresh flowers every morning for Rosa, climbing daily higher up the mountains as the summer flowers retreated, until at last there were few left but lilac crocuses and deep blue harebells. Innumerable sonnets too were written:

> What flowers for thee, dearest, what flowers for thee?
> Red roses for my Rose, and azure eyes
> Of gentian steadfast as thy constancy? . . .

Etc. I caught at every opportunity of meeting her and speaking with her. These were many, but not of a very satisfactory kind. We were living in a hotel, where every movement is watched, and none of the people of the house were ignorant of my wooing.

26 August. After breakfast Green and I walked to Interlaken, had lunch there, and walked back – a fair day's work. We whiled the time away, toiling up the valley of Lauterbrunnen, by repeating as many sonnets of Shakespeare as we could remember. Between us, I think we managed about half the whole number. I need not say that I knew more than he did.

At Interlaken I bought a little ring with a deep-coloured red stone in it, a jacinth I think, as a present for Rosa; and I also picked an oleander flower. These I brought back with me. In the evening she and her friend were sitting in the grass by the cabbage plot beneath the inn. I joined them. The friend was in her working dress, cutting up lettuces for salad. Rosa, as usual, was neatly dressed: a black velvet chaplet round her head, and the violet kerchief falling down her back and giving brilliance to her blonde hair. I gave her my oleander flower, which she took with a blush almost as deep as the colour of the blossom. Afterwards I noticed that she had placed it in the bunch of wild flowers which I bring her. After some desultory conversation, she got up, dropped a curtsey, and ran into the house with her pretty farewell words of 'Merci Monsieur!'

During this episode we were watched by all the English people on the balcony, and the guides and porters round the door. It amused me when I went inside to hear from Green that old brazen-faced Sir Andrew Aguecheek (a man called Harris staying in the inn) had remarked upon the scene with his stolid drawl, 'Quite pastoral!'

Later on, the moon had risen high above the Mittagshorn, and Rosa was out upon the balcony, reading a written paper by its light. I went, and asked her if she would accept the little ring which I had brought for her, and took her hand to place it on her finger. Then she stood up straight, and turned her face to the sky, and said, 'Je suis si jeune. Je n'ai jamais pris une bague d'un monsieur.' I still pressed her to take it; but again she said, turning to the calm still moon, and making heaven her witness: 'Je suis si jeune.' I cannot analyse the tone with which she spoke these words. There was a sadness in it, a melancholy, and apprehension of the future. 'Leave me alone,' she seemed to be feeling: 'Why stir in me the pleasures and the pains of love? They will come, but the time is not yet. I am here alone, without father or mother. Do not take advantage of my youth.' (These sentences I worked up two days afterwards into the sonnet 'Je suis trop jeune', published in *Vagabunduli Libellus*, page 151). The moon kept shining on her face, and she was sad. I saw that she did not blame me, only felt that she could not accept my token.

How selfish it is to be pining because I cannot get a girl's heart for one week – because I may not play with her and kiss her, and then leave her. She stays here and has the same life; we go elsewhere, and carry her kisses and her hand touch in our memory as talismans for evoking the sweetness of the past.

It was no scoundrel who penned the last paragraph: only my raw, sophisticated, literary, life-idealizing self. I did not love Rosa with sufficient masculinity of passion either to want to seduce her or to want to marry her. I might, except for her right feeling, have fallen into the former difficulty; and, except for her just perception of the situation, have blundered into the latter. I owe to her my deliverance

from two situations, one of which would have involved a crime, the
other a mistake.

> 27 *August*. Rosa has become part of me, as no woman, no one
> else perhaps before was. She has stirred true feeling, and has made
> Switzerland my soul's home. The memory of Mürren will endure like
> a great symphony, multitudinous with thoughts and motives – storm,
> sun, and mist and snow; unfathomable moonlight nights; calm
> mellow evenings and cold sunrises; the greenery of the pine-crowned
> alps, the glaciers and the precipices, the wrecks of avalanche and
> raving winds; all combined, controlled and brought into harmony by
> the thought of Rosa.

This was true enough; and yet I do not detect the right accent of
passion in all my romantic broodings on the thought of Rosa. She
did not compel me tyrannously, as Alfred Brooke had done. In the
very middle of my lunes about her, I foresaw the moment when I
should leave her by an act of my own will, and she would be to me
a gracious memory. Still I recognized the essential distinction
between this love for a girl and the love I felt for Alfred Brooke –
its superior naturalness and coolness.

> I receive the thought of Rosa into the inmost places of my heart; but
> how different is it from the thoughts of passion which have nestled
> there before! Her image is healthy, fresh, life-giving, bestowing some-
> thing which I had not earlier, and could not have obtained except
> through her. Those other dreams were self-created, self-sustained,
> enshrined in self, fed from self.

That paragraph of the diary indicates my perception of a radical
and specific difference between desire excited by a girl and the desires
I had previously indulged for boys or visionary beings in male forms
of beauty.

The last day I spent at Mürren was a Sunday. Herr Feuz, who
then sold alpen-stocks and little wooden models of Swiss cottages,
who was afterwards made postmaster at Mürren, and soon became
a man of substance, asked me to stand godfather to a little girl of
his, just born. Rosa and her friend Katrina were to be godmothers.
So of course I acceded willingly to his request; and when I informed
Rosa, her eyes lighted up, and she exclaimed, 'Ah! cela sera joli!'

The long evening which ensued was sufficiently *gemüthlich* [cosy].
I have spent many of the same sort since. But this was my first
initiation into real Swiss life. It seems that I enjoyed abundance of

A portrait in oils of John Addington Symonds,
Vigor, 1853

Sophie Girard

Mrs Sykes ('Auntie')

The drawing room at Clifton Hill House, Bristol

Clifton Hill House

Left: John Addington Symonds during his time at Harrow. *Right*: Dr Vaughan, *c.*1860

John Addington Symonds with Dr Symonds
and Charlotte

Above right: Maribelle

Right: Edith

proximity to Rosa, sitting on the sofa by her and putting my arm round her waist, and breathing burning words into her ears which brought a quick flush to her face. But she knew how to manage me, flung away, and returned again, half distracted by the situation. I attributed too much to circumstances, which now I know to be permissible and right in such Swiss holidays, though they often lead to serious results.

So ended the idyll. It is a story without an end, too stupid and insipid to be set down at length. And yet Rosa was a woman, as I have since learned to know, of no vulgar mould. She came and stayed with my wife and me here at Davos two years ago. She is still unmarried, still brilliant and beautiful, still perchance a little hard, forcible in character and intellectual precision. A girl of softer substance, as Katrina was, would not have resisted me; and Rosa was not unwilling to yield. But good sense and keen acumen kept the balance on her part; and I was nonplussed. I did not desire so passionately, love so unreservedly, as to throw myself upon her mercy with my heart and hand for life.

She has told me her own history, and it is not for me to reveal it. I know what prevented her from making a happy marriage with a young man whom she came to love. I know why she remained single; and I appreciate the kindness she has still preserved for me, her first impetuous wooer.

Of myself I may speak. When I was ill and weary in London, during the early summer of the next year, as I shall have to relate, I cast my thoughts out toward Mürren again, toward the beloved Alps, and sent my soul to Rosa. There is a little printed poem in my published works, which describes that state of feeling. ('Sehnsucht', *Many Moods*, page 42). . . . My love for her, whether it was the proper love of man for woman, or whether it might have become so under right conditions, was something real. Sense of relations and the intellectual light, glaringly cast upon romance, withered the only sexual love which I have felt for any being not of my own sex. . . .

It had been settled between Green and myself that we should go straight to Munich. But I could not tear myself away by one wrench from Switzerland. There had been some vague hope of finding a photograph of Rosa at Wintherthur. Thither then I made the long-suffering Green shape his journey, dreaming dreams myself and writing sonnets. (Among them 'In Absence', printed in *Vagabunduli*

Libellus, page 125.) Although I ransacked Wintherthur for photographers and photographs, of course I did not obtain what I wanted. Accordingly we travelled by Schaffhausen, Constanz, Ulm, to Munich. No sooner were the mountains left behind than my physical maladies began to revive. The life of cities decidedly disagreed with me. Head and eyes grew worse. I could not sleep properly and suffered terribly from exhaustion on waking from painful or erotic dreams.

I studied a good deal and had, on this journey, the sense to perceive the essential tawdriness of modern Munich. This I expressed in an article which I sent to the *Saturday Review*. (It appeared on 24 October 1863.) By the way, it is worth mentioning that I frequently used to contribute to that periodical.

A. O. Rutson joined us at Munich. We travelled, all three together, by Reckenberg, Nuremberg, Bamberg, to Dresden, where we put up at Fraülein Kretschmar's *pension*. Here I made the acquaintance of J. R. Mozley, Oscar Browning and Arthur Sidgwick.[13] Of the last I had heard a great deal from Rugby and Cambridge men – of his personal beauty, graceful manners and acute intelligence. I was not disappointed and formed a friendship which has lasted through my life, heightened for many years by a romantic admiration on my part. It was not quite wholesome for me at that crisis, for Arthur was enthusiastic about what I called Arcadia and this worked my feelings back again into the old channels.

Switzerland seemed far away during those weeks of concerts, picture-seeing, metaphysics and emotions at Dresden. Then came the day for returning to England. Green and I went to the book fair at Leipzig. I remember sleeping in one room with him next to the bedroom of two drunken German Jews. They were discussing the immortality of the soul till far into the small hours, shouting from bed to bed. At last they reached a point at which the argument turned on 'my mother's soul and thy mother's soul'. Green could stand it no longer. He jumped up, knocked at the partition door, and humbly began to beg *die Herren* to consider their sleepless neighbours. This caused an unexpected diversion. Both the Jews leaped out of bed and battered at the door, screaming the most obscene oaths, which contrasted ludicrously with their maudlin metaphysics and their mothers' souls. Luckily, the bolts of the door held fast and after cooling their blood, the Jews grumblingly retired to bed again and slumber.

Arthur Sidgwick joined me at Cologne and we went home together. I was received full fellow at Magdalen and spent a little time at Clifton with my father. Then, my head and eyes making any other occupation impossible, I set off again to travel. My father was so uneasy about my health that he made me take a courier as far as Genoa, where I met Rutson. Then I dismissed the man, who was an intolerable nuisance.

Rutson and I drove along the Riviera di Levante to Pisa, and thence to Florence, where we stayed until about 10 December, then travelled, mostly driving, through Siena, and Orvieto, Chiusi, Viterbo, and the Ciminian hills to Rome. Rutson was extremely kind but plaguily argumentative; and I was too chronically fatigued to stand the strain of his restless aimless intellectuality. At Rome he informed me that he was in love with my sister Charlotte; but he wrapped up his emotion in so many qualifying clauses, hypotheses and conditions of all kinds, that I did not much believe in its intensity. All my friends were falling in love with Charlotte. A. B. Webb[14] (afterwards a colonial bishop) did. H. G. Dakyns[15] (of whom I shall have much to say) did. And Green, though he spoke nothing for some years, was already thinking of her as the only woman he could wish to marry.

We reached Rome on 17 December. Rutson left for England; and W. R. W. Stephens came to stay with me. We took lodgings at the very top of a house in the Corso, extremely cold but healthy. Being unable to use my eyes for study, I read very little and learned no Italian. This was disadvantageous; and I shall remark, in the chapter on my literary development, upon the loss I suffered through ill health during the years which followed my degree at Oxford. On the other hand, I was able to walk as much as I liked, and could see everything which did not involve mental strain. Accordingly, with indefatigable curiosity, I drank in buildings, statues, pictures, nature – the whole of the wonderful Italian past presented in its monuments and landscape. I learned a great deal undoubtedly, which proved of use to me in after years. And the life I led was simple, reserved, free from emotional disturbances, pure as that of an anchorite.

How I dragged my illness and my ennui through that wonderful world appears from some stanzas written at Sorrento on 5 February. They are printed in *New and Old* under the title 'Looking Back'. It is noticeable, perhaps, that this poem, undoubtedly the pure spontaneous utterance of a prevalent mood, dwells upon Clifton and Willie, wholly omitting any mention of the Alps and Rosa . . . .

I was deeply wounded in the heart and moral nature, deeply wounded in brain and nerves; and yet I was so young. On 5 February 1864, I reckoned just 23 years and 4 months. And like Alfred de Musset, in his 'Nuit de Décembre', I could speak of my wanderings thus:

> Partout où, sous ces vastes cieux,
> J'ai lassé mon coeur et mes yeux,
> Saignant d'une éternelle plaie;
> Partout où le boiteux Ennui,
> Traînant ma fatigue aprés lui,
> M'a promené sur une claie.

The physical illness – that obscure failure of nerve force, which probably caused a subacute and chronic congestion of small blood-vessels in the brain, the eyes, the stomach perhaps, and other organs – was the first source of this ennui. But there was another and deeper source behind it, and of which in fact it was but the corporeal symptom. I had not recovered from the long anxiety caused by Vaughan's affair, from the blow of Shorting's treacherous attack, from the dumb effort to warp and twist aright my innate and aberrant passions. Then exercise, head work, superfluous agitation concerning religion and metaphysics – the necessary labour of an ambitious lad at college, and the unwholesome malady of thought engendered by a period of *Sturm und Drang* in England – depressed vitality and blent the problems of theology with ethical and personal difficulties.

Such, I think, were the constitutent factors of my ennui. It grew daily more and more oppressive. As the clouds had rolled away in the congenial atmosphere of Mürren, so now in the great cities of Italy they gathered again. I returned to England weaker than I had left it.

At Clifton in the early spring I saw much of Henry Graham Dakyns. He had come to be an assistant master at the recently established College. He was a Rugby–Cambridge man, the friend of Arthur Sidgwick whom I knew, and of Henry Sidgwick, whom I was destined to know. All these names will recur frequently in my memoirs. Of Graham, I need only say here that his perfervid temper of emotion, his unselfishness, his capacity for idealizing things and people, the shrewdness of his intellectual sense, and the humour of his utterance (style almost of Jean-Paul Richter),[16] made their immediate impression on me. In philosophy he inclined to Comtism, chiefly because of its altruistic theories. He was physically robust, athletic at football, courageous and spirited, but withal very nervously excitable and irritable. Gentle exceedingly and sweet in converse — ποθεινὸς τοῖς φίλοις ['longed for by his friends'].[17] Masculine to the back-bone.

Chapter Nine

Life in London, marriage, first attack of lung disease

Rutson rented the second floor of a furnished house, 7 Half Moon Street, Piccadilly. The first floor was vacant, and I enjoyed it for the year at, I think, one hundred guineas, or a trifle over. Thither I went to live in April, to eat dinners at Lincoln's Inn, and to make a pretence of studying law. My club was the Union, in Trafalgar Square, where, at that time, we had a very good kitchen, an excellent cellar of wine, and a society of country squires and city men. This club suited my tastes down to the ground; and when, by chance, I dined by invitation at a literary or academical club, I thanked my stars that I did not belong to one. It has always been my whim to keep my own affairs of the spirit as far as possible apart from the commerce of daily life – to pursue literature as a private pastime – to seek society and friendship among folk of different sorts, and while readily fraternizing with scholars and students, to avoid the boredom and bad taste and vitiated mental atmosphere of cliques, artistic circles, coteries. This, I know, has stamped my work with amateurishness. But I am well content to have achieved imperfect things in literature, and to have obtained a partial hearing from the public; because, through doing so, I have preserved intact my personal elasticity and freedom, my disengagement from professional and pecuniary considerations, my absolute incapacity for posing as a rival or competitor with any man, my privilege of being talked about in circles of the craft of authors, my contemptuous indifference to criticism, and my commanding sense of the superiority of life to culture. Life was what I always wanted; and of life I never had enough. Literature might go to the dogs, for me. As Sir Thomas Browne said of the terrestrial globe, I 'turned it round for my

150

recreation'. I liked it for its own sake; I loved it as my daily solace. But life stretched beyond, and life was what no art could seize, except (as Whitman says) 'by indirections'.[1]

Thus, in the early summer of 1864, I found myself set up in London. There was much, as I have hinted, in the situation favourable to my temperament. But the climactic and social conditions were adverse. My nervous malady, felt mostly in the brain and eyes, but also expressed by a terrible disturbance of the reproductive organs, developed with painful rapidity. I sat for hours with closed eyes listening to hired readers. I put myself under Bowman,[2] and paid him a guinea a day for dropping deleterious caustic under my nether eyelids. I went to Acton[3] and allowed him to cauterize me through the urethra. I did everything in short, except what nature prompted. Nature bade me indulge my sexual instincts; but these were so divided that I shrank alike from the brothel and the soldier. Nature whispered, Go again to Switzerland. I cast longing eyes to Rosa and to Mürren. I wrote for the *Saturday Review*: but now for the most part unsuccessfully; and for this reason, that I began to put myself into my articles, and these were, week by week, deleted by the editor. To write originally, not in the tone and form prescribed for the weekly, was a violation of the rule of the game. This I soon felt, and desisted. Then I set my thoughts about theology on paper in a commentary upon Goethe's Proemium to 'Gott und Welt'. (Printed in my private *Miscellanies*, pages 1–36.) I peered in purblind fashion at the minor Elizabethan dramatists. I read and thought and wrote at random in the club. I rode in the park, rowed on the Serpentine, and went sculling up the river with a waterman of Surbiton. Characteristically enough, I began to fall in love with this young fellow. And all this while, when it was possible, I accepted the invitations to dinner parties and balls which my father's numerous relations with good society amply afforded me. The opera houses, and the concerts at St James's Hall, were also a resource. With closed eyes I sat listening to the divine melodies of Mozart, the symphonies of Beethoven, to Gounod, Bellini, Donizetti, Verdi; to Rubinstein's impassioned pianoforte playing, and Piatti's violoncello, Joachim's violin; to the voices of Trebelli and Titiens, of Giuglini, and Patti, and Pauline Lucca.[4] Dear Mme Goldschmidt was very kind to me when I went down on Saturdays to stay with her at Wimbledon; and Mrs Clough at Combe Hurst; and my cousin, Sir Thomas Neville Abdy, at Harrow.[5]

The turbid chemical amalgam of my life had reached a point at which some sort of crystallization was inevitable. It only wanted a wire of resistance and support to be thrust into it. And this was speedily found.

My father, dissatisfied with Bowman and Acton, sent me to Sir Spencer Wells.[6] That excellent surgeon, with sound common sense, gave me a simple remedy for my eyes – vinegar and water for a lotion, and the prospect of recovery through time and perseverance. For my constitution, he recommended cohabitation with a hired mistress, or, what was better, matrimony. He impressed upon me the theory that marriage ought not to be regarded as a matter of idealized passion, but as the sober meeting together of man and woman for mutual needs of sex, for fellow service, and loyal devotion to the duties of social and domestic life in common.

This was a view in many ways distasteful to my nature both as man and artist. I felt that if I hired a mistress, or took a wife on calculation, I should be running counter to my deepest and most powerful instincts; shutting myself out from passion and ideal love, neither of which had been indulged, although my whole being panted for them. An older man, who had tried life, might do this safely, I reasoned. I, at the age of twenty-three, was far too young and too unformed for compromises. And I could not assume my good physician's plain practical standing ground with regard to the relations of sex. Illicit connections with a woman were out of the question. If instinct had to be followed, I must have found its satisfaction in male friendship. But this was just what I had resolved to suppress and overcome. His argument, therefore, made a strong appeal to my reason, when I considered the possibility of a suitable marriage. It seemed to be the one exit from my difficulties; and I found myself supported by my father and Sir Edward Strachey, when I talked the matter over with them. The temptation became powerful, to try.

Then, as by inspiration, the memory of Catherine North returned to me. She was connected with the best and happiest period of my past confused existence. To her I felt that I must turn. I was well aware what I was seeking from her, and what a poor self I had to offer. At least I could be frank and true with her. At least I might discover whether she would accept me, as I was, and enter upon life with me according to my modest views of matrimony.

The plan once formed, I put it into execution with characteristic impetuosity and single-sightedness. I did not stop to think or hesitate. I felt myself led and directed. To idealize the situation was for me only too easy, and to concentrate my energies upon it was obeying the impulse of my character.

I called at 3 Victoria Street where Mr North lived. He and his daughter received me hospitably, not forgetful of Mürren. They asked me to dinner. I hunted up common friends, especially Miss Mary Ewart.[7] All the social threads which connected me with the Norths, slender and distant, yet capable of being used, I put in requisition. And so I gradually made myself, during the later weeks of the London season, a house guest of the Norths. Catherine and I saw much of each other at operas and concerts. These were the places where we came to know each other best – and also in visits to her own house. The more I saw of her, the more I felt for certain that she was the woman whom I ought to marry – for my own sake. I did not foresee the complications of life in such a marriage. I deeply felt my own unworthiness of her. But at the same time, I saw no reason why I should not present myself as fairly as I could. In social position and birth I was hardly her equal. I carried an ugly surname. But I was well enough off in property and expectations. And I knew that, although my health had placed me under disadvantages, I was a man above the average in acquirements and ability.

It seemed to me, during the course of these July days, that she was not indifferent to me. The Norths told me they were going to Pontresina. I asked her elder sister, Miss Marianne North, whether I might be allowed to follow them thither, letting it be known that I should come for Catherine's sake. The answer was neutral, but such that I felt justified in joining them if I thought proper.

I went to Clifton and told my father what my plans were. He approved. I went to Norwich, for some forgotten purpose, and stayed with a clergyman of our acquaintance. I must have been in a sexually electrical condition; for his young wife nearly led me into an adulterous *amour* with her. Had it not been for my constitutional repugnance for mere casual acts with women whom I did not love emotionally, there is no doubt that I should have possessed her. The force of passion was in me, and the will to yield to her. And if she had been a male, some act would have been performed. As it was, the erethism caused by her presence and voluptuous incitements only disturbed my nervous system and repelled me with a disgust for her person. It is necessary to write this down; for it points, better than any analysis, the division at that time between sexual appetite in me (which was not natural and carnal, like Tom Jones's, for a female), and emotional sympathies and aspirations leading me to seek a woman for my life comrade. For a long time previously, I had treated the purely sexual appetite (that which drew me fatally to the male) as a beast to be suppressed and curbed, and latterly to be down-trampled by the help of surgeons and their cautery of sexual organs.

I kept a diary – one of those self-conscious, self-analytical, self-descriptive records, to which I was addicted – concerning all the daily details in this courtship of Miss Catherine North. But a sense of respect for my wife made me destroy it, while I preserved others of like import, which did not affect her personally. This is the reason why I am giving only a summary of my main life drama.

Well: I set off alone, early in August 1864, to overtake the Norths. I was going on the quest of Catherine. And I felt so uncertain of the issue that I carried with me a heap of books, chiefly Elizabethan dramatists, to work at in some corner of the Alps if my errand should prove vain. Paris, Basel, Zürich, Chur: I do not well remember how I did the journey. I only remember crossing the Lenzer Heide and the Julier in the banquette of the *diligence*, and feeling the aridity of Graubünden in painful contrast to what I had so fresh in memory of Mürren. With what different emotions I regard that journey now, known as the long road, in all its aspects of heat, dust and storm, of winter snow, of starlight and of daylight. . . . On the morning of 10 August, I found myself at the Hotel Krone (then a very modest inn, which Lorenz Gredig, now the millionaire, and his wife and children worked with their own hands). Loitering in the entrance before lunch, I met Catherine; and our life together began. No words, like 'idyll', must be used about it. This was earnest business on my part, charged with misgivings, not of her, but of myself, full of serious and fearful anticipations of the best. We walked out together with a party of friends to the little lake upon the way to St Moritz. And every day, we walked together – Marianne, or Pop, as she was called, allowing it. There is a bridge above the stream at Pontresina; and this became our meeting place; and here, one after-noon, I think, when snow was falling in thin flakes, I asked her to be my wife. Two days afterwards, we got permission from Mr and Mrs North to climb the Pitz Languard together without a guide. There we sat alone, undisturbed by tourists or by company, beneath the cloudless heavens, with all the Alpine world outspread before us – even to the distant Jungfrau, Mönch and Eiger, under whose snowy crags we met last year – and there we exchanged rings, I taking the one of lapis lazuli, inscribed with her initials J. C. N. which I carry on the little finger of my left hand now. That was a day of days. Few young people have been privileged to exchange vows to plight troth, to solemnize their future life in common, upon such an eyrie.

Surgit amari aliquid[8] ['There arises something bitter']. All was so sweet and unexpected so unbelieveable by me in this great happiness, that some bitterness must needs arrive. The best would have been to have died there on the top of the Pitz Languard – except that Catherine must have gone down alone and terrified. I had secured the great good of any man's life, a good too great for my imperfect nature, the love and troth of a woman gracious in her womanhood. Was I fit for her? I doubted not my power to serve her, and support her, and to care for her in every circumstance. I loved her ardently, and felt the thrill of something wonderful and new inrushing into my existence. But was it not too pure, too spiritual, too etherialized, this exquisite emotion? It would endure till death, I know. But I missed something in the music – the coarse and hard vibrations of sex, those exquisite agonies of contact, by which the God in man has subsumed into himself the beast and makes that God-like. These vibrations I had felt in dreams for male beings and in intercourse with Willie. Not discovering them now some qualms came over me. Was my love perfect for her, such a holocaust of self as she had a right to expect? The doubt troubled me. But I turned my thoughts to Dante and his Beatrice, and told my heart it did not signify. Better was it to love as I felt capable of loving her. Nevertheless, a word, dropped in my ear just before we left Pontresina, troubled this security. My old friend Charles Knight[9] the painter happened to be there. He knew, as all the English people knew, of our engagement. Penetratively and reflectively he said, 'The one thing in marriage is passion; without passion no man has the right to make a woman his wife.' Just the same words said a Davos peasant lad to me last night, '*Die Beiden sollten lieben, heftig lieben*' ['These two ought to love passionately']. Sexual passion, at the commencement of nuptial love, is not demanded of a woman; but it is demanded of a man. And while I had everything else, and have always had everything else to give Catherine – if needful, I would die for her willingly – I could not so conquer the original bent of my instincts as to feel for

155

her in the brutal unmistakeable appetite of physical desire. It must be added that I doubt whether this appetite ever entered into her affection for me. Only to this extent has our union been imperfect. But all the difficulties of my subsequent life, and a large part of hers have come from our not having originally started with a strong sexual attraction on either side.

We passed the Bernina Pass together to Poschiavo; and there these casuistical questionings occupied my mind to such an extent that I wrote a self-analytical letter to Rutson, *cacoethes scribendi*! [a frenzied itch to write]. I forget exactly what the letter contained; but the substance was my doubt of the coarser element of love in me for Catherine. Afterwards, this letter led to much unprofitable and disagreeable correspondence between him and me. Else it need not have been mentioned. I want in every detail of my inner life to be as exactly truthful as a mortal man can be.

Such clouds of thought were lightly puffed away. We crossed the Stelvio and went on our way to Venice. There to the Italian lakes and Turin. Homeward so to England. Mr North told me frequently upon this journey that Catherine had a terrible temper. I was not frightened, because I knew that I had moral deficiencies which would counterbalance her bad temper. Indeed I have often had to suffer from it as she has had to suffer from my faults. But age has mellowed her one defect, while it has developed all her noble virtues. Would to God that I could say the same of myself!

I think we were equally, and, on the whole, well matched. At any rate, for better and for worse, we were married at Hastings on 10 November 1864. It was a brilliant wedding; for Mr North, as Member, was much beloved; and irrespective of the town, the whole countryside including the Duke of Cleveland,[10] came to do us honour.

After our wedding my wife and I were driven to Brighton by a Norfolk coachman, who had been in Mr North's service many years.

It requires all the romance and passion of Romeo and Juliet to make a double bedroom in an English town hotel appear poetical. Marriage begins ill which begins with a prosaic tour through inns. The first joys of nuptial intercourse ought not to be remembered in connection with places so common, so sordid and so trivial.

I shall not forget the repulsion stirred in me by that Brighton bedroom or the disillusion caused by my first night of marriage. Disagreeable as it is, I cannot omit to tell the truth about these things, since they are all-important for the object I have in writing my memoirs.

I had never had anything at all to do with any woman in the way of sex. I had only a vague notion about the structure of the female body. I had never performed any sexual act with any one, and I did not know how to go about it. I firmly expected that some extraordinary and ecstatic enthusiasm would awake in me at the mere contact of a woman's body in bed, although I was aware that the presence of women did not disturb my senses in the ballroom or a carriage. I also anticipated that nature would take care of herself when it came to the consummation of marriage.

To my surprise and annoyance, I felt myself rather uncomfortable than otherwise by the side of my wife, oppressed with shyness, and not at all carried away by passionate enthusiasm. Dearly as I loved her, and ardently as I desired through marriage to enter into the state of normal manhood, I perceived that this thing which we had to do together was not what either of us imperatively required. I felt no repugnance at first, but no magnetic thrill of attraction. A deep sense of disappointment came over me when I found that the

> Corps feminin, qui tant est tendre,
> Polly, souef, si précieux[11]

did not exercise its hoped-for magic. What was worse, nature refused to show me how the act should be accomplished. This was due to no defect in me. The organ of sex was vigorous enough and ready to perform its work. My own ineptitude prevented me for several nights from completing the marital function; and at last I found the way by accident – after having teased and hurt both my wife and myself, besides suffering dismally from the humiliating absurdity of the situation. She afterwards told me that such manifest proofs of my virginity were agreeable to her. But all the romance and rapture of sexual intercourse, on which I had so fondly counted, were destroyed by this sordid experience. I also discovered that the physical contact of a woman, though it did not actually disgust me, left me very cold. There was something in it nauseous, and cohabitation in my case meant only the mechanical relief of nature.

Truly we civilized people of the nineteenth century are more backward than the African savages in all that concerns this most important fact of human life. We allow young men and women to contract permanent relations involving sex, designed for procreation, without instructing them in the elementary science of sexual physiology. We do all that lies in us to keep them chaste, to develop and refine their sense of shame, while we leave them to imagine what they like about the nuptial connection. Then we fling them naked into bed together, modest, alike ignorant, mutually embarrassed by the awkward situation, trusting that they will blunder upon the truth by instinct. We forget that this is a dangerous test of their affection and their self-respect; all the more dangerous in proportion as they are highly cultivated, refined and sensitive. Instead of the supreme embrace occurring, as it ought to do, and does in properly instructed people, as an episode, inevitable and consummative of the long chord of passion, it has to be stupidly sought out amid circumstances of abasement which generate repugnance.

I have known cases of marriage spoiled from the commencement by this idiotic system of let-alone education.

But enough of the subject. My marriage was not spoiled in any essential detail. After the removal of that preliminary obstacle, it remained what it had been before – an union of feeling and of fellow service, rather than one of passion or of *heftige Liebe* [passionate love]. The serious fault in it on my side has always existed, and could not be eliminated, because it belonged to the very groundwork of my nature. I was born with strong but slowly matured sexual appetites; and these were incapable of finding their satisfaction with a woman. Nuptial intercourse developed them by the exercise of the reproductive organs. It did not and could not divert them from their natural bias toward the male.

In the winter of 1865 we settled in lodgings, choosing Albion Street, Paddington, on account of its closeness to Hyde Park. I studied a little law, ate dinners at Lincoln's Inn, and did what private reading my weak eyes allowed. We then bought a house in Norfolk Square, number 47, chiefly induced by the quiet of the situation. Our friends George Miller[12] and his young wife, following our lead, bought the next house but one to ours. It was an unfortunate step; for the situation proved gloomy, and not by any means favourable to our health.

The greater part of the summer was spent at Clifton, where Thomas Woolner[13] made a marble bust of my father. I do not remember a more persistently rainy July than this. From certain symptoms in the left side which I remember, I probably laid the seeds of pulmonary disease during this month.

When we returned to London, it was to settle down at 47 Norfolk Square. For some time a strange state of affairs had been growing up between Rutson and myself. He was under the delusion (amounting to sheer hallucination) that he had himself cared for my wife, had retired in my favour, and that I had wooed and won her with full knowledge of his sacrifice. I shall introduce a succinct account of this extremely disagreeable episode, which was written when all the facts were fresh in my memory, and an open rupture between Rutson and ourselves had happened.* It is only necessary to mention the matter here, because it had a serious influence on my health. Rutson used to talk and argue upon these painful topics, like a veritable madman, for four or five hours together. He would waylay me on those autumn evenings on my way home from the Temple, and keep me sitting on benches in the parks, listening to the eternally repeated story of his wrongs. I felt such a debt of gratitude to him, and was really so sorry about his state of mind, that I bore in every way I could with these crazy humours; and caught a very bad cold, which settled on my lungs.

Meanwhile, on 22 October, our eldest daughter Janet was born. More than ever, after this, I neglected my health. The wet-nurse warned me one day that my incessant cough was what she bluntly called 'a churchyard cough'.

My wife had suffered, during the summer months before Janet's birth, from great depression of spirits and nervous disturbance. These symptoms, during her recovery from childbirth, became really alarming; and already now, after less than a year's experience of marriage, we both felt that it might be better for the happiness of each if we could avoid the necessity of adding to our family.

As soon as she could travel, a little before Christmas, we went down to stay at Clifton. There my father examined me one day, and pronounced that there was mischief of a very serious kind at work in the apex of the left lung. All thought of an active professional life had to be abandoned. I was subjected to energetic treatment and confined to the house for some weeks, at the end of which period my wife and I went to Mentone.

Before carrying the record of our doings further I will insert the last fragment of my wife's diary.

*See Appendix 3 – Editor.

[Symonds here inserted the following passage from his wife's diary, dated 30 January 1866, at Clifton. – Editor.]

We are here again, and we have a child, our little Janet, just three months old. She was born in London, last October, the 22nd, costing her mother much pain, but that is over now, and the little creature is very precious. But I am older, much older since I last wrote. Married life is not all romance and glitter, there is much in it that is, that *must* be painful, wearying; much, in cases where true love is, that is infinitely holy and beautiful. And in mine I have found this, love always perfect and enduring, making that good which otherwise would be scarcely endurable. If girls knew all that marriage means, there would be less 'marrying in the abstract' less of that foolish longing for the temporary glitter and variety of the thing, possibly for the romance also, which has so often disgusted me in my contemporaries.

I go back over the history of the past fifteen months, and I find just four that have been perfectly bright and enjoyable, the rest mostly full of sickness, heaviness and weariness (of body purely, by which the mind suffers and gets depressed against its better reason). I would gladly have a rest now, if only of a few months, but that it seems not to be, and I must only wait, and hope patiently, through another year. Perhaps it may not be so bad this time, but the pain and weakness of this last year have left me only half myself as I was at Pontresina, and I did long very much for a rest now. Is marriage worth all this? I think it is, where love so precious is given abundantly, but it is a point to be considered thoughtfully by those who are thinking of it.

Our first three weeks, we spent in the Isle of Wight, then came here for Christmas. Here we went through a course of dinner parties and entertainments from strangers whose very names were unknown to me, we were lions for a season, now we are old people again. Then we went to Hastings for Maggie's wedding, then to London, where we made a temporary home for our two selves in lodgings in Albion Street. Those were *very* happy months, the best since we married, we had no cares and lived in two tiny rooms, which were thoroughly comfortable, but wanted circumspection in walking about. I wish we could have stayed there always. But we had the prospect of a child, and it was thought advisable for us to get a house of our own, so we bought a house in Norfolk Square, and furnished it and went into it last June, and there our baby was born last November. Will that be our home always? I wish I could bring myself to look upon it contentedly as that, but I do not. We have lived in it so little, perhaps there has not been time to strike root in it yet. Those dreary two months of early winter after our baby was born gave me a repugnance to the house which I cannot shake off now though at a distance; perhaps it was our own weakness and physical depression that made it seem so big and gloomy; but its size and darkness, and chilliness seemed to haunt me then, and I cannot rub off the impression now.

A thousand times I have wished myself back in our sunny little rooms in Albion Street, but we have made our own lot and must abide by it. Perhaps when we go back to it, it may seem brighter. In summer it certainly did so, a July sun, blazing through the north-west windows, which all through the winter never catch his rays. I did not know till now how much winter sunlight had to do with raising or depressing one's spirits, at Hastings we had enough of it and to spare, in the flat also, and I never thought about it, or reflected on it. Here when it shines upon our window in the morning, gilding the leafless trees, and grey old city, I rejoice in it, like an Alpine grasshopper; it seems life-giving, better than tonics.

Am I growing hypochondriacal, fanciful? But for weeks after Janet was born, I never felt warm, always shivery, since Christmas when we came here, I have been a new creature, putting out feelers, and gathering strength abundantly. And now all the weary weary time is coming over again, . . . after one short month of rest; my God: grant me strength, and faith, that I may look forward to the time when my children shall be a pleasure to me.

All women do not mind this so, am I unreasonable? But it is hard that these first months of our married life should have so much of their brightness taken off by physical suffering. All this is egotistical, I speak nothing of Johnnie. He too has been ill, a bad cough of two months' standing, how caught I know not, partly sitting in a draught in his own study at home, partly in law chambers; it made us anxious, but his father has cured it, as it seems, entirely.

Now our life and plans are very uncertain, he is to give up law reading, and not to return to London for two months, the house is to be let, if possible, and we are to go abroad. I do not mind, a week ago I rejoiced in the plan, I do not love our house, and travelling will not be the enjoyment it used to be, but perhaps this time may not be so bad. And it will be good for Johnnie, and we two shall be alone together again among beautiful scenes which we both love, and without the hateful household cares.

9 February. Keeping a diary is in some respects a bad thing. It gives one a one-sided view of one's life, and *that* the morbid side. For when one is happy one does not write. All this last I wrote at twelve o'clock the other night, because I couldn't sleep and was miserable, and Johnnie was away in London, and my distempered thought *would* find vent somewhere. And I did myself no good by it, only went shivering to bed towards one o'clock, more wide awake and miserable than ever. And after all my worst dread was imaginary. For the weakness and sickness which I then thought was coming upon me again is not to be, I hope, at least for a season, and I shall have rest in myself. This is comfort.

If we can let our house for a few months, and so get rid of care, and go abroad for a season, how happy we ought to be. But I wish I could cultivate the home-feeling towards our house in Norfolk Square, instead of longing so intemperately to get rid of it; it would be wiser, more womanly. Wandering about is very well for a season, but our life has to be lived somewhere, and the home we have chosen to bring up our children in ought to have a different feeling to me from this that I have towards it. I almost wish I could be forced to live in it for a whole year, never quitting it, so as to be made to feel it inevitable that I should live there always, instead of this endless speculative retrospect, as to what *might* have been. And Johnnie is so good and patient to me always, and I am no comfort to him, only trouble. How weak I am, when I began life with such real, honest, earnest determination to be strong and a support to him, and now I am weak, querulous, cowardly, shirking my duties, and hating what ought to be such a happy life. How unfit I am to be a wife! And then a mother's duties are coming too by and by, and those are graver still. How little fitted I am to mould and form my little Janet's character, if my own is so weak and tottering.

Had I never realized the seriousness of life in the old time, that now it is come, I am to break under it, and be useless. There are so many people, that I used to dislike and despise who, I see now, are better, truer, wiser women in their lives than I. Oh my God, make me better, I cry, I struggle to be strong, and it comes not, I pray to thee, but it is blindly, faithlessly.

And all my life is full of good, full of blessing, if I could but get rid of this gnawing sordid dread of expense and responsibility. I try to hide it from Johnnie, for he hates it, and it is unworthy, but hiding it only makes it worse. He wrote me two letters from London, that ought to be printed in letters of gold, they are so good, so wise. If I could get up to his level, and so look down upon these petty cares of everyday life, how I should rejoice. But I am small, weak, not worthy to be taken up by two of his fingers.

This fragment from her pen sufficiently explains the situation, and will be of use in the interpretation of much which I shall afterwards relate.

We went to join my sister Lady Strachey at Mentone. Here began the long series of journeys to the Riviera in search of health, and also a new phase in my Italian experience. (The year 1865–6 was important for my literary development. I did a great deal of careful, yet instinctive writing, which helped to form my style, and much of which remains among my published works.) My wife's sister, Lady Kay Shuttleworth[14] had a villa at San Remo. The cure which my father had accomplished at Clifton was here confirmed. But it could not be radical. From the Riviera, we passed to Florence, Ravenna, Macugnaga, Val d'Aosta, Mürren, and returned to Clifton in July. Then again to 47 Norfolk Square; but this was soon abandoned, and the winter of 1866–7 was spent at Hastings with the Norths. Here I wrote an essay on the Greek idyllists and several studies of Elizabethan dramatists.

Chapter Ten

Early years of marriage; peregrinations of all sorts, interrupted literary labour

In March 1867 at Clifton, I caught a bad cold, from which I did not recover easily. Nevertheless we went back to 47 Norfolk Square. My father was so anxious about my state of health – I was suffering from the chronic trouble in my head, a permanent malaise and nervous sensibility, which made me incapable of steady work, together with a subacute pneumonia in the left lung – that he thought it best to send me off upon a journey at the end of May. My wife was unable to travel, expecting her second confinement in a few months. So my sister Charlotte, now Mrs Thomas Hill Green, kindly volunteered to bear me company; and very good company she was during our ramblings in Normandy.

I find a collection of letters written to my wife upon this tour, parts of which she copied out into a ms. book. They clearly indicate the state of mind and emotion at that epoch. . . .

It is not difficult to see why my head was tired. The hyperaesthesia indicated upon every page is only too apparent. As I find written in one of the passages, 'During all this journey I have been more excitable than dead.'

On the whole, I returned to England worse than I went. Such a fortnight was enough to fatigue anyone. Not only did I try to feel and understand everything I saw, but I scrutinized my own soul at every spare moment. And then how much I wrote! The letters were not intended for publication. Still they were composed with literary style and a large amount of compressed emotion.

After a short visit to Hastings, where we seem to have stayed until 23 June, we returned to London and lived at 47 Norfolk Square. I could not shake the lung mischief or the brain-weariness off, but grew worse and worse during the hot weeks, panting continually to be in Switzerland.

Henry Sidgwick, whose acquaintance I had recently made, was also staying in London – philosophizing, going to spiritualistic seances, and trying to support himself (for an experiment) on the minimum of daily outlay. Our acquaintance ripened rapidly into a deep and close friendship, which has been of inestimable value during the last twenty-two years. It would be difficult to say how much I owe to the rarely noble character, the wisdom, the extraordinary mental originality, the inexhaustible sympathy and kindness of this most remarkable man.

This summer and the year which followed were of such importance in my life that I must relate the incidents in some detail, and illustrate them by extracts from notebooks and letters in my possession.

I began writing poetry again during the hot summer weather; and all my poems were composed upon the subject of masculine love. The second half of 'John Mordan', 'Diego', 'Love and Music', 'The Headmaster',[1] together with a great number of dithyrambic pieces in the style of Walt Whitman, belong to those months. Yet I find myself constantly doubting my own literary faculty.

Art is very long. I have not yet vigour of nerve enough to give to composition that patient and incessant application which results in form. I have the molten fluid in my soul; but the strength to fashion the mould for it is wanting.

Whether I am a poet or not, I am haunted by certain situations and moral tragedies which demand expression from me. I suppose that this arises from what I have myself suffered in the past – emotional distress that has indelibly impressed my nature, and which reproduces itself in the shape of dreams or dreamlike images. Long ago I crushed the tendency to write these situations into poetry, as being injurious to my health of mind and body. Besides, I had no belief in my artistic faculty. Yet, for all this, the tendency to do so remains and gathers force; the ideas have never left my mind, but have acquired distinctness and durability with my growth.

There is a passive and an active imagination. The one creates, the other sympathizes. The one makes new things for the world, the other appropriates whatever has been made, informing the past with something of fresh life. To men as are not in a true sense artists, it is a solace thus to retrace the history of the world. Like Dürer's *Melan-*

choly, they sit brooding, their minds a mirror, their wings down-drooping, their arms sinewless, their back unbraced.

It appears to me now that I entirely misunderstood my own case. What was really happening was that I was pining away through the forcible repression of my natural inclination for the male sex. I could not keep my thoughts from running on this subject; I could not prevent myself from dreaming at night about it; I could not refrain from poetizing the passion in a hundred forms. What would have cured me would have been to indulge it .... Everything short of that I seem to have allowed myself because I could not help it. But this conduct resulted in a dangerous nervous erethism, especially since I was living as a bachelor in marriage. My wife, before the birth of her second child, suffered from a strong feeling of repugnance for the marriage bed; and after her delivery, we did our utmost to avoid another pregnancy. The third which ensued came by accident during the next spring, when the wretched conditions of this sort of life forced us to resume cohabitation. The precautions which we then used failed on one occasion; and it was in an old room of a Ferrard inn that Madge was begotten.

The circumstances here described aggravated my nervous and pulmonary maladies. I was in a perpetual fever. Early in the morning I used to rise from a sleepless bed, walk across the park, and feed my eyes upon the naked men and boys bathing in the Serpentine. The homeliest of them would have satisfied me; and I wrote my feeling out in a prose poem which will be reported in its proper place. Sometimes the literary expression of my incurable malaise assumed an almost hysterical form.

'I have in my heart's ear a couplet of Theognis:

ὄλβιος ὅστις ἐρῶν γυμνάζεται, οἴκαδε δ᾽ ἐλθών
εὕδει σὺν χαλῷ παιδὶ πανημέριος.

['Happy is the lover who does his exercise, and then goes home to sleep with a good-looking boy all day.']² This is thine, O man, to do! to supple strong limbs in not ignoble toil, to take fair limbs in amorous embrace, to sleep half-waking through long afternoons with beauty lulled upon thy bosom, thinking no wrong the while, and doing none, but cherishing thy youth with sweetness. Have I not seen it, felt it, lived it all? In dreams, in dreams, Iago! I who am a poet, in my barren fancy, embrace pleasure in dead dreams. Yes, this afternoon I held Lycidas upon the down of beds of dreaming, ἔστρωται τὸ λέχος [the bed is made ready], embroidered silk, with eiderdown for underprop of delicate flesh. Fair is the form ὀκτωκαιδεκάτος παιδὸς ἔτ ᾽ἐν χλαμίδι['of an eighteen-year-old boy still wearing the chlamys'].[3] Him I clasped slumbering very sweetly in the gates of dreams. From his closed eyelids I kissed the bloom of dreams, and from his parted lips I drank the balm of slumber. I was Hypnos gazing on Endymion in the cave of Latmos. Golden hair, and white neck, and breasts brighter than twin stars, and belly softer than the down of doves, and dewy thighs, and awful beauty of love's minister beneath the tuft of crispy curls, and slender swelling legs, and rosy feet, and long lithe languid arms. I had them all pressed to my body there, flank to flank – kissed every part and member of the lad – with wandering hand tasted them one by one, and felt the fervour of smooth buttocks glowing and divine. In a day dream: O Jupiter!

Four young men are bathing in the pond by the embankment. I pass; the engine screams and hurries me away. But the engine has no power to take my soul. That stays, and is the pond in which the bathers swim, the air in which they shout, the grass on which they run and dress themselves, the hand that touches them unfelt, the lips that kiss them and they know it not.

A dream of perfection. A face not necessarily of faultless beauty, but sympathetic to my taste, more amiable than all faces ever seen. It approaches. I gaze steadfastly. The face brightens, smiles with ineffable tenderness. We have surely known and loved each other in old times. We have waited very long, and now we shall not be separated again. Behold! already he has told me many things, and I have given to him of my treasures. Oh, what joy; oh, what a kiss! Da mihi centum, deinde mille! [Give me a hundred, then a thousand!][4] O friend, for thee, – I wake permeated by the sense of having communed in mind soul and body with the most beautiful and loveable being; not an atom of myself but has been touched and transfigured by his contact. For the time I have no vain longings, no flush, no painful corrosion of the flesh by aching wishes. I am new-born.

I sat in a lecture room, and listened to a rhetorician droning out dull periods with a deadened voice upon the familiar topic of the Dramatists I love so well. Yet the hour was not all barren of delight: for you, dear unknown boy, sat beside me, delicately made, with crisp hair curling round your forehead. Laughter dwelt in your eyes, and you looked as though you longed to be merry. – We touched each other. Little by little I used him to the feeling of my hand upon his thigh and knee. The tremors of his body ran magnetically through my right arm. I was penetrated with the streams of electricity that flowed from him. We exchanged no words. I do not even know the boy's name.

Give me love, love; to taste love, such as I imagine it, at length. Let me no longer hollow out my eyes and shrink my limbs with watchful longing. Let me not waste my days in wanderings, my nights in fevered visions of impossible delights. – Dreams soft and sweet as summer rain; dreams tremulous as music, tranquil as moonbeams; dreams restful as the grave, beautiful as Hesper, terrible as tidal storms of symphonies; dreams gloomy as Egyptian darkness, mournful as midsummer noon-tide, passionate as fading flowers.

To steady my brains in this hectic fever, and to distract my thoughts from unwholesome poetry-making, I now began, at Jowett's request, to translate Zeller's volumes upon Aristotle. (In the *Geschichte der Griechischen Philosophie.*) The task was extremely uncongenial and irksome. I worked at it with difficulty, and failed to produce anything worth looking at. Meanwhile the close attention I had to pay to small German and Greek type, and the constant recurrence to dictionaries, brought the chronic inflammation of my eyes again into an acute stage. I went doggedly on at intervals, until I had finished the whole text – not the notes – and then I flung the ms. aside for ever.

No wonder I grew weaker and more ill. Four photographs taken of me by Elliot and Fry in the month of July 1867 might serve as illustrations to a book on the physiognomy of phthisis. It was my one craving to be off to Switzerland. Instinct told me I should regain health there; for since those weeks I passed at Mürren in the year 1863, I had never failed to feel a peculiar well-being among mountains. Subsequent experience has proved that my constitution is specially adapted to Alpine air. This craving expressed itself in dithyrambic incoherent prose . . . .

I very rightly connected my present discomfort with past experiences of sorrow and repression. But I did not know how to cure myself. Perhaps I could not just then have cured myself in any way except the way I wanted – change of scene, return to the vital Alpine atmosphere. I find myself writing thus to Henry Sidgwick:

Now that you are gone, and I am not to see you again until we meet in the dim distance of the Riviera, I feel that much which I have told you about myself must seem painful. My past life has been painful in many ways, and I bear in my body the marks of what I have suffered. With you, with my wife, with friends like Arthur and Graham, or when I am writing verses, I can treat those troubles of memory with cheerfulness. But at times, when my nervous light burns low in solitude, when the fever of the brain and lung is on me, then the shadows of the past gather round, and I feel that life itself is darkened. Moreover, this great shadow, not of the past, whereof I spoke today, still threatens. [Probably, my sexual difficulties.] Oppressed thus, I am often numb and callous; all virtue seems to have gone out of me, the spring of life to have faded, its bloom to have been rudely rubbed away. I dread that art and poetry and nature are unable to do more for what Dante with terrible truth called *li mal protesi nervi* [the ill-strained muscles].[5] These darknesses, in splendid scenery, among pictures and statues, wherever in fact I ought to enjoy most and be most alive. It is only the intercourse of friends which does me really any good.

Large portions of these diaries and notebooks from which I am now quoting, consist of criticisms, reflections upon art, religion, morals, proving that, despite so much physical and mental malaise, I was forming my own mind.

Im Ganzen Guten Schönen resolut zu leben. [Resolve to live in the whole, the good, the beautiful.] *To me to live is Christ, and to die gain.* How much simpler is the latter phrase. It looks like a motto for children. But how much larger, really sounder, is the former. It is large as the world, a motto for adult souls. We cannot in this age believe that St Paul's utterance is the whole truth. We cannot burn our books like the Ephesians; we ought not probably to sell our goods and give to the poor. Those were impulses of incipient faith. We have now to coordinate ourselves to what is, and accept the teaching of the ages.

What is left for us modern men? We cannot be Greek now. Since the sixteenth century, what would Aphrodite Pandemos have been? The sculptors must have modelled her, white as leprosy, adorned with golden emerods. And the Spartan laws of comradeship, the Socratic doctrine of a noble life developed out of boy-love with philosophy, how would these show in the tents of Mrs Grundy? The ages and the seasons of humanity do not repeat themselves. The cypress of knowledge springs, and withers when it comes in sight of Troy; the cypress of pleasure likewise, if it has not died already at the root of cankering Calvinism; the cypress of religion is tottering, the axe is laid close to its venerable stem. What is left? Science, for those who are scientific. Art, for artists, and all literary men are artists in a way.

169

But science falls not to the lot of all. Art is hardly worth pursuing now, so bad are the times we live in for its exercise, so faulty our ideas, so far more excellent the clear bright atmosphere of antique Hellas. What then is left? Hasheesh, I think; hasheesh, of one sort or another. We can dull the pangs of the present by living the past again in reveries or learned studies, by illusions of the fancy and a life of self-indulgent dreaming. Take down the perfumed scrolls: open, unroll, peruse, digest, intoxicate your spirit with the flavour. Beyond, there is the Athens of Plato in your narcotic visions; Buddha and his anchorites appear; the raptures of St Francis and the fire-oblations of St Dominic; the phantasms of mythologies, the birth-throes of religions, the neuroticism of chivalry, the passion of the past poems; all pass before you in your Maya-world of hasheesh, which is criticism. And music? Ah, that is the best anodyne of all. In music we emerge from opium fumes, and narcotize the soul into a hypnotism which is spiritual. But, alas, not even slumbers of the critic and dreams of the music-lover are unstirred, are undisturbed by anguish. The world weighs on us. Nature and conscience cry: 'Work, while it is yet day; the night cometh when no man can work.' Heaven goads us with infinity of secrets and torments of innumerable stars. The spirit thrills us with its chidings. Hasheesh is good for a season, *faute de mieux*. But this is no solution of the problem. Criticism, study, history, artistic pleasure will not satisfy the soul. 'Therefore to whom turn I but to thee the ineffable name?' Ever onward toward infinity I voyage, demanding only what is permanent imperishable in the world of reality.

Drudgery too is a kind of goddess, worthy of worship for the gifts she gives ungrudgingly. A Cinderella-sister of Semnai Theai[6] is she, clad in homespun, occupied with saucepans, sweeping up man's habitation, a besom in her horny hands. She is accessible and always to be found. The anodyne of fatigue is in the greasy leather wallet at her girdle. All men should pay vows at her shrine. Else they will surely suffer.

I wonder what morality is; whether eternal justice exists, immutable right and wrong; or whether law and custom rule the world of humanity, evolved for social convenience from primal savagery. I am led in my actions by impulse, admiration, regard for the moments of happiness I have recognized as beautiful, dislike of what is vile, mistrust of low and impious men – but never by fixed principles. I do not know what these are, and I very much doubt whether anyone is guided by them. I pardon a vice for its sister virtue's sake. I feel coldly toward a virtue, because of its stolid insipidity.

The curious thing is that I never once thought of answering my queries by a direct appeal to life. I did not perceive that the touchstone had in my case to be an acted passion. This was natural perhaps; for I had so recently made the experiment of marriage that I could hardly acknowledge its failure. Certainly I knew already that what I sought in marriage would not all be found there: and I felt sure that no real life could be expected from the hasheesh of my intellectual work, from drudgery, from moral conduct. I recognized the fact that I was not truly living or alive, nay that I was very seriously dying. But experience could be freely inconsiderately attempted. When the moment came for inclination to assume her sway over my nature, then criticism, intellectual work, moral relations immediately regained the meaning of reality. They fell into their proper places. The man was restored to such health and energy as he could hope for after the exhausting errors of his earlier pilgrimage. But this clearing up of my subjective atmosphere had yet to wait. It was nearly three years before the clouds began to roll away under the keen breezes of what I still condemned as sin. . . .

Chapter Eleven

Peregrinations continued – Switzerland, Provence, the Riviera – settlement at Clifton, autumn 1868

On 30 July this year, 1867, our second daughter, Lotta, was born; and when my wife was fit to travel, we left London, never to return to 47 Norfolk Square for residence. That house has no pleasant memories for me, except, characteristically enough, the memory of a few days spent there alone with Norman in the spring of 1869. . . .

It appears that I finished the translation of Zeller's text during the [following] three months. But what is more important, I composed the first draught of an essay on Greek love.

I have been busy, and have greatly tired myself by writing an essay on Platonic love. To do so has been often in my mind, and some time ago I collected the materials for it, but had to lay the work aside. My object is to explain the feelings of the Greeks about passion, to show how paiderastia was connected with their sense of beauty, and how it affected their institutions. It is not by any means finished. I am once again compelled to lay my pen down breathless. The subject appeals too deeply to my sympathies, while its more repulsive aspects are painful. I stumbled on till I came to grief in my brain. You cannot understand how intolerable it is to be devoid of physical power – not to be able to use the eyes for assiduous study or the brain for prolonged processes of thought. I often think that if I had force enough to work over and over again at expression, I might produce more satisfactory results. This essay on Platonic love, for instance, I knew to be defective. But I dare not attempt the labour. My brain will not stand it; I lose my sleep; my stomach refuses to act; and obscure aching pressure on the top and front of the head grinds me down; my eyes become inflamed and feel as though they were filled with sand.

This essay remained in ms. for a long while. Part of it I used for my chapter, in *Studies of Greek Poets*, on the Greek spirit. The rest I rewrote at Clifton in 1874, and privately printed under the title of 'A Problem in Greek Ethics'. It is clear that the preoccupation with the phenomena of sexual inversion, which had been in abeyance at Glion, was now returning. I wrote some paiderastic poems of a more or less emotional description, and slight indications in the diary show that I was being tantalized from time to time by passing strangers.

All the evil humours which were fermenting in my petty state of man — poignant and depressing memories of past troubles, physical maladies of nerve substance and of lung tissue, decompositions of habitual creeds, sentimental vapours, the disappointment of the sexual sense in matrimony, doubts about the existence of a moral basis to human life, thwarted intellectual activity, ambitions rudely checked by impotence — all the miserable factors of a wretched inner life, masked by appearances, the worse for me for being treated by the outside world as mere accidents of illness in a well-to-do and idle citizen, boiled up in a kind of devil's cauldron during those last weeks at Cannes, and made existence hell. The crisis I passed through then was decisive for my future career. But I did not foresee the point to which it was about to lead me. I only knew for certain that I must change my course, and that I would never repeat, come what might, that infernal experience of the Riviera.

Among my papers of that period, written after I had escaped from Cannes, is an incoherent document, from which I can quote certain passages to prove how terrible the crisis had been. In another nature, acting under other influences, the phenomenon of what is called 'conversion' might have been exhibited. With me it was different. I emerged at last into Stoical acceptance of my place in the world, combined with Epicurean indulgence of my ruling passion for the male. Together, these two motives restored me to comparative health, gave me religion, and enabled me, in spite of broken nerves and diseased lungs, to do what I have done in literature. I am certain of this fact; and I regard the utter blackness of despair at Cannes as the midnight in which there lay a budding spiritual morrow.

I contemplated suicide. But

... death is not acceptable; it offers no solution. I loathe myself, and turn in every direction to find strength. What I want is life; the source

173

of life fails me. I try to rest upon my will and patience. Doing so, I faint; for there is no force in me to keep the resolves I form, and no content to make me acquiesce in present circumstances. When I attempt to drown my self-scorn in mental work, my nerves give way beneath me, and the last state is worse than the first.

Those who are dying of starvation, or have lost name and fame by some irrevocable crime, might think my troubles very light. They might envy me my well-filled platter, my fair repute, the love and the respect bestowed upon me. But, humbly thankful as I am for these good things, I cannot stifle the angry voice of conscience which accuses me of a void life, besotted in selfishness and slothful debility – they do not quench my internal thirst for peace and confidence and unity with the world.

Then came the goddess Drudgery I had invoked, and spoke to me, and I replied as follows:

It is my particular source of misery that I cannot labour; I am forced to be inactive by my health; I get mildewed with the melancholy of the impotent. If I could study for six or seven hours a day, the intervals might be devoted to a well-earned relaxation. But now the whole day has to be devoted to encouraging a cheerfulness and peace that rarely come. Relaxation is labour, and the untameable soul frets under its restrictions.

A little nervous strength might make all the difference – a loosing of the bands about my forehead, a soothing of the aching eyes, an opening of the clogged breathing-tubes.

Or some clear faith in things that are good and true and pure and eternal would make all the difference.

In my present state of entire negation I cannot get the faith without the strength, or the strength without the faith. Both remain outside my reach. I have 'Moses and the prophets' and the sign of Jonah's gourd.[1] But they avail naught. 'Virtutem video intabescoque relicta.' ['I behold virtue, and having abandoned her I perish.'][2]

The last night I spent in Cannes was the worst of my whole life. I lay awake motionless, my soul stagnant, feeling what is meant by spiritual blackness and darkness. If it should last for ever! As I lay, a tightening approached my heart. It came nearer, the grasp grew firmer, I was cold and lifeless in the clutch of a great agony. If this were death? Catherine who kept hold of me, seemed far away. I was alone, so utterly desolate that I drank the very cup of the terror of the grave. The Valley of the Shadow was opened, and the shadow lies still upon my soul.

I used to think that I had no conscience and no sins to be repented of. Now I find that I am all conscience, and the whole of my past life was sin. Yet I do not repent. To whom should I carry my repentance? On what does the law rest, that I should obey it? Who is the judge?

I have withdrawn myself from the influence of the ages, cut myself off from the heritage of mankind, dehumanized. With impulses toward evil, I have worn the cloak of good. I said to my soul: Compound, enjoy the idea of evil, act as though you love good. Thus you shall indulge your sin, and not be punished for it. Now I find that neither in heaven nor in hell is my portion. The perfect spue [sic] me forth, the damned will not receive me. I sought to save my soul, and I am losing it. I blew hot and cold; and now nor cold to brace nor heat to cherish, is my portion; lukewarm loathliness hath overspread me.

Then I turned to bewail my wretched state.

At dawn I start from waking dreams in which the present has been lost — old dreams of the impossible love. For a moment I know not what has roused me. Then suddenly I turn and see upon my shoulder seated the obscene vulture, Despair. It keeps its seat, and croaks there, through the day, until sleep comes again to wrap my consciousness in coils of dreaming fancies. It is terrible to be so ill and morally broken, senseless and thoughtless and desperate, amid this gracious nature, so dead beneath this generous and vital sun. I am in hell with Dante's slothful:

> Fitti nel limo dicon; tristi fummo
> Nel aer dolce che dal sol s'allegre,
> Portando dentro accidioso fummo.

['Fixed in the slime, they say: "Sullen were we in the sweet air that is gladdened by the sun, carrying within us sluggish smoke".']3 But is this my fault, is it not my martyrdom?

Next I had recourse to old religious ideas. If I were to cry to God, he must surely help me. 'But where is the Lord? The grave where they laid him is empty; the ages that believed in him have passed; like shadows they fade before a little streak of light. In the heavens I see innumerable worlds and incalculable interstellar spaces. On the earth I see atoms and recuperative cycles.'

Then I turn to my soul, to find bread in the blank mind.

Asleep, dead, deaf, deeper than the deepest shine of the Atlantic, lies my soul.

Now I perceive, since the shadow of that night fell upon me, what is the solitude, the impotence, of the soul of men. What is it that we

175

call a soul? If I have no soul, then let me die – for I cannot eat and drink; life has ceased to be more for me than the aching of my nerves. If I have a soul, I shall not rest till I have brought it into harmony with THE SOUL, the universe. I am in a dilemma, and all issues merge alike in this question of the soul.

I have not dealt as a coward in the game of life. Rejecting Christ, I rejected God, and took upon me the desolateness of atheism. In the sensuality of my imagination, I stopped at no point. I am as foul as one who has wallowed in carnal vices, albeit I refrained from acts. I have gone to the very bottom in my logic of audacity.

But abyss calls to abyss; and the abyss of misery has murmurings which harmonize with the notion of the voice of God. Will He speak to me after all? Not indeed until I crawl back – how swiftly I flew down – but back to where? The solitude of this despair assert Him. I am not alone.

Is it then possible that I have reached the last point of negation? Is there indifference ahead, and ahead of that again affirmation?

So I wrote, at Nice, just after I had left Cannes. The last question was prophetic. For I found indifference very shortly in the study of Marcus Aurelius, the *Imitatio Christi*, and Walt Whitman. Later on, I found the affirmation of religion and contentment in love – not the human kindly friendly *love* which I had given liberally to my beloved wife and children, my father and my sister and my companions, but in the passionate *sexual love** of comrades. Through the whole of my malady and my discourses on it, I had omitted the word 'love'. That was because I judged my own sort of love to be sin. But when, in the stage of indifference, I became careless about sinning, then, and not until then, I discovered love, the keystone of all the rest of my less tortured life.

It was at Monaco, at Bordighera, in Corsica, among the towns of Northern Italy, afterwards at Seelisberg and Mürren, then later at Clifton, all through the next eleven months of the year 1868, that I worked this part of my life problem out, and reached the state of indifference. My wife was always at my side, lovingly waiting on my irksome moods and illnesses, sustaining me with unwavering affection, knitting continually closer those holy ties which made and

---

*These lines seem to have been underlined by H. F. Brown. At any rate, in the margin opposite text's 'friendly love' he wrote 'affection'; and opposite 'passionate sexual love' he wrote 'lust'. He added, 'Let JAS words stand' (date smudged). – Editor.

make our union a blessed thing. . . . Pursuing the system adopted in these chapters, I shall here interpolate, by way of natural relief, some more or less descriptive passages from my diaries. Large portions of those mss. I cannot utilize here, since they have gone to make my sketches of 'Ajaccio', 'Ravenna', 'Parma', and 'The Love of the Alps'. And the more solid intellectual work of the period came to light in a study of Aristophanes, and in chapters upon Ariosto and Tasso written years after for my *Renaissance in Italy*. Perplexed and foiled, the literary faculty never wholly failed me; and while I thought that I was doing nothing toilsomely — *operose nihil agendo* [by laboriously accomplishing naught] — I was really laying the foundations for a good deal of my future work . . . .

I find, by notes in my diaries, that the congenital bent of my temperament was perpetually causing me uneasiness. All kinds of young men — peasants on the Riviera, Corsican drivers, Florentine lads upon Lungarno in the evenings, *facchini* at Venice, and especially a handsome Bernese guide who attended to the strong black horse I rode — used to pluck at the sleeve of my heart, inviting me to fraternize, drawing out of me the sympathy I felt for male beauty and vigour. The sustained resistance to these appeals, the prolonged reversion to mere study as an anodyne for these desires, worried my nerves; and sometimes I broke out rebelliously into poems of passionate longing. One of these written at Bordighera, has a deep significance for me, when I read it now. It shows how inevitably I was tending to a certain goal, in spite of all resistance, and how the resistance tended to diminish. It seems important enough to be inserted here. The first part of the poem as it now stands was written in the summer at Clifton, the third part at Venice in May. The whole bears the name of a singular and fetid fungus, which exactly imitates in shape the *membrum virile* when erect.

Phallus Impudicus

i

Deep in the dank obscenity of shade
Where day's Ithuriel lance was never laid;
But mouldering elders and unwholesome yews
Spread sun-proof, dense against heaven's healthy dews;
Where on the broken stone or roofless hut
Coarse shapes of shame and words of lust are cut;
While by rude feet the dull unlovely way

Is roughly stamped upon the oozing clay;
There, wandering an hour in woeful mood,
And saddened by the squalor of the wood,
I sat me down upon a stump to curse
The days of man that grow from bad to worse.

Thus idly pondering, my foot that stirred
Among the dead leaves, haply disinterred
From slime and rubbish a white swollen cone
Of mushroom birth smooth, silky, and full-grown
For bursting. At a touch the fibre thin
Broke; with a leap the life that lurked within
Sprang skyward; forth it shot a curving trunk,
And on the trunk an egg-shaped cone that stunk.
The strange thing vibrated, and lewdly thrust
Up from the gloom its mimicry of lust;
For here had nature, in a freakish mood,
Of mud and water framed a filthy brood:
Symbols priapic, phallic, prurient, crude
Of human needs and yearnings unsubdued.

Poisonous and loathsome both to touch and smell,
Rotten and rotting, wreaked the spawn of hell;
Emblems of heat unhallowed, foul desire,
Dry lust that revels in the fleshly mire,
Of dreams that start from rancid thoughts to taint
The soul with fevered joy too rank to paint,
Of men who deeds unclean around them spread
The sickening odours of a brothel bed.

ii

This was the manner of the lesson strange
I learned at Naples. – We were bound next day,
I and the tall Sorrento lad who drove
My carriage to the town, and stayed with me,
For England. In two chambers we were laid
That night; a door between. Time-measuring bells
Made through the still hours music in my brain;
And something with the bells melodiously
Kept time: some far off mystery of sense
I could not check, some hint of coming change,
Mingled with words which he had spoken, looks,
Turns of the body, gestures, flitting smiles.
Then, towards the dawn, I rose. The little light,
Through heaven's grey concaves feeling tremulously,

Melted the airy shadows, and made way
For morning; but as yet the skies were cold.
The door stood open: in I passed, and bent
Attentive on the mat before his bed.
What should I find? Tossed waves of tawny curls
Dashed from his broad brows, or full fervent eyes
Veiled by large eyelids, or the yellowing bloom
Of three years' manhood soft on cheek and chin,
With haply from the coverlid some flake
Snow-white of strong smooth throat? Ah no! The dawn
Pared me full-length within the curtain's shadow
From feet to brow a languid-lying form,
Swathed in deep slumber: thighs and rosy nipples,
Elastic belly, and soft sheltering velvet,
Short clustering down, luxuriantly wanton,
Round the twin marble man-spheres shyly circling,
Round the firm rondure of love's root of joy,
The smooth rude muscle, calm and slow and tender,
The alabaster shaft, the pale pink shrine,
The crimson glory of the lustrous gland
Lurking in dewy darkness half-concealed,
Like a rose-bud peeping from clasped silken sheath;
All this I saw; one arm along the flank
Out-stretched at ease, the other raised half-hidden
In the curls, fiery tangle. Only this:
Then to his slumber turned the youth, and sighed.

And this was all? Oh, this was everything;
For from that day I nurse a deathless fire:
I am aflame with beauty — not that faint
And vulgar phantom so miscalled by men.
Whom use and procreative instinct sting;
But the divine undying thirst that dives
Deep to the centre of all sense, and drinks
Masculine draughts of rapture epicoene.
Ah me! How sweet and bitter, drenched with tears,
And wild with laughter, and deep-dyed with blood,
Is this charmed life within my life, this joy,
Soul-born, soul-nourished, that consumes my soul;
That with strong visionary splendour pales
All sunshine, starlight, and soft moony sweetness
Of the world's real skies; that with excess
Of blossom mars my fruitage! — Do you loathe me?
Curse me? I smile and care not. Spurn and shun me?

Let all the world be sane; count me as madman!
Have I not seen, felt, fingered, tasted? lo,
Ye are madmen; it is I am sound.

iii

A man of goodly build, on whose square head
Scarce forty years had wintered, whose dark eyes
Flashed with a fitful lustre like cold skies
When flickering north-lights turn the horizon red,
Leaned on a bridge at Venice. His thin lips
Stirred fretfully, and with his hands he played
As though some fiend moved in the finger-tips.
Still, as I paused and marked him, down he cast
Enquiring eager glances where there stood
A group of fishermen in idle mood,
Half-clothed and sinewy: at times there passed
Those who, unheedful of the watcher, turned
To wet the wall; whereat the dark eyes burned
And the man's sinews shrank, ring within ring,
Straining to seize some brief lascivious sight.
While thus I mused and wondered what delight
For one so framed desire so crude could bring,
There came a youth, who stayed: it seemed the wind
Might waft him like a manlier Bacchus to
Another Ariadne; form and hue,
Fine as a female's, with coarse strength was twined,
Rank stuff of sex. The watcher by a word
Held him suspense; then downward dashed, and took
The young man's palm, and into parley broke.
What was proposed or promised went unheard.
The youth, I thought, blushed, frowned, at first said nay;
Yet in the end he walked with that strange man away.

We reached Clifton again in July; and here I soon resolved to settle.
The summer was divided between Clifton Hill House and Sutton
Court. I wrote many poems on Greek subjects – 'The Love-Tale of
Cleomachus', 'Theron', 'The Clemency of Phalaris', 'The Elysium of
Greek Lovers', 'Cratinus and Aristodemus'; all preluding to my
'Eudiades',[4] and all feeding the fever of my heart, which was also
kept alive by innumerable fair sights and passing episodes. I also
worked at the text of Zeller, and the edition of Clough's works.
September and October were spent at Hastings and in London. More
poems of the same sort: 'The Tale of Leutychidas and Lynkeus',

180

'Dipsychus Deterior', 'Diocles', 'Damocles the Beautiful'.[5] Essays of all kinds, descriptive and critical, were composed for publication. In fact I worked pretty hard.

On 17 November, Mr North was elected again MP for Hastings; on the 19th, we settled into 7 Victoria Square at Clifton; on 1 December I met Norman; on the* Madge was born.

This chapter must serve as introduction to the one which follows on my emotional development.

---

*Section missing in ms. Symonds left a space as though he intended to fill in the blank later.— Editor.

Chapter Twelve

Emotional development

It was my primary object when I began these autobiographical notes to describe as accurately and candidly as I was able a type of character, which I do not at all believe to be exceptional, but which for various intelligible reasons has never yet been properly analysed. I wanted to supply material for the ethical psychologist and the student of mental pathology, by portraying a man of no mean talents, of no abnormal depravity, whose life has been perplexed from first to last by passion – natural, instinctive, healthy in his own particular case – but morbid and abominable from the point of view of the society in which he lives – persistent passion for the male sex.

(December 1891: This was written by me at Venice in May 1889. I had not then studied the cases of sexual inversion recorded by Casper-Liman, Ulrichs and Krafft-Ebing.[1] Had I done so, I should not perhaps have dealt with my personal experience so diffusely as I have done in this chapter. What I wrote, I now leave as it stands. It forms a more direct contribution to the psychology of sexual abnormality than if I were to mix it up with the discussion of theories unknown to me at the time of writing.)*

This was my primary object. It seemed to me, being a man of letters, possessing the pen of a ready writer and the practised impartiality of a critic accustomed to weigh evidence, that it was my duty to put on record the facts and phases of this aberrant inclination in myself – so that fellow-sufferers from the like malady, men innocent as I have been, yet haunted as I have been by a sense of guilt and dread of punishment, men injured in their character and health by

*In margin of ms. – Editor.

the debasing influences of a furtive and lawless love, men deprived of the best pleasures which reciprocated passion yields to mortals, men driven in upon ungratified desires and degraded by humiliating outbursts of ungovernable appetite, should feel that they are not alone, and should discover at the same time how a career of some distinction, of considerable energy and perseverance, may be pursued by one who bends and sweats beneath a burden heavy enough to drag him down to pariahdom. Nor this only. I hoped that the unflinching revelation of my moral nature, connected with the history of my intellectual development and the details of my physical disorders, might render the scientific handling of similar cases more enlightened than it is at present, and might arouse some sympathy even in the breast of Themis[2] for not ignoble victims of a natural instinct reputed vicious in the modern age. No one who shall have read these memoirs, and shall possess even a remote conception of my literary labours, will be able to assert that the author was a vulgar and depraved sensualist. He may be revolted; he may turn with loathing from the spectacle. But he must acknowledge that it possesses the dignity of tragic suffering.

As a secondary object, I had in view the possibility of madness supervening on the long continued strain, the lifelong struggle of this tyrannous desire. Should the worst come to the worst, I wanted to leave an *apologia pro vita mea* – no excuse, no palliation of my acts, but an explanation of them; from the perusal of which it should appear that my ἁμαρτία [*hamartia*, flaw], my deviation from the paths of order, my stumbling up against the altar of Justinian's edict, has been, like that of Ajax or of Phaedra, something which the old Greek instinct recognized as fraught with fate or sent by God.

This being the case, I shall not shrink from continuing the analysis which I have undertaken, painful as it is to do so, and extraordinary as the needful confessions will have to be.

I have sufficiently described the character of my emotions during the period of adolescence. Up to the time of my marriage they were sentimental, romantic, without a touch of avowed sensuality. Even in daydreams about the boys I loved, no thought of anything obscene formed itself distinctly in my mind. I experienced, indeed, the strongest physical disturbance when I came into close contact with them. The touch of their hands, the laughter of their eyes, and the silkiness of their hair provoked the same agreeable sexual sensations as young men ordinarily obtain from the company of girls. And at night,

183

when I dreamed of them, the visions were erotic. But my wildest flights of fancy did not soar definitely beyond a kiss, a clasp, the virginal embrace which Daphnis gave to Chloe before Lycaenion taught him what the way of a man with a maid should be.[3] There was, of course, an indefinite background, made sufficiently apparent by the tumult of my blood, the quickening of my heartbeats, and the rising of my flesh. But these symptoms annoyed me; I strove to put them aside, and evaded the attempt to formulate their significance. I only twice kissed a male friend in those years – as I have already related in what I wrote about Willie. Good heavens! what an uproar in the city of my soul those kisses wrought, as we lay together couched in ivy and white wood anemones upon the verge of the red rocks which dominate the Avon!

I came to marriage then fatigued and fretted by intense desires, the worse for being still unconscious of their sensuality. Marriage, I thought, would satisfy the side of my nature which thrilled so strangely when I touched a boy. It did not, however; and the difficulties of my married life – difficulties connected with my wife's repugnance to childbearing and her constitutional indifference to sexual intercourse – whereby I spent many successive months as a bachelor beside the woman I had wedded, and with whom I strangely bedded – these difficulties prepared me for the three phases I have now to describe. The first of these corresponds exactly with what I have called 'the second main division of my literary life'. It was also the second main division of my emotional life, and it ended at the moment of my return to reside at Clifton in the autumn of 1868. In like manner the succeeding phase, or third in order, tallies with the third division of my literary life, when I left England for Davos in 1877; and the fourth begins with the new chapter of existence I opened among Swiss people.

The evolution of my emotional temperament comprehends four stages therefore. The first, of adolescence, sentiment, romance, has been dealt with. The three which followed will engage me now.

Being what I am, the great mistake – perhaps the great crime of my life, was my marriage. I ought not to have married when I did and whom I did. I ought not to have married at all. Yet I am able after nearly twenty-five years of matrimony to record my conviction that this marriage has not been a failure for either my wife or myself.

I called it a mistake in the first place, because I was urged to marry by my father, by my own earnest desire to overcome abnormal inclinations, by the belief that I should regain health, and by the confidence that I should not make a bad husband. I did not overcome abnormal passions. I did not regain health. In so far I mistook my path. I think, however, that I have been upon the whole a good husband; my wife emphatically says so now.

I called it a crime in the second place, because none of these reasons for marrying justify the step, because I married without passion or the feeling that this particular woman was the only woman in the world for me. Thus I deceived her practically, if not intentionally or deliberately. And I deceived myself, in so far as her temperament was incapable of sharpening the sexual appetites which in me had hardly any edge where woman was concerned.

Some sorts of self-deceit are crimes. They are the sign of a soul's willingness to accept the second best and to give the second best, instead of waiting through all suffering and all privation for the best in life.

There is no word of blame for my wife here. She has been at every point a good, true, honest, loving and devoted wife to me. She is a woman whom better and happier men than I am might have worshipped with sex-penetrated passion. No: if anyone in our marriage has been the injured party, it is she. The imperfections of our life in common are due far less to her temperament than to the fact that I could not love her in the way which makes a man enamoured of his wife's peculiarities. I married her without giving my whole self; and the best things which marriage has brought us both are friendship and our children. I do not believe that she has ever been acutely sensible of what we both missed – that supreme joy which made Romeo and Juliet happy in the jaws of death. But I shall go to the grave with an unsatisfied desire. Here am I fashioned in every fibre for passionate pleasure, and married to a woman who has borne me four children. Yet we have never had any really passionate moments together. And for the last eleven years, after shillyshallying with an ill-participated nuptial bed, we have found it best to live as male and female quite apart.

In spite of all this, my marriage has not to be regretted. So far as I am concerned, it probably saved my life from wreckage and prolonged my power of moral resistance. On the other hand I feel tolerably sure that she has not suffered as other women might from the imperfection of our sexual relations. She married late – at twenty-seven – and carried into matrimony the instincts of a virgin, for whom there is something ignoble in physical appetite and nauseous in childbirth. Any touch in literature upon the pleasures of the senses gives her pain. She shrinks from what men and women are, and what they must be, as from something common and unclean. 'That vulgar and trivial way of coition,' as Sir Thomas Browne puts it, has for her no attraction. Having realized by a life in common of twenty-six years how much better it is to be married than to remain single, having found satisfaction in my society and a sphere of activity in her domestic cares, she is satisfied. She could not have enjoyed the society of her daughters, whom she deeply loves, except through the troublesome process by which alone the human race is propagated. On the whole then, I estimate that our marriage, so far as it has gone, may be reckoned among the successful experiments of this nature – at any rate not among the more unsuccessful.

How far can anything in our mental and moral evolution be considered accidental? Nothing, I believe. And yet some of the most decisive turning points in life seem to depend on casual circumstance. I well remember three apparently trivial occurrences during the first fifteen months after my marriage, which aroused the latent trouble of my nature, and opened a new phase of conflict with incurable desire.

In the spring of 1865 we were living in lodgings in Albion Street, Hyde Park. I had been one evening to the Century Club, which then met near St Martin le Grand in rooms, I think, of the Alpine Club. Walking home before midnight, I took a little passage which led from Trafalgar into Leicester Square, passing some barracks. This passage has since then been suppressed. I was in evening dress. At the entrance of the alley a young grenadier came up and spoke to me. I was too innocent, strange as this may seem, to guess what he meant. But I liked the man's looks, felt drawn toward him, and did not refuse his company. So there I was, the slight nervous man of fashion in my dress clothes, walking side by side with a strapping fellow in scarlet uniform, strongly attracted by his physical magnetism. From a few commonplace remarks he broke abruptly into proposals, mentioned a house we could go to, and made it quite plain for what purpose. I quickened my pace, and hurrying through the passage broke away from him with a passionate mixture of repulsion and fascination.

What he offered was not what I wanted at the moment, but the thought of it stirred me deeply. The thrill of contact with the man taught me something new about myself. I can well recall the lingering regret, and the quick sense of deliverance from danger, with which I saw him fall back, after following and pleading with me for about a hundred yards. The longing left was partly a fresh seeking after comradeship and partly an animal desire the like of which I had not before experienced.

The memory of this incident abode with me, and often rose to haunt my fancy. Yet it did not disturb my tranquillity during the ensuing summer, which we spent at Clifton and Sutton Court. Toward autumn we settled into our London house, 47 Norfolk Square, Hyde Park. Here it happened that a second seemingly fortuitous occurrence intensified the recrudescence of my trouble. I went out for a solitary walk on one of those warm moist unhealthy afternoons when the weather oppresses and yet irritates our nervous sensibilities. Since the date of my marriage I had ceased to be assailed by what I called 'the wolf' – that undefined craving coloured with a vague but poignant hankering after males. I lulled myself with the belief that it would not leap on me again to wreck my happiness and disturb my studious habits. However, wandering that day for exercise through the sordid streets between my home and Regent's Park, I felt the burden of a ponderous malaise. To shake it off was impossible. I did not recognize it as a symptom of the moral malady from which I had resolutely striven to free myself. Was I not protected by my troth-pledge to a noble woman, by my recent entrance upon the natural career of married life? While returning from this fateful constitutional, at a certain corner, which I well remember, my eyes were caught by a rude *graffito* scrawled with slate-pencil upon slate. It was of so concentrated, so stimulative, so penetrative a character – so thoroughly the voice of vice and passion in the proletariat – that it pierced the very marrow of my soul.* I must have seen a score such *graffiti* in my time. But they had not hitherto appealed to me. Now the wolf leapt out: my malaise of the moment was converted into a clairvoyant and tyrannical appetite for the thing which I had rejected five months earlier in the alley by the barracks. The vague and morbid craving of the previous years

---

*'Prick to prick, so sweet'; with an emphatic diagram of phallic meeting, glued together, gushing.

187

defined itself as a precise hunger after sensual pleasure, whereof I had not dreamed before save in repulsive visions of the night.

It is difficult to say how far the exercise of sex in marriage helped to determine this new phase of the old instinct. I am inclined to think that it had much to do with the acuteness of the attack. Inborn instincts, warped by my will and forced to take a bias contrary to my peculiar nature, reasserted themselves with violence. I did not recognize the phenomenon as a temptation. It appeared to me, just what it was, the resurrection of a chronic torment which had been some months in abeyance. Looking back upon the incident now, I know that obscene *graffito* was the sign and symbol of a paramount and permanent craving of my physical and psychical nature. It connected my childish reveries with the mixed passions and audacious comradeship of my maturity. Not only my flesh, but my heart also, was involved in the emotion which it stirred.

The awakening spasm of desire had as little to do with either fancy or will as the return of neuralgia in a sudden throb of agony. God help me! I cried. I felt humiliated, frightened, gripped in the clutch of doom. Nothing remained but to parry, palliate, procrastinate. There was no hope of escape. And all the while the demon ravished my imagination with 'the love of the impossible'. Hallucinations of the senses crowded in upon my brain together with the pangs of shame and the prevision of inevitable woes. From this decisive moment forward to the end, my life had to fly on a broken wing, and my main ambition has been to constitute a working compromise. This afternoon walk to which I attach so great an importance must have taken place a few weeks before my eldest daughter Janet's birth. Soon after my wife was fit to move, we went down to Clifton, and there my father discovered that my left lung was seriously affected. During this visit I read Seeley's *Ecce Homo*,[4] which interested me by reason of its style and its philanthropy. And it so happened that I also read Greenwood's article 'The Amateur Casual' in an early number of the *Pall Mall Gazette*.[5] This brought the emotional tumour which was gathering within me to maturity. Almost without premeditation or plan I wrote the first part of the poem called 'John Mordan'. Since then I have suffered incessantly from my moral trouble, which I have beguiled by sundry feeble devices, and which has assumed forms of bewildering and often painfully distressing variety.

A distinct stage in what I may call the palliative treatment I adopted was marked by the composition of 'John Mordan'. I began to make verse the vehicle and safety valve for my tormenting preoccupations. A cycle of poems gradually got written, illustrating the love of man for man in all periods of civilization. Of these the two best are perhaps 'A Cretan Idyll' and 'Eudiades'.[6] The composition of the cycle lasted over the period between January 1866 and some time after 1875.

Nothing could, I think, have been much worse for my condition than this sustained utterance through verse of passions which I dared not indulge. It kept me in a continual state of *orexis*, or irritable longing. And for my literary career it was at least unprofitable. I knew that all those thousands of lines, into which I poured my red hot soul, would never see the light of publication. Consequently I gave way to the besetting foibles of my literary temperament – facility, fluency, or carelessness of execution. The writing of these poems was a kind of mental masturbation.

While thus engaged, and very early after the commencement of my cycle, I came across W. Whitman's *Leaves of Grass*. I was sitting with F. M. Myers in his rooms at Trinity, Cambridge, when he stood up, seized a book and shouted out in his nasal intonation with those brazen lungs of his, 'Long I thought that knowledge alone would content me.' This fine poem, omitted from later editions of *Leaves of Grass*, formed part of 'Calamus'.[7] The book became for me a sort of Bible. Inspired by 'Calamus' I adopted another method of palliative treatment, and tried to invigorate the emotion I could not shake off by absorbing Whitman's conception of comradeship. The process of assimilation was not without its bracing benefit. My desires grew manlier, more defined, more direct, more daring by contact with Calamus. I imbibed a strong democratic enthusiasm, a sense of the dignity and beauty and glory of simple healthy men. This has been of great service to me during the eleven years I have passed at Davos. I can now declare with sincerity that my abnormal inclinations, modified by Whitman's idealism and penetrated with his democratic enthusiasm, have brought me into close and profitable sympathy with human beings even while I sinned against law and conventional morality.

The immediate result of this study of Walt Whitman was the determination to write the history of paiderastia in Greece and to attempt a theoretical demonstration of the chivalrous enthusiasm which seemed to me implicit in comradeship. Both of these literary tasks I accomplished. The former has been privately printed under the title of *A Problem in Greek Ethics*. The latter exists in manuscript; and though I do not regard its conclusions as wholly worthless or its ideal as quite incapable of realization, I cannot take a favourable view of my achievement. My own thwarted and perplexed instincts rendered me incapable of sound or absolutely sincere treatment.

Such was the expenditure of time and intellectual energy demanded by this inexorable and incurable disease.

L'amour de l'impossible est la maladie de l'âme. It cannot be doubted that the congenital aberration of the passions which I have described has been the poison of my life. In the first place I shall die without realizing what constitutes the highest happiness of mortals, an ardent love reciprocated with ardour. This I could never enjoy, for the simple reason that I have never felt the sexual attraction of women. The following paragraph from a diary dated 23 March 1889 shows what I mean:

> I have been sitting opposite a young man in the *diligence* all day – a peasant about nineteen, with a well-knit frame and a good healthy face, exhibiting no special beauty but radiating intelligence and the magnetic force of the male adolescent. I looked at his hands – great powerful palms and fingers, fashioned to mould and clasp, yet finely shaped, and attached to sinewy wrists, where the skin had smoother texture, showing veins and the salience of sinews. Enough of his throat and forearms was visible to make one divine how white and wholesome was the flesh of the young man's body. I felt I could have kissed these hands hardened with labour, bruised here and there, brown in complexion – have kissed them and have begged of them to touch me. Then it flashed across my mind that no woman's hands – whether of duchess or milkmaid, maiden or married – had ever possessed for me such sexual attraction as these of the young peasant had.

A man who feels like that has failed as certainly in finding life's chief boon as a repulsive hunchback has. For no young man will return his passion. Then again what hours and days and weeks and months of weariness I have endured by the alternate indulgence and repression of my craving imagination. What time and energy I have wasted on expressing it. How it has interfered with the pursuit of study. How marriage has been spoiled by it. What have I suffered in violent and brutal pleasures of the senses, snatched furtively with shame on my part, with frigid toleration on the part of my comrades, and repented of with terror.

Nature is a hard and cruel stepmother. Nothing that I could have done would have availed to alter my disposition by a hair's breadth – unless perhaps I had been forced to fornicate by my father at the age of puberty. I doubt even then whether I could have been rendered normal. These sexual aberrations cannot of course be rare. The more frequent they are, the more grim is human destiny.

The whole of this which I have called the second phase of my emotional development was therefore passed in slow continuous assimilation of the passion which possessed me. I condescended to no act of lust and engaged in no clandestine intercourse. But I exercised the imagination with audacious freedom, and intensified desire by dwelling on delights beyond my grasp. I thought it permissible to indulge my sense of plastic beauty in men. With this in view I often visited public baths, and when I was in London, I used to stroll out in early morning or late evening along the Serpentine. There I feasted my eyes upon the naked bathers, consumed with a longing for them which was not exactly lust. The breath of lust had not passed over my earlier ideal of sentiment at that stage. . . .

I thought then that, if I were ever allowed to indulge my instincts, I should be able to remain within [Whitman's] ideal of comradeship. The dominance of this ideal, as will be seen in the sequel, contributed greatly to shape my emotional tendencies. It taught me to apprehend the value of fraternity, and to appreciate the working classes. When I came to live among peasants and republicans in Switzerland, I am certain that I took up passionate relations with men in a more natural and intelligible manner – more rightly and democratically – than I should otherwise have done.

The same period, however, was marked by the intrusion into my life of two friends, both of whom swayed me prejudicially, but in different ways. These were Roden Noel and Claude Delaval Cobham.[8] They had done and were in the habit of doing what I had now begun to desire. In every respect but this, no two men could have been more dissimilar than they were. Noel was married, deeply attached to his wife, a poet of high soaring fancies, a philosopher of burning nebulous ideas. He justified passion to his own eyes and preached it to others in an esoteric quasi-Manichean mysticism. He was vain of his physical beauty, which was splendid at that epoch; and his tastes tended to voluptuousness. The attraction of the male governed him through this vanity and this voluptuousness. He loved to be admired. He enjoyed in indolent sultana fashion the contact of masculine desire, the *attouchements* of excited organisms, the luxurious embracements of nakedness. Strange to say, the indulgence of these tastes did not disturb his mental equilibrium. Both as poet and thinker, he remained vigorous and grew in comprehension. Finally, I think, he overlived, absorbed, and clarified by religious mysticism the grossness of his passions. But for me the conversation of this remarkable man was nothing less than poisonous – a pleasant poison, it is true.

Cobham had no poetry, no religion, no philosophy. He disliked women. When I first knew him at Oxford in 1861, he professed himself an '*anderastes*'; and this he consistently remained through life.* He had a passion for soldiers, and enjoyed the most licentious pleasures to which two men can yield themselves. His imagination was steeped in a male element of lust, himself being rather patient than agent. In all other respects but this, he was what the world calls an excellent fellow – sympathetic, warm-hearted, ready to serve his friends, successful in society, cheerful, and not devoid of remarkable intellectual gifts. I have only met with one linguist more versatile in the acquirement of ancient and modern languages. This man told me that, while he was a boy of thirteen, a friend of his brother seduced him at his mother's house, and that he had never afterwards been able to conceive of love except under the form of rude and lustful masculine embraces. Both Noel and he were, I believe, among those individuals for whom this kind of passion is instinctive, not acquired. Only Noel remained superior in being sensitive to the attractions of the female.

---

*He was certainly what Ulrichs calls a *Weibling*.[9] (Note written in August 1889.)

Chapter Thirteen

Norman

It was not to be expected that this state of tension and of preparation should be protracted for ever. Residence at Clifton from the autumn of 1868 onwards determined a new phase of feeling.

In December 1868 my friend Graham Dakyns, a schoolmaster at Clifton College, invited me to dinner. Several members of the sixth form made up the party with ourselves; and among them was a boy who attracted me by his good looks, agreeable manners and excellent sense in conversation. He had a very remarkable face, rather long but finely cut, with deep-set dark eyes under level, marked brows, low white forehead, and a storm of flaky dark hair, laid in heavy masses on a somewhat small skull, and turning at the tips to dusky gold:

$$\tau\grave{\alpha} \ \mu\grave{\epsilon}\nu \ \acute{\epsilon}\nu\delta o\theta\epsilon\nu \ \mu\epsilon\lambda\alpha\acute{\iota}\nu\alpha\varsigma,$$
$$\tau\grave{\alpha} \ \delta' \ \acute{\alpha}\kappa\rho o\nu \ \acute{\eta}\lambda\iota\acute{\omega}\sigma\alpha\varsigma$$

['His locks, black beneath; those on top as golden as the sun.']¹ It was the sort of face which seemed made to be cast in bronze.

This boy, whom I will call Norman, though that was not his real name, played a considerable part in my life for the next few years. In order to approach him, I contrived that Percival, the headmaster of Clifton College, should invite me to lecture to the sixth form. Thus, to begin with, it was Norman's influence which led me to take a step decisive for my literary career.

In preceding sections of this book enough has been set down to characterize the nature of my feelings for young lads before the year 1863 – before I made a vigorous effort to shake off those enthralments, and sealed my vow by the decisive act of marriage. Six years had now elapsed, during which, as I have just said, the unconquerable instinct returned, was treated by me with literary and imaginative palliatives, and never found the least escape into experience.

I now deliberately engaged in an *amour* with Norman. It was romantic, delicately sentimental, but at the same time passionate and tinged with unmistakeable sensuality. During its whole course this leading type prevailed; but the sensual element was held in check. Nothing occurred between us which the censorious could rightly consider unworthy of two gentlemen.

Norman reciprocated my affection to a considerable extent. He was himself sensitive to the attraction of the male; but his mode of feeling corresponded to my own – that is to say, he already loved boys younger than himself. This prevented our union from becoming that of lover and beloved in the deeper sense of mutual satisfaction. Rarely, I think, in these conditions of aberrant sexual emotion, is the fine flower of a perfect relation developed. It is the misery of people born like us that, far more than in the case of normal passion, the one kisses and the other turns the cheek. The result was that I had to suffer from jealousy, from the want of any definite hold upon my adored friend, from the dissatisfaction of incomplete spiritual possession, and from the hunger of defrauded longings. I would have relinquished a large part of the physical intimacy which I enjoyed, if I could have felt more certain of his real affection.

Not that Norman was ever disloyal. The maladjustment lay in our circumstances, our respective emotions; and I believe that even if I had not been a married man, which of course complicated matters, the case would hardly have been bettered. Such as it was, this passionate friendship brought me an incalculable amount of delight. It also helped to emancipate my intellect and will, so that I date from it my entrance into a new phase of activity, the fruits of which soon afterwards began to show themselves in a full stream of literary performances. (Precisely as my first love, for Willie Dyer, in 1858, marked a new burst of energy, which carried me with academical honour through my years at Oxford.)

Having by me diaries of the years I spent with Norman, I shall adopt the method of describing this episode by means of selected extracts from those books. Norman was inextricably interwoven with my whole life – literature, friends, home affairs, my wife and father and father-in-law, travels on the continent, etc. – so inextricably interwoven indeed with all these things that I cannot present any adequate view of our intimacy without relating in some detail the events of that period. This I will now do following the diaries; and perhaps in this way will be gained a faithful general notion of the rapport existing in my nature at that time between the domestic, literary, emotional and active aspects of life.

On 18 November my father-in-law Mr Frederick North was re-elected Member for Hastings together with Tom Brassey, now Lord Brassey. On the following day I went to Clifton, where we had taken a furnished house for the winter, 7 Victoria Square. On 1 December I dined at H. G. Dakyns's. The party consisted of E. M. Oakley (a master at the college) and three sixth form boys, Norman, Bean, Howlett. I find the beginning of an epigram by Straton used as motto for this dinner party in my notes: '*Καὶ μισθοὺς αἰτεῖτε, διδάσ-καλοι; ὡς ἀχάριστοι*'. ['You teachers ask for pay as well? How ungrateful!']²

During the first half of this month Conington came to stay; and the project of my lecturing to the Clifton College boys, and to the Clifton ladies, on Greek literature, began to form itself in my mind. Percival, the headmaster of the college, readily adopted the idea, and it was only a question whether my health would stand the strain. I plunged at once into preparatory studies, reading Greek authors of all kinds, Max-Müller on language,³ Greek histories, and the various books upon Greek poetry. It occurred to Graham who took interest in my own poetry, that I should attempt the description of a Greek boy who responds to his lover and lives a noble life with him. Accordingly, I gave myself to this task, and between December 22 and 30 composed the tale in verse which is called 'Eudiades'. 'June days and nights in Athens', is the short note in my diary. Early in January 1869 Jowett paid us a visit; and on 15 January my daughter Margaret was born. Next day Henry Sidgwick came to stay, and we thoroughly investigated the subject of my poems on Erôs. His conclusion was that I ought to abandon them, as unhealthy and disturbing to my moral equilibrium. I assented. We locked them all up in a black tin box, with the exception of 'Eudiades', the ms. of which belonged to Graham Dakyns. Having done this, Henry threw the key into the river Avon on the 23rd.

There was something absurd in all this, because I felt myself half-consciously upon the point of translating my dreams and fancies about love into fact. And on 27 January occurs the entry, 'Norman dined with me alone: *κάλλιστος, ἄδρητος, εἰρωνικός* [most fair, untamed and deceitful]. I was launched upon a new career, with the overpowering sweetness of the vision of Eudiades pervading my soul.

Norman soon assumed ascendancy over my imagination, and my diary is full of him:

> *1 February.* Norman ascends like a star, but a troublous planet. And the prospect of these lectures to the 6th form involves a whole change of life. The black box is hidden away. The art which for three years has been so continuous a safety valve is now shut off. Can I pour the old wine into these new bottles?

Norman often came to dinner. We met in the college close and library; and sometimes I sent him presents of books. And then we began to write each other letters. It is clear from the confidences of my diary that I was impatient, lacking faith, eager to bring this life poem into bloom as quickly as the improvisatory poet brings his fancy. The boy responded readily, and felt my influence. I ought to have been satisfied. But I brooded too much on my own object; and we had not enough of life in common.

> *5 February.* Erôs, Storgê and Agapê are the '$\tau\varrho i\alpha$ $\pi\alpha\lambda\alpha i\sigma\mu\alpha\tau\alpha$' ['the three falls'].[4] If you begin with Erôs, and then seek the other two, you have a hard task; for you will not be satisfied unless they are as candescent as your Eros.

My intention to educate Norman and to stimulate his intellect, which seemed to me slack and indolent, soon assumed predominance. I began to coach him for his essays, and to read passages of good Greek and English authors with him. This led to little sweets of intimacy:

> *7 February.* As he read, I leaned on his shoulder, and his ear tip touched my forehead, and I felt his voice vibrate in his lungs, and I could see the subtle smile upon his lips . . . .
>
> Befooled am I, besotted, to live thus a poem when I have strangled my written poems. I used to think Butler's sermon on self-deception[5] unreal. I believe in self-deception now. I carry in my heart what I am afraid to analyse – even to define – what I hardly acknowledge to myself.
>
> O Love, why hast thou brought me to this barren shore again? Why was I born for this – to be perpetually seeking '$\tau\hat{\omega}\nu$ $\pi\alpha i\delta\omega\nu$ $\nu\epsilon\acute{o}\gamma\upsilon\iota o\nu$ $\check{\alpha}\nu\theta o\varsigma$' [the fresh flower of boys]?[6] I said unto my soul, be still! and to my heart, be silent! I sought and found wells of cool

196

waters, untroubled, ready to refresh me. I cried unto the Alps, receive and make me young again! I had peace among the great mountains. And yet, remorseless Love, I have not ceased to tremble at the 'ὄψις ἀστράπτουσα' ['the flashing spectacle'].[7]

At this point I wished with half my will to break the thread of Norman's friendship. But how was I to do so with justice to him? I should have to confess 'the unbearableness of his beauty', or to leave Clifton, or to give up my proposed lectures, or to be distant and yet on friendly terms. I felt incapable of taking any of these courses; and so things went their way, and the intimacy grew daily closer. Now I began to perceive that Norman was, and for some while past had always been, more or less sentimentally in love with one or other of his comrades. This added to my unrest.

Review-writing, reading of Greek, lecture-composing went steadily forward. I sent Norman letters, poems, violets:

> 13 February.
> ἴων πέπομφα στέφανον εὐωδέστατον
> ἔαρος ἀπαρχήν, σοὶ μὲν εὐωδεστέρῳ.

['The first-fruits of spring have I sent, a most fragrant garland of violets, to you who are even more fragrant than they.'][8]

On 18 February Mrs Clough came to stay with us; and I edited with her assistance the prose and verse remains of A. H. Clough. This, in addition to my other brainwork, told heavily upon my strength. We had considerable difficulty in deciphering some of the mss., and our opinions differed as to what pieces should be included in the collection. However, we always came to a final agreement, and about the end of March the two volumes were already getting into print. Mrs Clough's preface to this edition is dated June 1869.

Francis Newman was a frequent visitor to my house now; and just at the end of the month we had a delightful visit from W. J. Courthope . . . .[9]

28 February. Courthope and I went for a walk at 12.30, and met Norman in Clifton Park. We walked till 1 together, I too inebriated to talk sense or to be self-possessed. He was coming to see me, he said. Courthope liked him, and remarked that he had irony 'in his voice.'

Irony was a matter much discussed between Courthope and me at that time, and prized by us because of our admiration for Ariosto and Tassoni.

On 1 March my father left Clifton for Italy with my sister Charlotte. His health had begun to fail. It was the beginning of that long illness which ended in February 1871.

> 5 March. At 7 Norman came to dinner; elegant, self-possessed, in no sense disturbed by the three ladies he found there, willing to talk about things which interested him and, when silent, not uncomfortable, but slightly bored.

That evening I found out a good deal about his family. He is not nineteen yet. His father died some time ago; and his mother, who seems to be a weak woman, married a disreputable old clerical schoolmaster. They are always in debt and difficulties. All these things explained to me a great deal in Norman's character. He had a bad unhappy home, a depressing and demoralizing milieu.

> 7 March. Oh, this sleep toward morning, illuminated by a dream so piercingly sweet that it cannot be written. I can never in life be what I was last night in dreams; never so put my arm around another's neck, so thrill at the touch of another's throat and hand, so be fused into the soul's essence of one beside me, so know that eternity is perfected and shut and sealed and rounded in a single moment. There are sublimer, more lasting, better, more real things in life than this. I have experienced them. But except in such dreams life has never become art, no poem has been lived by me.
>
> 8 March. A black day. At eleven, dear little Margaret was christened in that abominable Clifton church; only Mrs Clough, Mary Hall,[10] Catherine, I, the nurses, Janet and Lotta being there. A lame lugubrious curate officiated, supported by two sepulchral clerks. The whole was like a ghastly desiccated ceremony – a mere husk. I was godfather. The vows stuck in my throat. It was like a total lovelessness and carelessness about the dear white quiet little daisy. And a slight forethought might have remedied this. I had been too busy, fretted with Clough's poems, indolently self-absorbed – Catherine too weak and helpless from her slow recovery. She forgot to ask Auntie and Aunt Charlotte, who were much disappointed. This made her miserable, and I was unhappy. A bleak east wind swept a leaden grey sky. Frank Newman came and prosed. Mrs Clough and Mary and I drove round by Failand in my father's carriage, discontented, ill-assorted. Mrs Clough and Mary are jealous of each other about us.

This is the description of certainly a black unpleasant day. But it has been amply made up to 'dear little Margaret' in after life. Soon after that day, I resolved to buy 7 Victoria Square.

15 March. I see that there are three grades in art: the first is living out a dream, such as I lived with Willie, and now am trying to live with Norman. Next comes the personal work of art, in which we dream and know it is a dream, and pour our yearnings and our passions into the dream, and give it form in words, trying to realize a vision of what we desire: 'εἰδώλοις κάλλευς κωφὰ χλιαινομένη' ['to be warmed by mere images of beauty'.][11] This is rather more like true art; and this I attained in 'Eudiades'. The third grade is the true impersonal work of art, in which we dream indeed, but create forms and stand aloof from them, and love them for their objective beauty, not merely because of some desire or longing of our own.

Norman continued to be much about the house. My wife did not take to him greatly. She was not exactly jealous of him then, though she became so afterwards, as was only natural. I shall have to enter into details about this, when the time comes. On my side the intimacy became more and more engrossing, and I felt that I was taking some hold both on the lad's mind and his affections.

Arthur Sidgwick came to stay with Graham on the 30th. 'I have not met him since we were at Glion in 1867. He is unaltered: as of old indolent in manner and voice, crystalline in thought and speech, abundant in silence, deep in feeling, real all through.' Arthur lectured me upon the right way in which I ought to approach my work with the sixth form – in a philanthropic spirit and so forth – repressing my emotional tendencies: very sound sense. 'Arthur's strong clear spirit influenced and penetrated me. I do not compare him at all to Graham. Graham, like music, intensifies what is within those whom he loves.' Graham showed him 'Eudiades', and Arthur pronounced it 'degrading to whoever wrote and whoever reads'. I said that, for aught I cared, 'Eudiades' might be burned. Graham, however, claimed it as his own, and the attempt to destroy the poem came to nothing. Arthur sent me a pencil note: 'He refuses to burn Eudiades. *Liberavi animam meam*.' Of course if I had really cared to have the poem burned, I could have done so. But I was indifferent on the subject, and withal nettled by Arthur's high and mighty ways. He had read and approved of many other poems by me in a like vein – 'A Cretan Idyll', 'John Mordan', 'Diego' etc. And I did not see why he should suddenly turn round so.

Still his advice sank pretty deep into me; and when I discovered that Norman had not been to see me of late and had not written because he was laid up with that depressing malady the mumps, I had a revulsion of feeling against my own egotistic maundering. I thought I ought to change my tone toward him, and wrote the following letter under date 1 April.

> I am going to confess to you something in my hatred of concealment. I know you enough, I think, to trust your good sense and good will. It is this. In my letters to you I have sometimes adopted an artificial and sentimental mode of expression. Please forgive me for this; and if you have found it a fault, attribute it to the awkwardness of commencing friendship, and also to the literary habits of one who has sought to gain a kind of freshness by using a language of his own determination. I have not said a single insincere thing to you – nothing that I do not mean and stick to. But somehow I feel that I need to ask your pardon for the strong language of attachment I have used. I believe and hope you understand me. But I would not have you think me a weakly sentimental man whose words go further than his feelings or his acts. Such is not the case. Nor would I have you mistake me for one of those who seek the impossible in friendship. I should like to tear my soul in shreds for those whom I love; and just now I would give you a very large portion of it. How easy it would be to die, if those dear ones could be made the better by my death! But this is vain talk. God has appointed for each of us a work; and none can lighten that work. I must do mine. And, as for you, if I can help you honestly and loyally, should you allow me so to do, I will do my best – so help me God!
>
> There. I have trusted you and confessed. If henceforth I seem to play on the surface or to deal in trivialities, remember this which I have now said. Be often with me; accuse me, call me to task, if you think that I am doing wrong. Make me explain myself when I am obscure. On this ground be my friend, and give me love.

It appears from the diary that I duly received from Norman a highly satisfactory answer, and that our friendship was placed upon a sober understanding. Without diminishing in passion for the boy, I turned my thoughts steadily and with a will to forming his taste and training his intellect.

Under the same date, 1 April, I find a long letter to Arthur Sidgwick transcribed in the diary. Some extracts from this throw light upon the situation.

> In consequence of what you said to me this morning, I have made the following resolution; I will not enter upon my schoolwork next term in any but a philanthropic spirit. I will not seek in that work a mere form of emotional excitement.

I must, however, add that I never fancied for a moment that at Clifton College – of all places in the world, when there are Venice and Naples! – I should be able to live out an aesthetic ideal. I need not be told that life is not art, not even Goethe's or Shakespeare's art, far less such feeble art as mine. We do not meet Margarets and Juliets in real life – nor yet Myronides and Damocles the beautiful.[12] This such experience as I have already gained from Willie Dyer, Alfred Brooke, Rosa Engel, Letitia Malthus, one whom I care not here to mention (Mrs Butler), and another whom I will not mention (my wife), or from the dishonour of Shorting, or from the debasing spectacle of Pretor, has taught me.

Had I wanted to live a poem, I should have chosen Venice, and not Clifton. Be sure therefore that I shall not engage in my lectures on Greek literature in any maudlin spirit.

As to my cycle, I determined in August to suppress these poems; and now the deed is done. I shake from my wings those drops of morning dew. What matters it if ephemerals like 'Eudiades' perish? This brain holds a dozen Eudiadeses. And you were quite at liberty, so far as I am concerned, to burn it.

But about 'Eudiades' I have still something to say. This poem was written with an attempt to realize a historical situation. You asked me what I meant by the temptation of the lovers. I chose to depict one of those young men of Plato's *Phaedrus*, who recoil from acts which were permissible in Hellas. But I admit there is an element of pathos in the poem, which makes it what you called 'orectic' [appetitive] and therefore inartistic.

Lastly, you thought perhaps that I ought to have mentioned Norman. I humbled my pride this morning, as one friend should do to another. But I could not speak of Norman. And even now it is chiefly pride which makes me write about him – lest haply you should say I have omitted aught. Well: I promise that, through Norman, without the flapping of an aesthetic tail in puddles of imagined sin, I will fail or conquer.

What I lived through last winter on the Cornice and in Corsica, placed me where the feet of dying men tread. I do not forget those months, nor can I ever forget them. This is enough. For the rest, I am very sick and sorrowful. I conceal my deepest smart. If my words are bitter, try to pardon them. I have today drunk wormwood. I have talked of my malady, and let you probe my soul.

O my brother, whom I love, whose life I have in these hours touched with keen delight, before whose strong swift sweet spirit I have bowed the neck of my soul, bethink thee yet awhile! Hast thou solved all things in the acid of thine understanding? Who came to Job and found him on a dunghill, scraping his sores with potsherds?

In the strained eager way of young life, all these talkings and letter-writings and diary-scribblings were accomplished on that April fool's day 1869; and when I met Arthur on 2 April at Graham's, there was no rift in the lute of our friendship. I find records of much merry conversation and good fellowship together till the day when Arthur left, and Jowett, who was always turning up at Clifton then, took his place in my thoughts and 'daily dreadful lines' of diary.

So the days went by, and I visited Norman in his home, and made acquaintance with his aunt, and walked with him on Sundays in Leigh Woods, and learned more about his family, and wrote my lectures on Homer and Achilles, and heard concerts and debates at the college. Here is a scrap, which afterwards became a poem:

10 April. There is a breath of Venice in this first spring day. I forget myself and fancy that it has a smell of seaweed in it, and that toward sundown the awnings of my gondola will be flapping Lido-wards. Here the chestnut buds are bursting into fans, and there is a gummy scent about the palings of town gardens. We lounged in the Close, where cricket was uppermost. Then I lay half an hour upon the cliffs above the Avon. Two sulphur butterflies flew past. Late at night, stars seen through the white bud-blossoms of a horse-chestnut, birds half-asleep, and the perfume of poplar sheathes unfolding.

I had a long talk with my wife. The points were these: 'our common wish to beget no more children, chiefly for her sake; the consequent difficulty of my position; my increase in health since I knew Norman, the uncontrollable bias of my nature in this direction, and my firm resolve to keep within the limits of good sense and taste; my illness at Cannes last winter, and its threatened repetition in January; all intensification of my life intensifies my love for her'; which latter point was certainly true.

On 20 April I went to Cambridge, and stayed with Henry Sidgwick at Trinity. . . . I showed my diary to Henry, who said, 'It fills me with terror and pain. I admire your spiritual gifts so much, the versatility of your intellectual interests, your power of poetizing life. But this thread of etherealized sensuality.' In spite of the uneasiness which I too felt, and which these remarks accentuated, I was pledged to meet Norman in London. My foot was in, and could not be drawn out. So I arrived at 47 Norfolk Square upon the 24th, and lived in the big house alone with Norman for six very delightful days. We enjoyed some continuity of intercourse at last, and this week was one of the best we ever spent together. He had never been in London before. The opera, the theatres, the picture galleries, the Crystal Palace, my club, the Abbey and St Paul's, all delighted him immensely. . . . We heard *I Puritani* and the *Trovatore*, saw *School* at the Prince of Wales's, and Sothern[13] in *Home* and the *Night-Watch* at the Haymarket. Norman gave me unmistakeable signs of his affection.

> *30 April.* Last night, *summa cacumina tetigi. In meis obdormivit brachiis, non sine basiis frequentissimis.* [I have touched the heights; he slept in my arms with many oft-repeated kisses.][14]

There was no harm in this either to him or to me. The records of my diary during those six days are free from the self-introspection and etherealized sensuality of the previous months. I had found satisfaction in proximity with Norman, and was natural without wishing to be licentious. Health came to my heart and mind in his expansion. That Henry should be pained and terrified was intelligible. That I should feel the perplexities of the situation was inevitable. Yet it was to me as clear as day that the fruition of my moderate desires brought peace and sanity and gladness. If the mode of intercourse I now enjoyed with him could have been prolonged, our friendship might have been ideal. None but those who understand abnormal temperaments will admit this, because they have not the evidence of their own experience to disprove and annihilate the misconceptions of prevalent opinion. But the fact is so.

On 30 April we travelled down to Bristol together. Norman went home to his aunt and I drove over to Sutton Court, where I found Catherine. It was a lovely spring – a spring of cowslip meadows, primrose lanes, and hyacinth dells, through which I walked with her.

> *2 May.* Catherine and I talked long together about Norman and about our life during our walk upon those heavenly hills. I told her how I felt adequate to living a life of passion without the flesh, and to meeting the difficulty of celibacy in marriage. [We had resolved on that, though it proved impossible in the sequel to adhere continuously to our resolution – J.A.S.] Never again must we be as we were last spring in Italy – companionless, uncomforted, though side by side – dragged down by the burdens of the flesh. [That was when she was

suffering acutely under the gloom and depression of pregnancy –
J.A.S.] She is not made to be a companion to me, and to be a childbearing woman at the same time. But now she will be a companion
in the highest sense, when she is relieved of these necessities. She
comprehends the situation, and understands me completely about
Norman – probably because I understand myself.

Events have proved that these prognostications, on the whole,
were just. It is certain that what her nature required was to be
delivered from the peril of pregnancy, and that a celibate marriage
caused her no discomfort. It is also certain that we have grown to
be closer friends and better companions in proportion as we eliminated sex from our life. When, at a later period, Katharine was born,
we went through another nine months of antecedent wretchedness.
And the last eleven years have been the happiest. But, on the other
hand, the mode of existence laid out on that May day at Sutton
Court had its trials for both of us. She could not help being jealous
of Norman, especially when she found some letters written by me
to him in strains of passion I had never used to her. On my side, I
was exposed to perturbations of the senses and the inconveniences
of sexual abstinence while encouraging my love for Norman. Nevertheless, I did not break the promise I had made and though I desired
him sensuously, I slipped into nothing base.

On 7 May we came to live at Clifton Hill House, while our own
house, 7 Victoria Square, was being made ready.

7 *May.* Clifton is full of vague yet powerful associations. When will
this Circe cease to brew enchantments for my soul? The trees and
streets and distant views of down and valley kept saying to me, as I
walked to Graham's, Put upon your soul the dress which we have
woven for you; you will have to wear it, whether you like or not;
palpitate, aspire, recalcitrate as you may, here it is ready for you.

And indeed a fresh period of unrest, agitation and unwholesome
self-analysis opened. Next day I began my lectures to the sixth form,
which were continued through that term, and went on for more
than two years regularly. By means of them I was brought acquainted
with many boys, who have been my best friends – J. E. Pearson,
A. Nash, C. W. Boyle, T. H. Warren, A. R. Cluer, and H. F. Brown,[15]
not to mention a host of others. Their society gave me great pleasure;
and I am sure they will say that mine was both pleasant and beneficial. We used to dine and walk and talk together, stroll about my

garden, sit among the trees of Leigh Woods. They brought me essays to read and I discoursed on an infinity of topics. Though I dearly loved them, and felt the physical charm of one or another, I entered into no relations like that I had begun with Norman. The duties of a teacher prevented this; and besides, I felt that it would be a mistake to repeat what I gradually came to recognize as more or less a failure. Consequently, these friendships grew up without jealousies, sentimentalities, and etherealized sensualities.

12 May. The nights are still strange. I have had the same dream during the last ten nights. Half-waking I clasp the sleeper at my side, and kiss sleepy lips. Is it Erôs himself? At first the prolonged dream makes me think so. Then my senses uncoil themselves from slumber and the fraud of dreams. Awake, I know it is she whom I have sworn not to touch. On my side I roll heavily and sigh. And Erôs? Where art thou?

This indicates no healthy state of things.

Clifton Hill House was far away from Durdham Downs, where Norman lived. He came often to see me, and did a good deal of work in my study. But I attributed all his unexpected absences to indifference, and became fretful. The good time of London seemed so far away. Then my family and I moved into our house in Victoria Square, which was nearer to the college and the Downs. But the work and play of the summer term absorbed Norman's time; and I noticed also that, under the sweet influences of the season, he had begun to love, as was his former wont, a boy. Norman was all right, giving me what he had the power to give, and this ought to have satisfied a less exacting man. Here is an instance.

24 May. Norman came at 9 p.m. with questions on political economy. We read together, and just before he went, he thought I was not going to kiss him. He stopped and put his face close to mine. Then we walked in the twilight to the Downs.

At the end of the month my father returned from Italy, rather better in health; but frequent illnesses had plagued him during his absence, and he was no longer the same vigorous and splendid man he used to be.

Here is a passage from the diary, recording a conversation I had with Norman's cousin:

15 June. I went out with him, and we began to talk about Norman. This topic so interested both of us that we walked, in a keen wind under a clear green sky, deepening to feldspar blues with stars in it, on to the cliff edge above the Avon at the sea walls. His admiration for Norman is touching and beautiful. He says that all admire Norman, who can do what he likes with people. But his 'nearly perfect' character is spoiled by indolence, procrastination, want of definite will and ambition, readiness to let things take their course. He has not the energy of passion. He needs to be stirred up. . . . Then about the evil influences of his home in Derbyshire. His father and two elder brothers threw themselves away. His mother is not much to be respected. Her second husband is an old scamp. Must Norman go the way of the rest, who are fascinating, clever, weak, indolent and self-indulgent? He has sincere enthusiasm for his school. He is really affectionate toward those of whom he has been fond: is fond of me: I can do much with him. – So I jot down some of the things which the cousin said. I wish I could write them as nicely as the cousin said them.

This extract throws light upon the situation. I was going astray by a keen desire to attach Norman, not merely through affection, but also through service and the ties which come of intellectual and moral life in common. He, of his nature, remained wavering, inconstant, readily affectionate, fascinating and conscious of his fascination, but not attachable. I imperiously craved too much. He indolently and kindly gave what there was to give. I wanted an ideal thing. It was not in him to respond; and probably I was not the man to draw him to the point I wished. The simple course would have been to have just taken the most which I could get, and to have plied the yielding side of his character toward sensuality. But this was precisely what I refused to do. At that period of my life I still clung to ideal conceptions, and I had fallen upon a friend who could not help me to realize them. Neither had blame.

There came a thunderstorm about these things with Catherine. We made a reconciliation and new bonds of friendship, which proved the essential rightness of our wills and wishes. But it was a moment of tempest:

18 June. No one but she will know what burdens I have borne, imposed upon me by my temperament, and how I have been disciplined to the service of my congenital passion. I cannot write down what I have told her. And if I did, whom would it profit to know that this wretch, clasped from his cradle by a serpent, sought to elude its folds – that he ran to the waters of oblivion, but the stream dried

up and the snake followed – that the thick leafage of close study was lightning-scathed, so that the glittering reptile eyes shone through – that the high tree of marriage was hewn down beneath him, so that he fell into those serpent jaws again – that the sinews of escape, the eyesight of occupation, the brain force of activity through will, were paralysed, and he was never free from the creeping coiling length of his soul's murderer. – To have the imaginative and sensuous side of passion disconnected in one's nature from the rational enduring solid part of love, and never to feel the former in its truest sense for women, but only for dreams or the incarnations of dreams in male beings, selected for the moment, not thoroughly respected or believed in; is this common?

Common enough, I answer now, but very tragic and pathetic.

Just then, so oddly was my life mixed, that I began to write the essay on Aristophanes, which is one of the best, I think, of my *Studies of Greek Poets.*

18 June. What is painful about Norman is this – that as far as the selfish and lower parts of the desires expressed in my diary go, I have been satisfied; but the purer, nobler, more disinterested desires which have sprung up in personal contact with him are unsatisfied. Of physical closeness I have as much as I can want. Of spiritual closeness I get little – I am not even allowed to exercise my paedagogic faculty for his good in any definite way. I have learned how valueless, how worse than valueless, how degrading in my own eyes, is mere physical closeness without truly passionate or spiritual closeness. Yet, were there but passion on his part or spiritual unity, how would not hand touch, lips, scent of hair, be dignified? Do I dream? Are the two things really separate? I have spiritual closeness with Catherine. . . .

I had arrived now at seeing that I could not exactly establish the sort of comradeship which I desired. But Norman's society remained very sweet to me; and it speaks well for the relations we had established that they suffered no change for the worse. I took him with me in July for a journey on the Continent, through Paris and Berne to Mürren, then over the Grimsel and Furka to Hospenthal, down the Gothard to Amsteg and up into the Maderanerthal, to Axenstein and Rigi Scheideck, Engelberg, and back by Basle to Clifton. We were alone, and enjoyed ourselves as much as we had done in London. The good times returned. I have many pleasant memories and records of that journey – the little wooden rooms of inns in which we slept together, generally in the same bed; the long walks upon the mountains, down the valleys in sunshine and in rain; the hay stable where we couched together through a night by the Trüb See, intending to climb Titlis (but the Fohn swept down and a thunderstorm deluged the whole region); the sleepy voluptuous days at Axenstein; the kisses and embracements and the long delicious hours between walking and sleeping; the wet days spent in the Maderanerthal. . . . One little entry from the diary may be inserted here:

21 August. Jam summa cacumina voluptatis tetigi, et flosculos quales desiderabam plena manu in gremium recepi. Hic tamen morari nequeo. Flores flammiferi, in cineresque abituri, cor cordium ne comburant graviter metuo. [I have reached the highest heights of pleasure, and the flowers for which I was longing I took by the handful into my bosom. But I cannot tarry here. For I am very much afraid that these flame-bearing flowers, soon to depart to ashes, may set my heart of hearts ablaze.][16]

I was thoroughly satisfied with what I used to call physical closeness; but I dreaded what that might lead to, if the spiritual and intellectual relation between us remained imperfect. . . .

We reached Clifton on 4 September and I settled down again to domesticity and work. Began writing on Pindar, and lecturing to boys and ladies. On the 23rd I had news that Conington had died almost suddenly; and on the 28th a telegram announced the serious illness of Mr North. Catherine was with him. On the 29th I reached Hastings just an hour too late to see him alive. After seven days spent at Hastings, I returned to my lecture work at Clifton, where my father was ill again – obliged to go to Brighton. Meanwhile there were people on visits – Roden Noel, John Nichol,[17] Mrs Clough.

On 20 November I heard two pieces of news, first that Percival was defeated by Dr Hayman as a candidate for the headmastership of Rugby,[18] and second that Norman was elected a scholar of Balliol. This was highly satisfactory to me, as well as to everybody – except that it implied a speedy separation. In fact it was settled that he should go up to Oxford at the beginning of the Lent term.

Life went on as usual: I lecturing and devouring the Greek traged-ians with their fragments, one after the other, and writing lectures on them, which were afterwards turned into studies, writing poems (among them 'Amoris Amari Genius'), visiting my father at Brighton, going to concerts and dinner parties, giving parties at home,

Symonds at Am Hof.

A portrait of John Addington
Symonds in Venice

Right: The Bridge of Sighs, Venice

A portrait of Angelo Fusato
in Venice

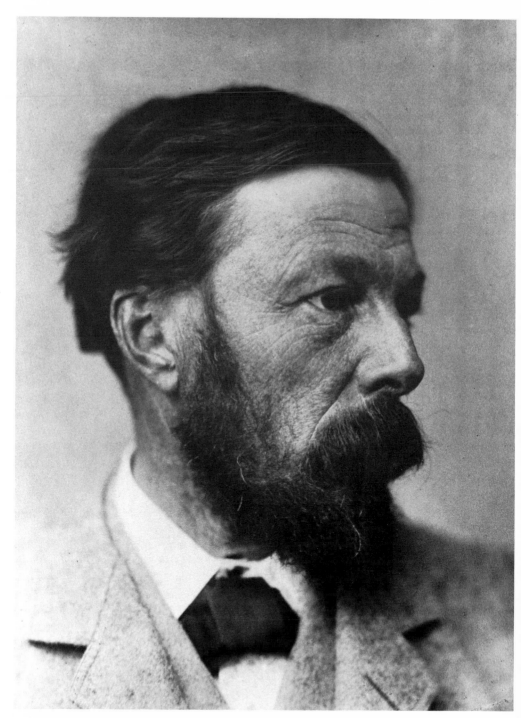

John Addington Symonds, 1886

entertaining the boys, seeing much of Norman in the evenings, and often noting in my diary little phrases like φιλάματα μελίτος ἀδυμελεστέρα [kisses sweeter than honey],[19] receiving visits as usual from Jowett and Henry Sidgwick – carrying on the round of life, in fact, until the day approached when Norman was to go to Oxford.

How it happened I do not know; but he spent the last two days and nights before this parting as a guest in our house. I shall copy out what my diary contains about this visit. It happened to coincide exactly with the date of his first coming to my house in the previous year.

28 January 1870. Norman came to me on Wednesday night at 11. I made James (my servant) make him a bowl of hot milk and bread which he likes. After he had eaten it, I said, 'You are a snake to whom one offers innocent libations.' Then again, looking into his face, 'How could you think it strange that I should go on loving you passionately?' – 'Most people don't; it comes by fits and starts.' – 'Then they are not like me.' – 'You are not like most people.'

I have had two perfect midnight hours with him: one on each of the two past nights. The house was still; the windows of his room were curtained; the fire burned dim, but warm; a candle shaded from our eyes gave twilight, so that we could see. We lay covered from the cold in bed, tasting the honey of softly spoken words and the blossoms of lips pressed on lips. Oh, the strain of those delicate slight limbs and finely moulded breasts – the melting of that stately throat into the exquisite slim shoulders – as of the Genius of the Vatican – the στέρνα θ' ὡς ἀγάλματος κάλλιστα [and his most lovely breast, like that of a statue].[20] I find it hard to write of these things; yet I wish to dwell on them and to recall them, pen in hand: – the head that crowned all, pillowed with closely cut thick flocks of hair and features as of some bronze statue, sharp and clear – the chiselled mouth, the short firm upper lip, the rounded chin, the languid eyes black beneath level lines of blackest brows, the low white forehead over-foamed with clustering hair and flakes of finest curls.

I stripped him naked, and fed sight, touch and mouth on these things. Will my lips ever forget their place upon his breast, or on the tender satin of his flank, or on the snowy whiteness of his belly? Will they lose the nectar of his mouth – those opened lips like flower petals, expanding neath their touch and fluttering? Will my arms forget the strain of his small fragile waist, my thighs the pressure of his yielding thighs, my ears the murmur of his drowsy voice, my brain the scent of his sweet flesh and breathing mouth? Shall I ever cease to hear the metallic throb of his mysterious heart – calm and true – ringing little bells beneath my ear?

I do not know whether, after all, the mere touch of his fingers as they met and clasped and put aside my hand, was not of all the best. For there is the soul in the fingers. They speak. The body is but silent, a dumb eloquent animated work of art made by the divine artificer.

Beneath his armpits he has no hair. The flesh of his throat and breast is white as ivory. The nipples of his breasts are hardly to be seen, they are so lost in whiteness and so soft. Between them, on the breastbone, is a spot of dazzling brightness, like snow or marble that has felt the kisses of the sun. His hips are narrow, hardened where the muscles brace the bone, but soft as down and sleek as satin in the hollows of the groin. Shy and modest, tender in the beauty-bloom of ladhood, is his part of sex κύπριν ποθοῦσαν ἤδη [now longing for passion] – fragrant to the searching touch, yet shrinking: for when the wandering hand rests there, the lad turns pleadingly into my arms as though he sought to be relieved of some delicious pang.

If I could only paint him, as he lay there white upon the whiteness of the bed, and where he was not white, glowing to amber hues, and deepening into darkness of black eyes and hair – dawn of divinest twilight – only one rose upon his flesh, and that the open, passionate, full-perfumed mouth, the chalice of soul-nourishing dew. Norman is all in all and wholly 'μελίχλωρος' ['honey-golden'].[21]

Ah, but the fragrance of his body! Who hath spoken of that scent undefinable, which only love can seize, and which makes love wild mad and suicidal?

Now come the nonchalances and superb abandon of repose. How his head drooped on one shoulder, and how his arm lay curved along flank and thigh, and how upon the down of dawning manhood lay his fingers, and how the shrinking god was covered by his hand!

A year has passed since Norman first came to dine with me. I think that the flower of the apricot hath crowned the misty brows of this past year, and that its feet have trodden on sweet Calamus. Truly, the reeds have pricked the tender feet of the year, so that the months are pearled with drops of blood.

The slender well-knit body of a lad: why is it so beautiful to me – more beautiful than Aphrodite rising from the waves, or Proserpine upon the meads of Enna? Why do I love the star of the evening better than the moon? Why are white violets in March (when flowers are few, and the wind blows dust along dry lanes) dearer than the rose gardens of Shiray or the anemones of Bordighera?

After the long claspings of the first night with Norman, I dreamed. I dreamed of a lane of cypress trees and firs and cedars. Roses bloomed on the ground and in the underwoods, in the thickets, in the open. Roses climbed the cedar trunks and trailed in odorous garlands from the topmost pines. They wreathed the cypress spires into thyrsi; they burned in dark tangles of bay, myrtle, ilex, rosemary and box. The air was heavy with their perfume. Wandering and soaring roses made milky ways, and flaming, through the boskage.

And now there is an end. Norman will breathe the same air with me no more. His bed in the upper chamber of the house upon the Downs knows him no more. He is a scholar of Balliol; into Oxford rooms and walks and gardens he will carry his perfume (as of some white violet) for other men.

For me there is nothing left tonight, but to smooth and kiss the pillows where we lay together. The room is cold and cheerless now. Go down into your study, by the fire, and think of him.

Where is he now? A first night in college rooms is an experience. He will accommodate himself to circumstance more easily than most men do. But I know how cold it must be in his bedroom – how very cold the sheets are (college sheets are always cold) – how hard and narrow the bed is. He will assuredly feel solitary. He was never alone at school here, or with me abroad. I wonder whether, one moment, he will wish for me – for my arms making him warm, for my soft speeches wooing sleep!

Oh child, child! What would I not give to have you here? Your waist between my knees, as you knelt and I sat in the armchair before the fire. Or your head upon my shoulder. Or to be myself upon the floor, with my face in your lap. Or to be sitting on your knees. What would I not give, for once and for one moment only, to lay my body on your body, and to drink your mouth.

What would I not give, even for a single instant, to be knotted with you, limb with limb, arms, breasts and bellies open and eyes drinking fire of eyes.

With this *Chant d'Amour* I ought perhaps to close the chapter. The diary never rises to the same height of lyricism again. But there remains much to be told, without which the lyric cry would be a cry of shame.

In spite of the more than etherealized sensuality of the passionate farewell to Norman on his way into the world which I have just transcribed, it is a fact that neither then, nor afterwards, nor before, did any one of those things take place between us which people think inseparable from love of this sort. I was content with contemplation, contact, kissing. The candour with which I have set down everything about myself, and the admission which I here make of having at a later period indulged in such acts with other men, ought to be sufficient guarantee of my truthfulness.

(After writing the above paragraphs I happened to come upon one of the few letters which I have preserved of Norman's correspondence. It is dated 26 November 1886. He describes in it some of the temptations and the evils of his boyhood. Then he proceeds: 'A most pandemic state. The combined influence of Percival *and yourself* did something to cure me of this.' The words I have italicized show that, in spite of all appearances, and in spite of what I have described myself, he, after the lapse of sixteen years, looked back upon my influence as salutary in the very matter of love between male and male. The original letter, though it is very private, I shall enclose among these papers.*

Well. Norman went to Oxford, where he in due course of time took his degree after a fairly distinguished career. I was not dissatisfied with his performance, though more might perhaps have been expected of him; for I had come to recognize that his brain lacked energy and that his temper was indolent. What distinguished him intellectually was justice of perception, lucid intelligence and good sense. These qualities made him, when still a boy, appear more remarkable than he really was. They helped him to be a sound scholar. But they did not contain the stuff of growth.

We continued to correspond and I saw a great deal of him in vacation time. In the summer of 1872 I took him for another Continental tour – this time to Zermatt, across the Theodul pass into Val d'Aosta, then to Milan and Venice, and home by the Etzsch-thal, Finstermüng and Vorarlberg. We enjoyed this journey in a social comradely season for amorous caresses had gone by. That I still regarded him as a lover appears from this last extract from my diary:

21 June 1872. Yesterday was the eve of St John, and a night of full moon, wonderfully clear, a Bezaüberungsnacht [night of enchantment]. We have invented sitting on the house roof (at Clifton Hill) during this summer time. The limestone flags are broad and white and dry and warm. The northern heavens hold faint twilight; toward the south-west sails the moon, golden, globed, high over fold on fold of hill and wood, on which lie swathes of mist. Down in the valley sleeps the city, a sub-lunar world of constellations, with the

*See Appendix IV. – Editor.

sharp white spire of Redclyffe and the massive cathedral tower among its limes, and lamps shimmering upon the water winding in and out among the houses. A sound of trains, throbbing and panting like dragons with lolled-out tongues, is heard far off. Our garden slumbers below – smooth lawn – velvety headed trees – solemn shadows and silvery lights. There, on such a night, in such a scene, Catherine took Norman to her heart, and pledged herself to love him like a son. She knows everything about him and me. We have both suffered much through him – she most – but she has borne and believed all; and now she has accepted him with more than toleration.

I must add that, soon after our return from this foreign tour, on 19 September 1872, I received the first copy of my *Introduction to the Study of Dante*. Thus my entrance into authorship took place exactly at the moment when a final reconciliation of opposites was effected in the matter of my love for Norman. He became a schoolmaster, married, and is now the father of children.

I always retained a tender affection for him. . . .

Reviewing this episode of my love for Norman, twenty years after it commenced, I am able to perceive very clearly that the real malady of my nature was not in the passion I felt for him, but in the self-conscious morbid and sophisticated way in which the passion expressed itself. The passion was natural; and he responded to it naturally, so far as temperament, age and constitution of his emotional self permitted. I was always fidgeting and fiddling away in my self-scrutinizing mood at aspects of the passion – posing in the looking-glass, weighing him in balances. I approached sincerity and truth mainly in those 'native moments' of self-abandonment to what the moment offered, which have been described above. I approached truth again in certain rare efforts to suppress my instincts. But the large tracts of time employed upon self-analysis and fretful suspicious jealousy were thrown away, except in so far as they tended to clarify my reason, to disgust me with such shillyshallying, and to prepare me for the franker comradeship of my later experiences.

I do not take myself greatly to blame for all this folly. It was merely the inevitable outcome of my life through ten years of adolescence and early manhood, during which I had done everything in my power to sophisticate my inborn bent of feeling, to warp my nature, to clog myself with chains of circumstance. I could not move freely, or take things as they came. I was a compound of antagonistic impulses, fostered by a radically vicious training; and when I now came to close quarters with my desire, I could do nothing but pursue my desire through a jungle of unwholesome casuistry, self-deception, and mortified ideals. This episode closed the period of idealism; and certain experiences which I shall relate in another chapter led me to seek a new solution upon lower and more practical lines of conduct.

Chapter Fourteen

Intellectual and literary evolution

Since I have reached the point of my embarking on the great wide sea of literature, it is right that I should attempt to form some estimate of my natural and acquired faculties for this branch of art.

From nature I derived a considerable love of books, an active brain, a fairly extended curiosity, receptivity to ideas above the average, an aptitude for expression, sensibility to external objects in the world of things, and intense emotional susceptibility of a limited and rather superficial kind.

My power of application was always small. What patience I may now possess in the acquisition of knowledge or in the exercise of my talents, has been gained with difficulty. Quick and intelligent at the outset, I grew very slowly, and arrived comparatively late at the control of my faculties for any definite purpose. The larger part of my early years was spent in apparently ineffectual dreaming.

Few people are contented with their memory, because all of us feel the inevitable limitations of a faculty on which we are continually making extraordinary demands. The more we have of it, the more we expect from it, and at the same time there are few who train it systematically. In my own case I am certain that my memory was originally weak and unreliable. I remembered nothing definitely which I had not either seen or acutely felt. Names, dates, numbers, historical events entered my mind with facility, abode there for a short space under the control of a deliberate volition, and vanished again as though I had never possessed them. I could get a subject up with tolerable ease. But I could not retain my knowledge of it. This gave me some advantage in preparing for examinations; and like the sieve used in the story of the forty thieves, my memory caught in its meshes a piece of gold here and there. Having an active brain and a lively curiosity, I was always acquiring information; while the defect of my retentive power made me continually lose the larger portion of it. In this way my intellectual furniture grew to be a vague, ill-digested, inaccurate mass, rich in possibilities but poor in solid stuff. I have never been able to overcome the congenital inferiority of my brain in these respects. Yet being aware of the deficiency, and resolving to make the best of things which might be worse or better, I learned to utilize the strength and to supplement the weakness of my memory. I saturate my mind with rapid reading, devour multitudes of books, and make voluminous notes, feeling sure that I shall obtain a general conception of the subject under consideration. Then I return again and again to the leading documents, check every impression of fact by reiterated comparison of my notes with their sources, verify dates and quotations, force myself to attain accuracy by drudgery. Few writers, I take it, have undergone so much preparatory labour as I am obliged to go through.

For numbers I have absolutely no head. I do not visualize them except in the most rudimentary way. At best I can see the digits scrawled upon a slate. I am unable to remember the multiplication table; and it is notorious in my family that I constantly make mistakes between a ten and a hundred, a hundred and a thousand, so feeble is my grasp upon the value of the symbol 0. If I have not been involved in pecuniary difficulties, it is because I am conscious of this imbecility, and refer on every occasion to written memoranda. The same consciousness made me early in life scale my expenditure considerably below my income, in order that I might have always a fair margin of cash to fall back upon.

I cannot learn anything systematically. Grammar, logic, political economy, the exact sciences offered insuperable obstacles to my mind. The result is that I know nothing thoroughly. And I do not think this is so much due to laziness as to cerebral incapacity. My brain was always impenetrable to abstractions. When I attacked them, I felt a dull resistance, a sense of benumbed and benumbing stupor stealing like a fog over my intellect. I have had to circumvent abstractions, to present them in the concrete, and to return upon them by the path of metaphor or symbol, before I was able to approach them in the form of pure thought.

I have already observed that visible objects — forms, colours, aspects of nature, faces, buildings, statues, pictures — leave keen and durable impressions on my sensibility. What I have once regarded with curiosity I retain. And more than that, I remember the atmosphere of these things, the feeling they exhale, their specific quality so far as I am able to perceive it. This has helped me in the line of graphic writing, and has given me such certainty of touch as I possess.

The same may be said about the other senses – touch, taste, hearing, smell – but in a less degree. In spite, however, of this retentive receptivity to objects of sense, I am not strong in the faculty of observation – that faculty which makes the novelist, the man of science, and the higher artist. Perhaps I lack patience or interest in things for their own sakes. What I observe and treasure up comes to me casually, by no premeditated effort, but because it attracts me and is correlated to my tastes or sympathies.

Emotional states, whether painfully poignant or fragile in their evanescent lightness, I remember with unerring accuracy. This, I think, has been useful to me in the exercise of criticism; and had I been a greater master of expression, it would have made me a no common lyric poet. As it is, I possess a certainty with regard to past conditions of feeling which I find valuable when attempting to pronounce judgement upon works of art or literature or to recall the sentiment evoked by places.

At the same time, just as I am no deliberate observer, I cannot claim to be an analyst of emotion. Retentive receptivity is the quality I claim. Combined with a moderate estimate of my own powers and a fair share of common sense, together with an active curiosity, this receptive and retentive susceptibility to various objects and emotions has given a certain breadth, a certain catholicity, a certain commonplaceness to my aesthetic conclusions. Being sufficiently conscious that I am far from normal in my personal proclivities and instincts, I have perhaps the right to give this explanation of my sanity as a critic. No doubt another explanation could be offered. Those who study these memoirs will be able to say – and to say with justice – that they now understand the balance of my mind in matters of the higher criticism, the even-handed justice of my verdicts, the irritatingly comprehensive way I have of looking upon things they value more than I do. 'In his lifetime the man never spoke out,'[1] they will assert. 'He cherished an engrossing preoccupation, an absorbing and incurable proclivity, which found no outlet except in furtive self-indulgence, which had to be suppressed and hidden out of sight, although it flamed within him in the foreground of all vision, rendering him comparatively indifferent and therefore apparently equitable to everything which lay outside that fiery circle of his inmost self.'

My powers of expression were considerable, yet not of first-rate quality. Vaughan at Harrow told me the truth when he said that my besetting sin was 'fatal facility'. I struggled long to conquer fluency. Still I have not succeeded. I find a pleasure in expression for its own sake; but I have not the inevitable touch of the true poet, the unconquerable patience of the conscious artist. As in other matters, so here, I tried to make the best of my defects. Concentration lies beyond my grasp. The right words do not fall into the right places at my bidding. I have written few good paragraphs, and possibly no single perfect line. I strove, however, to control the qualities I knew myself to have, to train and curb them, to improve them by attention to the details of style. If I have achieved any success in literature, the secret of that success lies in persistent effort, combined with a steady determination to preserve the spirit of delight in labour and the spontaneity of self.

Passion and imagination, in the true sense of these words, were denied me. I was not born without capacity for passion. But I had to tame it down and subdivide it for reasons which*

I may conclude this topic then by saying that spontaneous passion and creative imagination have hitherto been sterilized in my work. The one point of my nature on which they might have taken hold and flourished, was that central love of the soul's malady, which remained for ever inaccessible to their approaches. Wheeling round and round the stubborn rock of agony and heartache, finding no foothold there, breaking and bruising their wings against its barren adamant, the pair of soaring eagles retired to self-built cages. There they have drooped a lifetime. It has been my destiny to make continual renunciation of my truest self, because I was born out of sympathy with the men around me, and have lived a stifled anachronism. What I have achieved in literature might be compared to the fragments of an aerolite scattered upon the summits of some hard impiteous peak.

Of moral qualities exercised in the same field of work, I may claim the following. First, humility, developed by the sense of inefficiency

*Sentence left incomplete in ms. – Editor.

which overclouded my earliest efforts. Secondly, pride and self-respect, developed during the same period of baffled aspiration. Blending their forces, these qualities rendered me indifferent to criticism, comparatively cold about the fortune of my books, alien to cliques and coteries, contented to compose for my own pleasure in a spirit half sanguine and half pessimistic. I have never expected success or been fretful when I did not gain it, never cared very much for praise or blame, never curried favour or sought to disarm opposition. In the third place, I think I may ascribe to myself justice and open-mindedness, enabling me to take a broad survey of the fields I had to traverse. But perhaps this virtue is rather the outcome of indifference than an active sense of what is righteous. Fourth, I have been gifted with obstinacy, in the face of physical and other disadvantages. This might also be described as courage or tenacity, or a determination to make the best of things, or a want of fastidiousness, impelling me to push my work forward in spite of obstacles, and without caring greatly how much it suffered owing to adverse circumstance. Fifth, I find in my character a freedom from jealousy and envy. This has perhaps been tainted with indifference: so that the maxim *noli aemulari* [do not get involved in rivalry] bears upon my lips something of contempt for things which are really more important than I choose to hold them. Experience of life, often extremely bitter, at times unexpectedly blissful, has taught me that there is nothing extraordinarily great in the greatest of achievements, nothing mean in the meanest of occupations: briefly that human life is not to be estimated by what men perform but by what they are. I have learned that rank can be vulgar, genius fretful and ignoble, virtue unsympathetic, vice heroic and amiable. I have discovered the best society and finest courtesy in cottages, the most lovable comrades among peasant folk, the soundest wisdom in those who never heard the name of culture. What essential difference indeed is there between making books or boots, manoeuvring for a mayorship or a premiership, driving in a donkey-cart or a barouche, embracing a duchess or a dairymaid, dining off ortolans or porridge? Struggle for place, contention about title, strivings to eclipse our neighbours in wealth or fame, appear to me essentially ignoble and subversive of man's equipoise. It is the duty of each to perform his own function as faithfully as he can; his privilege to obtain his pleasure where he finds it; his dignity to suffer pain as cheerfully as he is able. But petty wranglings, rivalries, heart-burnings about nothings corrupt

219

the source of happiness. What is there worth fighting for that lies outside ourselves, our own capacity for joy? The span of the greatest, as also of the least of us, is too insignificant, the span of the universe is too incalculable, for a mortal to waste his precious breath in competition. Money-makers are bound indeed to do so; and we need not be too scornful in judging Rothschilds. But children of the spirit ought not to descend into the arena of their mud. It is enough for them to produce the best work they can, and not to be annoyed when others produce better than God allotted for their own share. The final question is what a man enjoys. Perhaps Titian and Pictor Ignotus enjoyed equally. Perhaps the latter enjoyed more than his decorated and justly famous fellow craftsman. In either case fame had little to do with their pleasures and pains. What Clough called 'a Stoic-Epicurean acceptance' seems to be the wisest attitude: the temper of mind which accommodates itself to everything, and finds everything passably good. For me, my deepest preoccupations have been so far beyond the sphere of art and letters, my desires so painfully unrealizable in life, that literature has always seemed to me a noble pastime – what Aristotle called a 'διαγωγή'[2] but not of sufficient importance to involve a free man in ambitious toils. Under the dominance of these moral qualities I have pursued literature, not as a mission, not as a vocation, not as a profession, but to please myself and to occupy the leisure which would else have been for me the λίαν σχολή [too much leisure][3] of Prometheus on his crags of Caucasus.

This account of my natural faculties, so far as I am aware of them, will serve perhaps to explain why I have produced so much, why I have entered into no literary contests and enrolled myself under no banner of a sect, and also why my work is marked by something approaching to amateurishness. The review of what education and circumstance have done for the development of these faculties will cast further light upon the same questions.

The chief fault of my education as a training for literature was that it was too exclusively literary, and favoured my own indolent unambitious inclinations.

Neither at Clifton nor at Harrow nor yet at Oxford did I learn any one thing thoroughly. I failed to grasp the elements of mathematics, absorbed nothing of physical science, acquired a bare smattering of two modern languages, and, after spending long years upon Latin and Greek, emerged a wretchedly inadequate scholar.

The Harrow system in my time was a bad one. I venture to say this because I can challenge anyone to produce a list of five really eminent men turned out of Harrow between the years 1854 and 1859. I have chosen a lustre, and have demanded only one eminent individual for each year of that lustre. Can they be found? I think not. Yet Harrow numbered at that period an average of 500 students; and these were recruited from the aristocracy, the landed gentry, the professional and mercantile classes. No school could have desired a wider selection, including specimens of the most favoured and the most energetic stocks which England generates. The stuff was excellent; the handling of the stuff was miserable. In theory, athletics balanced study. We were supposed to combine gymnastic and music – Plato's phrases – in the healthy all-round exercise of human faculties. But athletics degenerated into lawlessness, licentiousness and rowdyism. Study dwindled into mechanical and easily evaded task work. The athletes were exposed to sensual vices and the brutification of their intellects. Physically beautiful, and fit for noble purpose, they had no moral discipline. The students were starved through the inadequacy and negligence of their instructors, stupefied by unintelligent routine, numbed by the goddess Dullness which spread her sleepy money-getting wings above the place. There was no master-spirit to infuse energy into either of the dual branches of the system, to combine both in a vital organism and to provide a proper scope for individuals. In spite of its theory, so plausible in aspect, the little state of Harrow was rotten to the core. Learning could not flourish there. No tough studies were encouraged. Even the lighter graces of humanism shrank beneath the touch of dullards like Drury and Harris, egotists like Middlemist, zanies like Steel, pragmatical martinets like Rendall, scholastic souls like Westcott, sphinx-natured shams like Vaughan. In a blundering sort of way the docile boys were made to recognize the force of drill and duty. That was nearly all we gained. We learned to work for work's sake. Of solid knowledge we acquired next to nothing. It must also be admitted that the prevalent somnolence, the reign of intellectual dullness, had its paradoxical advantages. Our brains, except through our own fault, were not over-taxed. No effort was made to turn us into youthful prodigies. I am perhaps not in the position to speak justly about Harrow. English public schools deliberately sacrifice exceptional natures to the average; and I was in many respects an exceptional nature. Still, judged by the low standard of an English public school, I think that I am justified in saying that Harrow failed conspicuously as a nursery for the picked youth of a great nation. What I owe to Harrow is first the contamination of my moral sense, and second the hardening of my character by premature initiation into the bear-garden of mundane life. Neither of these things is exactly what an ambitious and very expensive system of education aims at. Of substantial knowledge I owe nothing to the system. Still I acquired the habit of work there. I think I should have acquired it anywhere, and with less expenditure of useless labour under more congenial conditions. At Harrow I learned to be acquainted with work, 'as the tanned galley-slave is with his oar': not because I liked the work appointed, or felt that it was well appointed; but because it offered a pause and respite in the utter wilderness and desolate conditions of the godless place.

On leaving Harrow for Oxford, I very soon began to feel the stirring of a more vigorous intellectual life. The conditions of society and the methods of study suited me; and I derived great benefit from the friendships I made with men of distinguished talents. I worked harder than I had done at Harrow. Yet I pursued no rigorous course of study – nothing which deserves the name of *études fortes*.

Jowett was the leading spirit in the college at that epoch; and under his influence even philosophy was studied mainly from the rhetorical point of view. The temper of his mind unfitted him for systematic thought. He mistrusted the dominance of rigorous method, and disbelieved in metaphysic. So far as he possessed a philosophy, it consisted in a criticism based on common sense (shrewdness, knowledge of the world and men) applied to the history of ideas. He abhorred precise definitions and shrank from logical dilemmas. One of his favourite ways of solving a difficulty was to state its several aspects and to fall back upon an appeal to instinct. Aristotle's φρόνιμος [rational person] seemed always present to his mind. Under his influence we were taught to write upon a vast variety of debatable topics, and to acquire a wide but superficial familiarity with what the several schools of Greece and Rome and modern Europe had thought about the universe. The aspirants after honours learned to deal cleverly with words and phrases, and to criticize without possessing substantial knowledge. This sophistic training, in which I delighted, developed my literary faculty and filled my memory with a really considerable amount of facts, ideas, and speculative points of view. But the absence of any robust intellectual gymnastic encouraged my natural propensity toward amateurishness. Just after taking my degree I found myself able to write articles on all kinds of books and many sorts of questions for the *Saturday Review*. The editor Cook[4] said that they were admirably packed with matter. All this, however, did not make me a scholar in the higher sense of that word – the sense attached to it by Pattison.[5]

The fact is that I was not qualified by nature to be a scholar in this higher sense, and my education did nothing to correct my bias. Plodding along at the curriculum, and taking vivid interest in those subjects which suited my literary bent, I obtained a zeal for study and contracted habits which made study and production of one sort or another the pleasure and necessity of my subsequent existence. But I did not acquire the method of rigorous investigation. In the same way I learned to think, and largely increased the activity and subtlety of my brain. But I did not gain a due sense of what may be called the search after truth. I was too easily satisfied with plausibilities, and content to grasp the *à peu près* instead of waiting till I had seized the very heart of things.

Some of my contemporaries were by nature provided with strong political interests. Outside the curriculum, they grew and flourished and evolved their personalities by reading the newspapers and taking part in the Union debates. It was the momentous period of the great American war and the Lancashire cotton famine. Others pursued an ideal of more or less effective genius. But many of us, among whom I was, had proclivities without any commanding bias. We wandered only too helplessly between duty to the curriculum and indulgence of undisciplined instincts. I could mention men who might have been musicians or painters, but who wasted their time at Oxford in aimless strumming on the piano or in silly sketching.

I, for my part, went philandering about music, heraldry, the fine arts and literary studies, doing nothing thoroughly and acquiring no fundamental science. I wrote poetry, weak in form and morbid in feeling. I dreamed away hours in ante-chapels. I mooned in canoes along the banks of Cherwell or among yellow waterlilies at Godstow. I joined the volunteer rifle corps, and neglected drill. I entered Maclaren's gymnasium, and got no further than jumping and vaulting. I rode across the country, larking on half-broken hacks and taking no pride in becoming an expert horseman. I indulged day-dreams about choristers, and acted trivial dramas of love and hate and reconcilement with my less respectable friends. My suppressed emotional life was indeed a great hindrance – perhaps the chief hindrance to my making myself a scholar or an artist. It absorbed an enormous amount of time and engaged the larger part of my nervous energy. It preoccupied my thoughts and rendered me com-paratively indifferent to the acquisition of knowledge. Engulfed in it, I refused to take either science or art seriously. They appeared secondary in my scheme of life, which already placed life before learning and above art. Yet the literary faculty was so strongly pronounced in me that nothing which I did or thought was wholly thrown away. I passed brilliant examinations with comparative ease, impressed examiners with my style and mental versatility, and acquired the reputation of being what was called 'an able man'. What was more important, I learned to write, to command my powers of expression, and to utter with some precision what I felt and thought. The different kinds of writing which I was continually practising developed my gifts in this direction. These were elaborate essays on philosophical and historical subjects, English verses of many sorts, answers to questions in examinations, and lastly the copious private diaries I kept.

Meanwhile, the society of friends and counsellors whom I was free to choose, kept exercising a salutary influence over my mind. Among these I place my father in the first rank. Growing into ever closer sympathy with him, I learned immensely from his fine and varied culture, his high ideal of purity in language, and his liberal philosophy of life.

Jowett, when I came under his influence, enjoyed peculiar prestige among the young men, owing partly to the stir which *Essays and Reviews* had made. When I went up in the autumn of 1858, my father gave me a letter of introduction to the awe-inspiring don. I found him dozing in an armchair over a dying fire. It was about 5 p.m. His rooms were then in Fisher's Buildings, looking out upon the Broad. The study was panelled, with an old-fashioned mantel-piece of carved wood. He roused himself, glanced at the letter, and said dreamily, 'I do not think I know your father.' Then, after an awkward pause, he rose and added, 'Goodbye, Mr Symonds.' I had gone with all a boy's trepidation to present myself, intensified by my own repugnance to any semblance of uncalled-for self-assertion.

This dismissal, therefore, hurt me exceedingly; and I do not under-stand it, for I know that my father had a slight acquaintance at that time with Jowett.

I saw nothing more of him for at least a year. But shortly before I went in for Moderations, he sent for me, and asked me to bring him Greek and Latin composition. The few evenings during which he coached me made me feel for the first time what it was to be *taught*. He said very little and gave me no tips. But somehow he made me comprehend what I had to aim at, and how I had to go about it. The contact of his mind enabled me to use my reading in Greek for the purpose of writing. We learn not so much by what is dictated to us or by set instruction as by sympathy and effused influence. I am sure that the iambics I produced for those few lessons were better than the thousands I had laboured at before. And yet I had been working under men technically reported better scholars than Jowett – Westcott, Vaughan, Conington.

When I began to read for Greats, I took him an essay on some philosophical or historical subject every week. The work for this essay, including a great deal of miscellaneous reading and a sustained effort to write effectively, absorbed the larger portion of my energy. I neglected everything, except my sentiments and fancies, for its production. And, in a certain direction, I grew vigorously under this discipline. I used to wait with intense eagerness, after reading my composition aloud, for Jowett's remarks. They were not lengthy. 'That is very good, Mr Symonds.' 'That is not so good as what you read last week.' 'You want to aim at condensation.' 'There are faults of taste in your use of metaphors and illustrations.' 'You have not taken the point about utilitarianism.' 'That is an admirable statement of Plato's relation to the pre-Socratic philosophers.' 'Very good, very good, indeed.' 'You write too much; you ought to write less and with more care; you can write well, and you have some power of thinking.' I can hear him letting fall these sentences, bent before his fireplace in the tower room of the New Buildings.

One evening Jowett sat staring at the fire, and would not speak, and did not seem to want me to go. At last he said, 'When I say nothing, people fancy I am thinking about something. Generally, I am thinking about nothing. Goodnight.' On another occasion he broke silence with this abrupt remark: 'Mr Swinburne is a very singular young man. He used to bring me long and eloquent essays. He had an illimitable command of language; but it was all language;

I never could perceive that he was following a train of thought.' On a third evening, he stopped me before I sat down to read: 'I cannot listen to your essay tonight. I have just had news that Clough is dead.' This was the first time, I believe, that I had ever heard of Clough. Jowett went on, 'He was the only man of genius – whom one felt to be a man of genius – I have known among the younger men of Balliol.'

Jowett's breakfast parties were even more paralysing than his coaching hours. Nothing is anywhere more depressing than a breakfast at which conversation is expected. In the great tutor's rooms the young men came together, torpid, stiff, shy, awkward. He sat, sipped tea, ate little, stared vacantly. Few spoke. The toast was heard crunching under the desperate jaws of youths exasperated by their helplessness. Nevertheless, it was a great event to go there – although nobody shone, neither host nor guest.

Jowett had the knack of killing the innocent foundlings of his own or his companion's brain by some crushing and yet inconclusive observation. One after another, topics fell stillborn from our lips. The stock story of the undergraduate who, passing the gate of Balliol, remarked, 'A fine day, Mr Jowett,' and getting no answer relapsed into silence during an hour and a half of peripatetic exercise, to be greeted on re-entering the gate with, 'A poor remark, that of yours, Mr Jones' – this story is hardly a caricature of the truth.

In course of time Jowett became a frequent visitor to my father's house at Clifton. There I learned to know him more familiarly, and derived great benefit from his sparse utterances. They were so long waited for and so eagerly welcomed that they made a deep impression. Jowett's mixture of shrewd sense, acute criticism and evasive subtlety of thought (which preferred to compromise conclusions instead of forming them this way or that), determined me against dogmatism – even had I been inclined to dogmatize, which I do not think was the case. Jowett no doubt gave a sceptical and sophistical direction to those of his pupils who accepted his ways of dealing with problems. I used to be reminded of Montaigne's motto when I had done talking to him: '*Ni comme ceci, ni comme cela, ni même autrement.*'

He positively disliked to '*trancher la question*'. He felt that truth, so far as truth can be approximately attained, consisted in a balance of opposites, an adjustment of contradictory points of view, the exact sum and total of which remained nebulous. I do not even now know whether this is not the utmost which can be expected from the human mind, at all events in our present stage of evolution. Metaphysical, moral and religious problems hardly admit of definite solution.

The yearly journeys on the Continent which began in the autumn of 1860 did much to determine my literary bias. Before I left Oxford, I had acquired a superficial knowledge of Belgium, the German cities, a considerable part of Switzerland and Tyrol, Lombardy and Venice, and some portions of France. Travelling with my father, I had been shown everything of historical interest which the towns we visited contained – their architectural monuments, pictures, art galleries, museums of antiquity, and so forth. I kept a minute diary; and the habit of recording aesthetical impressions on the spot greatly helped to form my critical and descriptive style. The training which began among the engravings and portfolios of our Clifton home was now extended and confirmed by these extensive rambles. The love of nature which had grown up in the leafy thickets of Leigh Woods became a passion in the valley of Chamonni, on the Simplon Pass, at Isola Bella, on the lagoons of Venice and the terrace of Novara. My faculty was thus being powerfully, if not systematically, developed for the kind of work to which in afterlife it was devoted. I started, at the close of my academical career, with a really considerable stock of ideas and a large fund of knowledge about the arts of antiquity, the Middle Ages and the Renaissance, as well as a pretty vivid conception of the landscape features of the principal European countries. This miscellaneous culture, it is true, was amateurish. Yet it possessed the quality of catholicity and spontaneity. I learned to appreciate art in a large and liberal spirit, without prejudice, prepossession or dogmatism – and what was better, without looking through the spectacles of any master. Such as it was, my knowledge had been acquired in moments of delightful leisure, on holiday trips or in the comfort of our home. I have never dissociated culture from enjoyment or regarded art as other than a pleasurable adjunct to the serious life of men and nations. Thus it is possible for me now to trace a continuous quality, a specific note, in all that I have thought and felt and uttered about art and nature. This quality, this note, is a certain carelessness about details, a want of thoroughness, combined with a vivid sense of things as they affected me. My literary work has been a prolonged *causerie*, deficient in scientific research but abundant in suggestiveness. I do not think that it smells of the lamp or smacks of the workshop. If temperament and education failed to make me in any strict sense a scholar, they enabled me to become a lover of beauty and an impartial sympathetic student of its manifestations.

In my last year at Oxford an opportunity was afforded me for displaying the first fruits of this culture. The Chancellor's prize for an English essay was given to a composition on 'The Renaissance'. I competed and won the prize. The two streams of my previous mental training converged and blent in this production. I applied the skill I had acquired in handling philosophical and historical themes to the matter of aesthetical evolution. The essay is immature and crude, based to a large extent on superficial and uncritical study of Michelet. Yet it possesses the merit of freshness on the one hand and of width of survey on the other. The touch on works of art and literature is that of one who has enjoyed them and feels at home among them. The subordination of both Renaissance and Reformation to a single intellectual movement of the modern spirit shows a right sense of the problem and a comprehensive view of history. I have thought it worthwhile to dwell upon this performance because it no doubt directed my thoughts to the chapter of European *Cultur-Geschichte* which I afterwards expanded into the seven volumes of *Renaissance in Italy*.

While reading for the final schools I began to study the Elizabethan drama. I needed some distraction and relief after the hard work of the day was over. This I found in poetry. What first attracted me to the minor dramatists I do not remember. I think I had an instinct that my style would gain by drinking at the well of English in its earlier abundance. At any rate I seized on Beaumont and Fletcher, and sucked the sweetness of their romantic dramas with the avidity of a bee rifling the treasuries of honey-laden blossoms. Marlowe and Webster followed. Gradually I collected and perused the whole mass of Shakespeare's predecessors, contemporaries and successors. Reading led, as it has always done in my case, to writing. I planned and executed a literary history of the drama. But when it was finished, in the course of about four years, I threw the whole aside. I judged and judged rightly that my powers were not mature enough, my style not fixed enough, for so ambitious a performance. One volume on *Shakespeare's Predecessors* (which ought to have been followed by two others on his successors and contemporaries, had

228

publishers and public allowed) remains the principal fragment of this original design.

After I became Fellow of Magdalen, the question of a profession had to be seriously entertained. It is singular, I think, that I should not have been aware that my real bent was literary. I felt indeed that literature was my chief pleasure; and I had no confidence in my power to engage in any other work successfully. But my father displayed an intelligible dislike to my engaging in this career where mediocrity is tantamount to failure. – *Mediocribus esse poetis, non di non homines non concessere columnae.* ['Not god, not man, not the bookshops have allowed poets to be mediocre.']⁶ – I was too modest to feel sure of attaining to eminence as a writer; nor did I feel drawn to any definite line in literature. I wavered still between poetry, criticism, journalism, miscellaneous culture. Besides, we both of us knew beforehand that literature, as a profession, is not lucrative; and though I already possessed a competency, I could hardly marry and support a family. A man who sets up at the age of twenty-one to be a man of letters exposes himself to other risks, moreover. He may easily drift into sloth and dilettantism and self-indulgence. Good sense therefore indicated some other form of work. With my usual docility I resigned myself to studying law, though I thoroughly disliked the prospect and felt sure that I should never succeed either as a Chancery or a common-law barrister.

Looking back upon the past, I see now that immediately after my probationary year at Magdalen, I ought to have applied myself to palaeography and learned the modern languages – in Germany, France, Italy. This would have added to my training what it lacked, and the want of which has made itself painfully felt in my published works. But I was incapable of a decisive step. Constitutional indolence and the dislike of doing anything upon a systematic plan would probably have rendered such a process of exact self-education nugatory in my case. I became a student at Lincoln's Inn, ate dinners, and in due course entered a pleader's office. But I only trifled with law. Butterworth, under whom I worked in Paper Buildings, used to tell me that Goldwin Smith had come to read with him – 'and it was like setting a razor to chop wood'. He meant, I think, to hint politely that, though I might not be a razor like Goldwin Smith, I was equally unfit for drawing declarations and drafting pleas.

*   *   *

229

At this critical point all plans and prospects for the future were confused and overclouded by the collapse of my health. It had never been robust. At Harrow and Oxford I was always on the verge of falling into invalidism. Irritable nerves and a morbid condition of the reproductive organs, due to the peculiar erethism of my sexual instincts and the absurd habit of antenuptial continence, rendered me physically a very poor creature. Then I continuously overworked myself – not by steady application to severe studies, but by the strain of emotions combined with my specific tendency to approach knowledge from the aesthetical and literary side. I lived in a perpetual simmer of intellectual and emotional fermentation. The pain and distress of Shorting's attack upon me during my first months at Magdalen broke me down. I received a blow then from which I have never recovered.

In some obscure way my brain became functionally disordered. They called the affection hyperaesthesia, and gave it all kinds of names. My dilettante habits were now no longer a matter of choice but of necessity. I wandered about Switzerland and Italy, coquetted with journalism for a month or two, then married and pretended to read law in the Temple. After my eldest daughter's birth my lungs gave way; and from this time forward their condition determined my movements. We wintered on the Riviera, toured in Switzerland, passed some part of each year at Hastings and Clifton, keeping our London house but never settling down there. At last we gave it up, and bought a house at Clifton, 7 Victoria Square, in which we managed to reside rather more continuously.

The period of six years between November 1862, when my health broke down at Magdalen, and November 1868 when we went to live at Clifton, forms the second main division of my literary life. What I managed to do was done under great difficulties, and in a desultory fragmentary manner. Moving from one place to another, without access to libraries, and always in depressed health, I could not undertake any important work or engage in any regular scheme of study. Intellectually I lived from hand to mouth. The weakness of my eyes rendered systematic reading impossible; and I depended in a great measure upon my wife's unfailing kindness. She read aloud to me for hours together. Curiously enough, the lung troubles which now threatened my very existence seemed to relieve the misery of my brain. Gradually that organ regained tone, although I suffered frequently from attacks which proved that the disorder had not been lived down. Sustained mental labour was out of the question. I worked by fits and snatches.

Not having the strength for what the French call a 'work of long breath', I contented myself with swallow flights. I wrote a great deal for the *Cornhill*, the *Pall Mall Gazette*, the *North British* and the *Westminster*. In this way I composed some of my Italian sketches – 'Orvieto', 'The Cornice', 'Siena and St Catherine', 'Ajaccio', 'Christmas in Rome', 'The Love of the Alps', 'Provençal Towns', 'Ravenna', and others which have been incorporated with the productions of a later period. They were transcribed almost literally from the diaries I left during our winter and spring wanderings. Some of the studies of Greek poets also belong to this time. Among them I may mention 'Aristophanes', 'Empedocles', 'The Idyllists', 'The Gnomic Poets'. I also wrote those essays on the English dramatists of which I have already spoken. My little book on Ben Jonson in the 'English Worthies' series is mainly a *rifacimento* of the elaborate study I then made of him. Much time was wasted upon the translation of Zeller's history of Aristotle and the Aristotelian School.* This I undertook at Jowett's suggestion. Jowett, I may say in passing, has a singular way of setting his friends to do work undoubtedly useful but for which they are not suited. To make me translate Zeller instead of Cellini or Boccaccio, was nothing short of a *gaucherie*.

So far, I have spoken of literary work which was designed for publication. It only represented a portion of my persistent, though hampered, activity. Writing for myself alone, I produced the larger portion of my poetic cycle – on the love of comrades. In another chapter I shall have to relate how and why I came to undertake this ambitious enterprise in verse – an enterprise as unprofitable as it was hopeless. Some of the best pieces in the cycle, 'John Mordan', 'A Cretan Idyll', 'Hesperus and Hymenaeus', 'The Schoolmaster', 'Love and Music', 'Diego', were composed during this period. Others belong to the next phase of my literary life. But I never expected them to see the light of day. Their theme forbade that. And I suppose that my best claims to be called a poet will be consumed in the flames to which they are probably destined. Also I designed and partly executed a history of Greek love. This has been privately

*See page 168. – Editor.

printed; and it is one of the few adequate works of scholarship I can call my own.

The study of Greek literature in sources commonly accessible and in sources more recondite, which was forced upon me by this labour, bore fruit afterwards in my books on the Greek poets. The treatise itself, unexceptionable as I feel it to be in moral tone and literary taste, ought at some time or another to be given to the world. Yet I have not had the courage to do so. While it was passing through the press of Messrs Ballantyne and Hanson – ten copies only being printed for the author's use – a compositor wrote to upbraid me for my iniquity. Such is the state of scientific investigation in our island, while we allow Jowett to translate the *Phaedrus* of Plato and encourage our youth to explore the Greek classics.

This period of six years was in one sense miserably misemployed. I ought properly at that time to have been invigorating my mind by *études fortes*, and laying the foundations for a really *magnum opus*. Bad health and perpetual change of place forced me to fritter my energies away. Yet the peculiar conditions of my life were not without some counterbalancing advantages. I learned in that long tract of weariness and leisure – that λίαν σχολή,[7] as Prometheus called his time on Caucasus – to take a just measure of man's endeavour in the world. Enforced abstinence and baffled ambition implanted in me a wise indifference, a Stoical sense of ἀδιάφορα [indifference].[8]

I said to myself, *entbehren sollst du, sollst entbehren*. ['Thou shalt abstain, renounce, refrain.'] I saw contemporaries pass me in the race of life; and taught myself not to envy this man's strength or that man's skill, the art of Jack, the health of Tom or the prosperity of Harry. In a word, the stern school of adversity delivered me from many pettinesses which beset most men of letters; and in a genial, if somewhat scornful, mood I determined to do what I could, however little and however worthless that might be. I wrote for distraction, for enjoyment, for myself; and did not cumber my soul with what society or critics thought about me. Hampered by so many disabilities, I slowly but surely emancipated my soul from academical and middle-class prejudices. The callings and the works of men appointed to different places in the world assumed proper proportions in my tired and disillusioned eyes. To wear the poet's crown, to win the fame of scholar, seemed to me on a par with driving a straight furrow through the cornland or steering a ship to port through perilous waters under stormy skies. I was disciplined into democracy with all its sympathies and all its hauteur. Moreover, in proportion as I ceased to study systematically, I learned to think and feel originally. In my prostration I grew to be self-confident without losing humility. Daily experience told me what a slight difference there is between a man handicapped as I was and a man as privileged as Southey. I mention Southey because he is the sort of man of letters I might have become if I had not been thwarted by circumstance. On a lower level, it was no small gain to acquire the knack of pursuing my studies, such as they were, in hotels, in railway carriages, on steamboats, in lodging-houses, in lonely Alpine chalets. The life of the spirit, a thin thread, it is true, but tough and elastic, was carried on continuously under conditions which would have appalled an armchair student or the habitué of a public library.

What the Italians call *sprezzatura* sustained me. I adored beauty, I enjoyed mental energy, but I held opinion, as Farinata[9] held hell, *in gran dispitto*. Then there was the close communion with nature in many fascinating and appealing places. This surely was some equivalent for the loss of methodical investigation, of physical vigour, of combative ambition, and of opportunities for strenuous study. Lastly, I ought not to neglect benefit derived by a man of my temperament from the slow dumb imbibition of a few books – Whitman, Theocritus, Shelley, Wordsworth, Milton, Marlowe, Dante, Browne – in hours of inertia face to face with Mediterranean seas or Alpine summits.

The next period may be reckoned from November 1868 till August 1877, at which date I removed to Davos Platz. These nine years were spent at Clifton, first at 7 Victoria Square, and after my father's death in 1871 at Clifton Hill House. It was decisive for my career as a man of letters. At the commencement of this period I continued my previous occupations. That is to say, I wrote a great deal of poetry, continuing and completing the poetic cycle, so far as this was ever finished. Two of the best pieces, 'Eudiades' and 'The Lotos Garland of Antinous', belong to the first year of my residence at Clifton. I also contributed descriptive articles on Italian towns to the *Cornhill*, and occasionally published something in the *Westminster*. Though I still suffered from a chronic weakness of the eyes, I regained to some extent the power of reading, and began dimly to project a history of Italian culture. With this object in view I studied

Sismondi and made analyses of Muratori's *Dissertations*.[10] My thoughts were being gradually drawn to Italy.

The most important event, however, was my acceptance of a lectureship to the sixth form of Clifton College. I chose for my subject Greek literature. This brought me into close relations with the boys. The interest I took in them made me work with energy and enthusiasm. Once more I read through the Greek poets, and wrote copiously, assimilating at the same time the criticisms of Müller, Mure[11] and many scattered essayists. These lectures proved successful; and I was asked to repeat them for classes formed by a society for the higher education of women. I have always thought that the large amount of time and vigour devoted to this work of lecturing prepared me for the definite career of authorship. I became conscious of my own powers and learned the art of rhetoric – the art of putting forth my knowledge impressively, attractively and systematically. Writing connectedly on so vast a theme as Greek poetry, always with the view of exposition, trained me to attempt a work of long breath and ripened my faculty of *vulgarisateur*.

In 1870 I agreed to lecture to women on Dante. This involved a study of the *Divine Comedy*, *Vita Nuova*, and *Canzoniere*. I wrote the bulk of these lectures in a little tavern at Heiligenblut during the month of June, and remodelled them at Clifton while Europe was ringing with the fall of the French Empire at Sedan.

In February 1871 my father died. As yet I had published nothing with my name attached to it – except the Newdigate prize poem on the Escorial and the Chancellor's prize essay on the Renaissance. It has always touched me with a thrill of pathos to think that my good kind father died before I came before the world as an avowed author. His ambition for his only son had been checked and thwarted. He had suffered deeply by my failure in health at the close of a brilliant academical career. Yet he never uttered one peevish word to make me feel his disappointment. Shortly before his death he expressed to me his conviction that I should never acquire the physical force to do anything like solid work. 'You have one of those constitutions,' he said, 'with just enough nervous strength for the common require-ments of life. You cannot draw upon the fund of energy without imperilling your health.' In fact he had resigned all expectation of my making a mark in the world – and herein he was amply justified, for I had now reached my thirty-first year, with nothing to show but a somewhat misty reputation as a writer of articles. Yet what I still contained of slumbering force was now on the point of bursting out into sudden activity. And nobody would have watched the efforts of the next eighteen years with more sympathy and satisfaction than he would have done. Modest as my achievement may have been, I am sure it would have gratified his fatherly pride and have compensated in his old age for the disappointment of the past. *Dis aliter visum est.* ('The gods thought otherwise.']12 And so strangely are we mortals made that God forgive me if I do not believe my father's watchful supervision would have hampered my energy. He exerted an extraordinary influence over those who came within his sphere. Always benevolently exercised, this was none the less despotic. I doubt whether I could have written as freely and published as spontaneously as I have done, had I been conscious of his criticism.

Anyhow, the year of his death coincided with a new and far more energetic phase of my literary life. For the rest of that year things went forward much as usual. In the spring of 1872, however, I made arrangements for publishing my lectures on Dante under the title of *An Introduction to the Study of Dante.* The book was favourably received upon the whole, and added to my reputation. (It has since been translated into French, *Dante, son Temps, son Oeuvre, son Genie,* Paris, 1891.) At the same time I collected and published a volume of my father's miscellanies (Arrowsmith, Bristol, and Macmillan), and prepared Conington's remains in two volumes for the press (Longmans). Both of these latter works I scamped – not wilfully or culpably, but because I was still indifferent to the technique of literature. I allowed my own articles to scramble into print as they could, neglecting proofs and not resenting misprints which would now make my blood boil and the hair bristle on my head.

In 1873 I published the first series of my *Studies of Greek Poets* (Smith and Elder). It consisted of essays reprinted from the *North British* and *Westminster Reviews,* together with an equal number based upon my Clifton lectures. The success of this book was marked. In London I found that everybody I cared for had been reading it. Miss Thackeray said to me at a dinner party, 'We have all been thrilling over your *Greek Poets.*' Swinburne wrote to congratulate me on 'this delightful book – in the true sense of the word delightful'. But the main event of the year was the composition of a long series of lectures on 'The Renaissance in Italy'. Since this formed the kernel of my future labours, the fact deserves mention.

I worked very hard in my study at Clifton Hill House, and filled four or five thick books of manuscript with fervid declamation.

In 1875 I published the first volume of *Renaissance in Italy*. It was entirely rewritten from lectures; and the defect of the method is clearly observable in its structure. I believe that I should not have obtained the initiative for a ponderous work unless I had begun by lecturing. The irritability of my brain rendered me peculiarly intolerant of sustained labour. But a rhetorical tone survived my best attempts to rehandle the material which had been designed for declamation. Changes of style and purple patches deformed the unity and gravity of a serious historical work. Private sorrows and disappointments, which I shall elsewhere explain, induced me to undertake the heavy task of *The Renaissance*. Relief from thoughts which had become intolerable, and longings recognized as unassuageable, had to be sought in brain labour. That being so, I did not sufficiently count the cost or approach my theme in a calm artistic spirit.

I worked furiously, recklessly, at this period, devouring books upon Italian history, art, scholarship and literature, writing continually, and pushing one volume forward while another was going through the press. The same year 1875 sent out the second volume of *Studies of Greek Poets*, a large number of which were prepared from lectures or written expressly to fill up gaps in the series. The last essay in this volume, on the Greek spirit, was a first attempt to deal philosophically with moral and religious problems. It adumbrated a confession of faith, and stood in my way when I foolishly came forward as candidate for the Oxford Professorship of Poetry in the summer of 1876.[13]

This year, 1876, was wholly occupied with the composition of the second and third volumes of *The Renaissance*. That on the 'Revival of Learning' displayed a far superior command of literary method than anything which I had yet attempted. Both volumes were printed in the following winter. But meanwhile my father's dying prediction had been fulfilled. The tax upon my nervous strength during four years of intense and feverish industry exhausted my constitution; and the old pulmonary disease assumed a serious and threatening aspect. In February 1877 I was prostrated with a severe attack of acute bronchitis; and my physician Dr Beddoe (to whom I dedicated *The Renaissance*) informed me gravely that extensive mischief had been going on for some time in the left lung.

... I spent the month of May in unprofitable wanderings about Lombardy and Venice. Chronic fever was upon me; and I had the recklessness of disease – the curious fretful energy of someone tormented by a persistent yet unlocalized drain upon his vitality. On this tour I discovered Campanella's sonnets and began to translate them in railway carriages, determining to turn them together with Michael Angelo's into English. Terribly ill at last, I managed to reach Clifton early in June without a collapse. During a night spent in great misery at Turin I was probably on the verge of calamity. Fortunately I reached home; and the next day, while riding on the Downs, I was surprised by a sudden and violent haemorrhage from the lungs.

This accident abruptly put an end to the period of my literary activity at Clifton, and led to a change of life. As soon as I could move, we left home for Davos Platz, intending to winter on the Nile. I derived so much benefit from the Alpine climate during the months of August and September that I determined to stay there for at least a year. In course of time I discovered that there was little hope of my regaining strength enough to bear a return to old ways of life in England. We resigned ourselves to Davos, where we have now spent nearly eleven years.*

A new period of mental work under very peculiar conditions now began. My intellectual energy was rather increased than diminished by the change. But I had to subsist upon such books as I could collect for myself. To carry on *The Renaissance in Italy* seemed at first impossible. I felt that residence at Davos Platz put an end to any hopes of my becoming a scholar in the exact sense. I could no longer look forward to utilizing public libraries, to examining original documents and to working up a subject with the fullness demanded by scientific criticism in our day. The forces which since my boyhood had been directly and indirectly moulding me for a particular kind of writing were once more operative. I had to remain a man of letters in the looser sense of that term, choosing such useful or enjoyable occupation as could be carried on without a large stock of books. Literature more than ever came to be regarded by me as a διαγωγή [pastime, avocation]. On the other hand the bracing climate and the solitude of the mountains helped me to acquire a

*Written in 1889. – Editor.

more forcible style, enabled me to be as active as I liked without damage to my health, and added to the vigour of my brain. Accustomed as I was to compromise by the whole previous tenour of my life, I cheerfully accepted the situation, and fixed my thoughts upon compensating advantages instead of chewing the cud of mortification. What I felt most was the separation from friends of like interests and pursuits. I had to do without the stimulus which comes from conversation. Whatever work I did must be accomplished in solitude, without sympathy. As it turned out, the continual production of books in that stern Alpine region – the contrast between my life there among peasants and invalids with my growing reputation as a man of letters – acted somewhat unwholesomely upon my moral temperament. This topic will be dealt with in another chapter.

During the last quarter of a century I have never ceased from scribbling and have produced, as I have shown, a large quantity of various work. Yet on striking an average of my yearly receipts, I find that I have earned only about £250 per annum. I could not put my gains at this figure, were it not for pay derived from lectures, magazines, newspapers, and the *Encyclopaedia*. At least two-thirds of this income has been spent on books and journeys necessary for my undertakings. This shows sufficiently how poor a trade is literature. Equal abilities and equal industry devoted to law, medicine or the art of painting might have secured me an income where tens would have been replaced by hundreds. But I could not do otherwise than I did. I had to follow the bent of my talent, and that directed me into unpopular channels of literature. Had I possessed a faculty for novel-writing, the case would have been different. Had I been gifted with conspicuous genius, I should no doubt have been adequately remunerated. I am content, however, with things as they are. The pleasure and the solace I have derived from letters during a life which without them would have been cramped and crippled and condemned to stagnant sloth, are sufficient rewards. Moderately supplied with the goods of this world, I have never felt the pinch of want, and I do not envy more fortunate contemporaries.

I have often endeavoured to formulate my conception of the influence, physical and moral, which this literary work prolonged for a quarter of a century exerted over me. In the first place it greatly contributed to my enjoyment, since it gave me that pleasure and exhilaration which is the concomitant of any energy unimpeded in its exercise. I always liked writing, and never disliked reading. In the second place it afforded me an occupation which could be carried on with more or less convenience under the peculiar conditions of my unsettled life. Had I not already formed myself for literature when I was compelled to settle at Davos Platz in 1877, I doubt whether I should have even partially recovered health. The habit of writing rendered me independent, and sustained my spirits under circumstances which would have been unutterably depressing to a barrister or merchant checked in his career. In the third place it brought me a fair amount of distinction and a certain kind of consideration.Without being ambitious or overvaluing the sort of reputation I have gained, I am not insensible to this advantage. I feel with satisfaction that a large number of people both in England and America are favourably predisposed towards me. My natural shyness – a shyness in which there is quite as much pride as of awkwardness and conscious inability to shine – has been diminished by knowing that I have made my mark and won a name. When the committee of the Athenaeum elected me to that club in 1882, I became aware that I had the right to consider myself one of the men of our time.

On the other hand I cannot pretend to think that literature, in the way I have pursued it, is exactly wholesome for a man of my peculiar temperament. '*Travailler pour la gloire,*' says George Sand, '*est un rôle d'empereur ou le métier d'un forçat.*' I have never indeed laboured for glory, because I have always thought less of results than of pleasurable exercise and innocent pastime. Yet study and composition are none the less exhausting to the nerves, when taken from this point of view, than when a man is consciously ambitious. Often I have felt myself as tired and worn with writing 'as the tanned galley-slave is with his oar'. Reaction follows; and the fatigue of labour craves the distraction of amusement. Trying to evade the congenital disease of my moral nature in work, work has drained my nerves and driven me to find relief in passion. The subjects with which I have been occupied – Greek poetry, Italian culture in one of the most lawless periods of modern history, beauty in nature and the body of man – stimulate and irritate the imagination. They excite cravings which cannot be satisfied by simple pleasures. Long after work is over, the erethism of the brain continues. The little ocean of the soul is agitated by a groundswell. The pulses beat, the nerves thrill and tingle. To escape the tyranny of the impossible vision which keeps the mind upon a rack, 'libidinous joys' present themselves under seductive colours, and the would-be hierophant of artistic beauty is hurried away upon the wings of an obscene Chimaera. For anyone who may have read my sonnets in *Animi Figura* and *Vagabunduli Libellus* this state of emotions needs no further exposition. They are to a great extent autobiographical. The sonnets entitled 'L'Amour de l'Impossible', 'Intellectual Isolation', 'Stella Maris', and 'Self-Condemnation' were penned under the stress of poignant and present suffering. One of my most penetrative and sympathetic critics, Mr Hall Caine,[14] writing in the *Academy*, pronounced his opinion that there was no exit for the hero of 'Stella Maris' but in madness. Alas! he did not know perhaps that he had given voice to my soul's darkest apprehensions.

It may be questioned whether the pursuit of literature as διαγωγή – as that mode of life which secures its end by employing energy and occupying leisure agreeably to the individual – renders a man really happy. The underlying preoccupation of my life has been a tyrannous emotion, curbed and suppressed for the most part, but occasionally indulged with spasmodic violence. Literature takes the second place; and for this reason, although I have persevered in it for solace and escape from fretting care, I have never been able to regard it very seriously. In a certain sense I do not condemn this habit of mind. It enables a man to keep in view the truth that literature exists for life, not life for literature – a truth which less half-hearted men of letters do not sufficiently recognize. It delivers him from the conceit of authorship by constantly reminding him how trivial any literary successes and achievements are in comparison with the solid good things of a comely and contented existence; how little talent or even genius weighs in the scale against character, strength of will, goodness and tranquillity of mind; how men ought really to be reckoned not by what they think or write or create in art, but by what they are and what they have enjoyed. This attitude, however, is not without counterbalancing disadvantages. It precludes that centralizing force of enthusiasm which springs from self-dedication to a single great conception. The literary *viveur* cannot hope to become a scholar or to produce a monumental work. In so far as he shares the scientific spirit of our age – in so far as he is sensible of possessing faculties above the average and is open to the animating ideas of the modern world – he will have to endure a lifelong recurrent regret for sterner paths abandoned and for nobler triumphs of the spirit carelessly forgone. His activity is necessarily divided, and his vigour attenuated by distribution.

Who shall be contented with his life when he looks back upon it? Contentment is not the appanage of high-born natures. They must be like Marlowe's heroes:

> Still climbing after knowledge infinite,
> And always moving as the restless spheres.

It is not possible upon this path or that to satisfy the insatiable within the mind. That is the frank pledge of the soul's infinity — if not of personal immortality. It were as easy to drink the ocean up as to exhaust man's capacity for curiosity and desire for enjoyment. Therefore the only contentment we dare hope for here is that which comes from being satisfied with limitation and inured to imperfection. From this point of view it signifies extremely little at our life's end whether we have been a Virgil, a Titian, a Gibbon or a literary *viveur*. In the scheme of the universe all sorts and conditions of men have their inevitable place and their irrefragable right to exist. Nothing is known to us about their relative importance or the issues of their several activities.

Chapter Fifteen

Religious development

Religion is so important a factor in man's intellectual life, and has so direct a bearing upon the growth of the emotions, that I ought not to omit some account of my development upon this side.

I have already observed that I was not gifted by nature with any strong sense of God as a person near to me; nor was I naturally of a pious disposition; nor yet again endowed with that theological bias which qualifies the metaphysical thought of philosophers like my late brother-in-law, Professor T. H. Green.

The groundwork of my mental temperament might rather be described as literary, aesthetical, with a certain bias to scholarship and curiosity.

In boyhood I received the usual kind of training in religious matters at home. I learned the Catechism, the collects of the prayer-book, and considerable portions of the Psalms and Gospels. My aunt, Miss Sykes, used to read the Bible with us every morning; and on Sundays we always went twice to church. In a previous section of this book I described the dreary impressions made upon me by the place of worship we frequented, and the dislike I felt for the dry uninteresting evangelicalism of the Knight family. There was nothing in my early surroundings to evoke the religious sentiment by any appeal to my peculiar nature. And yet I believe that I went to Harrow with as strong a sense of moral allegiance to the deity, as God-fearing and as willing to receive religious influences, as most boys of my age.

Just at the time of my confirmation, a period when young people of thoughtful disposition are compelled to take stock of their religious feelings, I made that discovery about Dr Vaughan's relations

242

with Alfred Pretor which so strongly influenced my character. It was impossible but that a boy *in statu pupillari* should greatly exaggerate the importance of this matter. I could not be expected to regard the failings of our headmaster with comprehensive justice. The shock of the discovery, and the casuistical reflections it engendered, had the immediate effect of dissociating piety from morality in my view of the religious life. There existed no doubt that Dr Vaughan passed for an eminently pious man; and it was equally clear that he indulged habits in secret which he denounced as sins from the pulpit. Brooding upon this discord in his character, I began to suspect human nature at large of hypocrisy and inconsistency. A scepticism, cynical and jaded rather than logical or aggressive, checked the further growth of faith; just as a frost may throw back budding vegetation. I broke into dangerous paths of speculation, and questioned the ground principles of social ethics. Intellectually, I was too languid to become rebellious. But I went on unhealthily musing, poring over my difficulties, consulting no one, and allowing them slowly to sap and soak into my spiritual tissue.

This state might be compared to the gradual infiltration of disease through previously normal lungs in the first stages of consumption. About the same time my aesthetic sensibilities awoke to one side of ritualism. I delighted in church music, church architecture, church millinery. What this eventually led to was a passionate attachment to a chorister. I did not acquire any kind of reliance on the Anglican creed, the loss of which could cause acute pain. What I took for a religious movement in my heart, I soon discovered to be a form of sentimentalism.

My father's mental and moral influence began to make itself powerfully felt during my Oxford life. We were drawn together by the painful catastrophe to which I have alluded, and exchanged thoughts upon the deepest problems, with a freedom unusual perhaps in the intercourse of father and son. Some of his most intimate friends had been, and others still were, thinkers of the Broad Church School – John Sterling, the Rev. Frederic Myers of Keswick, F. D. Maurice, Francis Newman and Professor Jowett. Their ideas filtered through my father's conversation into my head, together with the criticism of his own clear logic. The conversation of the three last whom I have mentioned, and also of that subtle thinker, Sydney Dobell, familiarized me with lines of speculation antagonistic to any narrow interpretations of Christian dogma. The

243

creeds which cling so firmly to many minds hung loose on me. As they dropped off and melted away, they did so without appreciable suffering or keen regret. I felt, indeed, the difficulty and the danger of living in the world without a fixed belief in God, Christ, the scheme of redemption, the immortality of souls assigned to reward or punishment. I sympathized much with Arthur Clough. But I soon perceived that it would be impossible for me to rest in that halting place which men like my father, Maurice, Jowett, Stanley, had constructed for themselves and fitted up according to the particular tone and bias of their several dispositions. I understood and respected their position, especially my father's. Still I felt that their qualified adherence to Christianity and the Scriptures had something illogical in it, which might be explained and excused by the circumstances of their emergence out of rigid orthodoxy into liberalism. I was starting from the point which they had reached; and I should be compelled to go further.

This does not mean that I became irreligious. On the contrary, I now for the first time began to comprehend what religion is, and to feel about for some faith whereby my own soul might be supported. I took to examining my thoughts and wishes with regard to the mysteries of the universe, God, nature, man. This I did seriously, almost systematically, during more than two years of reading for the Final Schools at Oxford. The studies on which I was engaged, Plato, Aristotle, the history of ancient and modern philosophy, logic, supplied me with continual food for meditation; and in the course of long walks or midnight colloquies, I compared my own eager questionings with those of many sorts of men: Conington, who professed himself a submissive Christian through terror; Hugh Pearson, one of the mellowest of the orthodox Broad Churchmen; T. H. Green, the sturdy and yet imaginative philosopher; C. C. Puller, already fascinated by the gospel of Auguste Comte; W. R. W. Stephens, a man of simple faith; A. O. Rutson, George Bright, J. S. Philpotts, Albert Dicey, Charles Parker, James Bryce, Edwin Palmer.[1] A book called *Essays and Reviews* attracted extraordinary attention at that time; and a vehement contest about the endowment of Prof. Jowett's chair was raging between the liberals and conservatives of the university. Theology penetrated our intellectual and social atmosphere. We talked theology at breakfast parties and at wine parties, out riding and walking, in college gardens, on the river, wherever young men and their elders met together.

The lines of speculation which I followed led me to believe that some radical change in the current conceptions of the Divine Being was necessitated by the changes taking place in modern thought; and that this would eventually substitute the ideal of a god immanent in the universe for the ideal of a god external to it, creative of the world machinery and providentially controlling it. Goethe's 'Proemium' to the poems called 'Gott und Welt' supplied me with a formula adapted to my own emotional and rational forecast of this new phase, on which I thought theology must enter. Just after leaving Oxford, I wrote a commentary on those stanzas (privately printed in my *Miscellanies* pages 1–36), which expresses the point of view I had then attained by the process I have been describing.

During my readings in the Greek philosophers, I came upon the Hymn of Cleanthes: 'ἄγου δέ μ᾽, ὦ Ζεῦ, καὶ σύ γ᾽ ἡ πεπρωμένη.' ['Be my guide, O Zeus, and you, O Destiny.']² This suggested the moral attitude of willing submission to universal law, which will have to supply a groundwork for the conduct of the individual under the conditions of the new faith I had conceived. The study of Marcus Aurelius now absorbed me. Eagerly and spontaneously, I grew to be penetrated with what has since been called 'the Cosmic Enthusiasm'.

While this religion, composed of scientific pantheism and of Stoical morality, was forming in my mind, I read Seeley's 'Ecce Homo'. The enthusiasm of humanity expressed in that essay took no hold upon me; just as Comte's worship of the *Être Suprème* (so eloquently advocated by Richard Congreve in my frequent walks with him about the Roman hills) had been rejected, and as Renan's seductive portrait of '*le doux Galiléen*' was somewhat contemptuously laid aside. They struck me as ineffective attempts, each in its own way and on its own line, to save something valuable from the mass which had to be rejected. The first was a survival of evangelical piety transmuted into philanthropy; the second a survival of Catholicism, in curious conjunction with scientific agnosticism; the third a survival of the old religious sentiment, denuded of dogma, replaced by means of scholarship and romantic emotion upon a treacherous ground of poetical sympathy. The respectability of such efforts to modulate from the old to the new, and of many other efforts made by many eminent persons, I could not and did not wish to deny. But I felt that I should not be saved by any of these palliatives. My soul needed something more sincere than the first and third of those I have named, something less pretentious and grotesque than the second. It was surely better to abide upon the rock of expectation I had found for myself; however stern, arid, unhomely, the landscape might appear; however dolefully the waves and winds of the eternal storm raged round it. I therefore stuck to the determination of singing my hymn of praise in Goethe's 'Proemium', of breathing out my prayers at night in the verses of Cleanthes. The religion of the Cosmic Enthusiasm appeared to me the only creed compatible with agnosticism forced upon a candid mind.

Nothing but the bare thought of a God-penetrated universe, and of myself as an essential part of it, together with all things that appear in their succession – ether and inorganic matter passing into plants and creatures of the sea and beasts, rising to men and women like myself, and onward from us progressing to the stages of lives unrealized by human reason – nothing but the naked, yet inebriating, vision of such a cosmos satisfied me as a possible object of worship. When this thought flooded me, and filled the inmost fibres of my sentient being, I discovered that I was almost at rest about birth and death and moral duties and the problem of immortality. These were the world's affairs, not mine. Having lost the consolations of faith in redemption through Christ, and all that pertains thereto, I had gained in exchange this, that I could

> lay myself upon the knees
> of Doom, and take mine everlasting ease.[3]

So far I had travelled on the path of self-construction, when I came across the writings of Walt Whitman. I find it difficult to speak about *Leaves of Grass* without exaggeration. Whitman's intense emotional feeling for the universe, his acute sense of the goodliness of life in all its aspects, the audacity of his mood – as of one eager to cast himself upon illimitable billows, assured that whether he sank there or swam it would be well with him, confident the while that sink he could not, that nothing can eventually come to naught: this concrete passionate faith in the world, combined with the man's multiform experience, his human sympathy, his thrill of love and comradeship, sent a current of vitalizing magnetism through my speculations. The formulas of Goethe and Cleanthes fell into their proper place. The Stoical philosophy, like Aaron's dry rod, put forth blossoms. The rock of expectation I had found, and where I meant to stay, began to sprout with herbage, rustle with forests, echo to the notes of singing-birds, and gush with living fountains. The waves and winds of the eternal storm around it changed their message. If they spoke not to my soul of peace, they roused me to the sense of 'liberty, immensity, action'. In short, Whitman added conviction, courage, self-reliance, to my sense of the Cosmic Enthusiasm. What is more, he taught me, as no enthusiasm of humanity could do, the value of fraternizing with my fellows – for their own sakes, to love them, to learn from them, to teach them, to help and to be helped by them – not for any ulterior object upon either side. I felt, through him, what it really is to be a member of the universe I sought to worship.

About this time I began to study Darwin's theory of zoological development, and absorbed, so far as suited me, from him and Herbert Spencer the philosophy of evolution. With the metaphysical idea of that philosophy I was sufficiently acquainted through my readings in the works of the Greek sages, Bruno, Spinoza, Goethe, lastly Hegel. But I perceived at once how the latest aspect of the theory and the partial proof of it squared with my religion and gave it substance. I derived, as I suppose all men must do, only so much from these teachers as might feed a self-forged faith.

So then, having rejected dogmatic Christianity in all its forms, Broad Church Anglicanism, the gospel of Comte, Hegel's superb identification of human thought with essential Being, and many minor nostrums offered in our time to sickening faith – because none of these forsooth were adapted to my nature – I came to fraternize with Goethe, Cleanthes, Whitman, Bruno, Darwin, finding that in their society I could spin my own cocoon with more of congruence to my particular temperament than I discerned in other believers, misbelievers, non-believers, passionate believers, of the ancient and the modern schools. This is the way with all of us who, like the caddis worm, build houses around them. Men of a different stamp follow the ways of the hermit crab, and creep into solid shells which shelter them against the sea and assaults of neighbours. It comes to the same thing in the end; only the caddis worm is the pupa of that winged ephemeron the Mayfly, born to be eaten up by trout; while the shell into which the hermit crab has crept may last long after its tenant's lonely death, until at last it perishes beneath the stress of elemental forces, pounding waves and churning sands.

But these things are metaphors; and there is a want of taste and sense in straining metaphors too far. Speaking simply I chose for my motto 'to live resolvedly in the Whole, the Good, the Beautiful'.

247

I sought out friends from divers centuries – Marcus Aurelius, Cleanthes, Bruno, Goethe, Whitman, Darwin – who seemed to have
arrived, through their life throes and ardent speculations, at something like the same intuition into the sempiternally inscrutable as I
had. They helped me by their richer or riper experience, by flights
beyond my reach, by knowledge denied to my poor studies, by
audacities which thrilled the man in me. I addicted myself to their
society because they accepted the Whole, and were not trafficking
or pettifogging about a portion. They threw themselves upon the
world and God with simple self-devotion, seeking nothing extraordinary in this life or the next, accepting things as they beheld them,
attempting to mould no institutions, leaving the truths they had
discovered to work like leaven, aiming at justice and a perfect clarity
of vision, discarding economies and accommodations of all kinds,
casting the burden of results upon *that* or *him* who called them into
being, standing unterrified, at ease, before time, space, circumstance,
and any number of sidereal systems.

Because these men were so, I elected them as the friends with
whom my spirit chose to fraternize. From being in their company I
derived solace, and their wisdom, like in kind, was larger than my
own. It is good for the soul to dwell with such superiors; just as it
is also good, in daily life, to live with so-called inferiors, to learn
from them and love them.

I do not seek to preach this faith which animates me. As a necessary part of my autobiography, I have described how I came to form
a certain religious creed. No one more than myself is capable of
criticizing its inadequacy to satisfy other minds. Certainly no one
but myself knows how tentative and far from stable it is, how like
a gaseous fluid, in the mind of him who lives by it. After admitting
so much, I may anticipate ridicule by comparing my faith to something which lifts a balloon in air, to the fermentation of a fungus,
to the sulphuretted hydrogen in a rotten egg. Still, being what it is,
this faith has enabled me to do my duty in so far as I have done it
by my family and friends; it has brought forth my literary work,
and has sustained me active under the pressure of many grievous
and depressing maladies. Through it, I think, with God's blessing, I
have been enabled to pull through consumption preying on my vitals
during the last quarter of a century. It penetrates almost everything
I have sent to press under my own name. It will be found notably
in the last essays of my *Renaissance in Italy*, in the epilogue to

Palumba, in the last sections of *Animi Figura*, in the whole of my latest work, *Essays Speculative and Suggestive*. The perorations of all that I have written are inspired by this faith, as the substance of all my labour was for me made vital by it.

How frail and insecure is any faith! I might adapt a memorable sentence of Walt Whitman's and exclaim, 'Belief is to the believer, and comes back most to him.' We know that the solidest stronghold of faith, dogmatically built up, mortised on granite, mortared into battlements, garrisoned by multitudes of men militant, will crumble with the lapse of ages. The form passes away; and only the enduring relations which it represented, partial adequacies to the wants and truths of human nature, remain. These survive, accumulate and are continually being worked into the form and substance of new creeds. The question for a man who has dared to innovate in any age is whether his religious instincts are at all concordant with the coming belief. If they should be, he may reckon among pioneers. If they are not, it will not signify for him so long as he has lived by them. God is the only judge; and God 'reveals Himself in many ways'; God is known to us as everlasting variation, albeit 'God is the same and his years do not change.'

Let then the one man who has found his faith speak to the rest of human kind, as a linnet sings to linnets.

The ever-during idea, independent of dogmas, of creeds, of cocoons spun by the individual in order to protect his germ of spiritual life against the cold – that idea, out of which religions spring, is the same now as when Kant expressed it in his pregnant imaginative phrase: nothing stirs the sense of awe in me except the stars at night and the soul of man. The soul and the universe, their apparent contradiction and their ultimate solidarity; that is the ideal substance out of which all creeds are carved. In both and each of the factors, as these present themselves in apparent duality to us, God remains the only reality, the unifying constituting life. To transcend, to circumvent, to transact with the law of the world, is impossible. To learn anything final about it is probably denied the human intellect. Yet the very consciousness of these limitations and disabilities forces the soul back upon religion. It does not so much matter which faith a man adopts or what he fashions for himself. Yet hardly can he live to any purpose without faith.

In conclusion, as regards myself, I am compelled by the spirit of veracity which dictates every paragraph of these memoirs, to put on record that the religious emotion I have described has not made me submissive to the human laws of conduct condensed in any code at present known to me. I have allowed myself to be an innovator, taking the principles of human sympathy and self-respect as my guides. At only one point have I come into collision with conventional morality; and on this point I have felt it to be both my right and duty to act as I thought best.

In practical rules of conduct this ethical attitude resulted in the following formula.

The indulgence of any natural craving so as to injure the whole organism of the man, is sin.

The young man who has used his stomach and the apparatus of taste connected with it for more than the purposes of healthy nutrition, is on the wrong road.

The young man who has used his heart and lungs and all the sensations of vigorous virility that flow from their exercise for more than the proper strengthening and evolution of his physical force, is on the wrong road.

The young man who has used his sexual organs and all the exalted passions implicit in them for more than sober steady satisfaction of imperious desire, or for more than the consolidation of a durable love, is on the wrong road.

In each of these cases he runs the risk of disturbing that equilibrium of the man which is virtue and health, the violation of which is vice and disease.

The violated organ, whether stomach, brain, heart, lungs, or reproductive apparatus, is equally a deity offended by the youthful sinner.

Fortunately for the human race, each of these organs is capable of very considerable wear and tear; so that we may sin with regard to each of them until seventy times seven, in calm expectation of the mercy of offended deity.

But each has a point of strain which cannot be overpassed. And some of them, notably the alimentary and the reproductive apparatus, have dangers from deterioration through infection which constitute a secondary point of weakness.

The Greek virtue of temperance, σωφροσύνη, was a recognition of the equilibrium which man should aim at in the maintenance of his chief glands through sober use of them.

In a large measure it was a virtue based on physical foundations.

But it implied a delicate consciousness possessed by man of his essential functions, of the necessity under which he lies of correlating and harmonizing the exercise of each for the service of the whole, and the subordination of all bodily organs to the one purpose of a sustained life in health.

Christian theology has to some extent confused this simple and clear intuition. It has encouraged us to condone injuries done to the brain, while it has weighed fantastically on the least indulgence of the sexual apparatus. The vices of the stomach pass for venial; while the ruin of the human being through activity of the heart and lung is hardly considered.

Why this should be is clear enough. Historical Christianity, framing itself as a practical discipline for semi-barbarous masses of the Occidental nations, regarded the chief perils of the average man. That average man is not inclined to superfluous cerebral energy, or to more muscular exercise than is good for him. He is very much prone to indulge his sexual appetites, because the sexual organs are the centre and main point of his structure; and these he indulges to his own injury and to the subversion of social order. This main instinct must therefore be kept under control. His stomach also has a large demand to make upon him. But gluttony is not obviously injurious to the individual, since the stomach is a capacious vessel and tolerant of much misuse; nor is gluttony, except as indirectly, pernicious to the social organism.

On the score of σωφροσύνη then, Christianity sought to protect and govern the sexual organs in the first place, for the welfare of the individual and the benefit of the race. In the second place it took the stomach under its discipline. Brain, heart and lungs were left to shift for themselves.

And in the established moral order there was good reason for this. Physical exercises, carried even to the point of sinning, imply ethical qualities of great value and virtue both for the individual and for society. The same may be said about cerebral exercises in even a higher degree, for these are rarer and imply a more distinguished quality of nature. Both together elicit brave fruits from humanity, and serve the end we seek. The maximum of good result is to be expected from them. The minimum of bad may be anticipated – since the vicious indulgence in either strenuous physical exercise or in severe mental labour is exceptionally rare, while such indulgence

251

in both may elicit something beneficial to society by the sacrifice of the sinners.

Having made these allowances, the supreme justice which nature teaches, and which is summed up in the words 'Live only in the whole,' compels us to revert to that old Hellenic standard of σωφροσύνη. He who overworks any organ, whether brain, heart, lung, stomach or sexual apparatus, sins. The indulgence in excessive brain exercise, in excessive muscular exercise, in excessive or innutritious feeding, in excessive or libertine sexual pleasure, is wrong. The hierarchy of functions which compose us and on which society depends, forces man to regard one indulgence as more pardonable than another. Thus the indulgence in sex is so bound up with the first object of our physical being, propagation, that it cannot be viewed as more than venial. The indulgence in muscular activity is so serviceable as an example to the race at large that it appears almost to rank with virtues. The indulgence in cerebral tension is so rare and aims at such high objects that even when it maims or kills, it passes for 'the last infirmity of noble minds'. The indulgence in food is either so harmless or so ignobly detrimental to the individual alone, that it is almost overlooked.

Yet all excessive indulgences in all of these regions are sins against the nature of man considered as a whole, and playing his part in a larger whole.

Rightly understood, properly expounded, the doctrine of the equality of all these sins in the sight of an inexorable God of natural law would go far to restore mankind to the pristine ideal of human excellence imagined by the Greeks.

Am Hof
14 April 1885

Chapter Sixteen

The transition to Davos Platz, and life there

In the winter of 1875–6 my health, as usual, began to fail. Dr Beddoe recommended me to go to the Riviera. My wife and I accordingly settled at S. Remo in February. There I wrote a large part of the second volume of my *Renaissance in Italy*. It has also to be mentioned that I took a fancy there for a curly-headed quarryman from the hills beyond Savona. This *amour* did not advance far beyond Platonic relations. The summer was spent in hard work upon the third volume of the *Renaissance*; and at the end of it I went with H. F. Brown and James Pearson to the Valais. Here I found that my physical vigour was considerably abated. I took severe colds which left me exhausted; and I remember suffering considerable fatigue after a walk with Brown from Saas over the flanks of the Fletsch horn to the Simplon Hospice. Work meanwhile advanced with a regularity and rapidity which told of feverish and diminishing nervous energy.

In February 1877, I think, I gave three lectures on 'Florence and the Medici' at the Royal Institution. This took me of course to London; and, as it happened, an acquaintance of old standing asked me one day to go with him to a male brothel near the Regent's Park Barracks. I consented out of curiosity. Moved by something stronger than curiosity, I made an assignation with a brawny young soldier for an afternoon to be passed in a private room at the same house. Naturally, I chose a day on which I was not wanted at the Royal Institution. We came together at the time appointed; the strapping young soldier with his frank eyes and pleasant smile, and I, the victim of sophisticated passions. For the first time in my experience I shared a bed with one so different from myself, so ardently desired by me, so supremely beautiful in my eyes, so attractive to my senses. He was a very nice fellow, as it turned out: comradely and natural, regarding the affair which had brought us together in that place from a business-like and reasonable point of view. For him at all events it involved nothing unusual, nothing shameful; and his simple attitude, the not displeasing vanity with which he viewed his own physical attractions, and the genial sympathy with which he met the passion they aroused, taught me something I had never before conceived about illicit sexual relations. Instead of yielding to any brutal impulse, I thoroughly enjoyed the close vicinity of that splendid naked piece of manhood; then I made him clothe himself, sat and smoked and talked with him, and felt, at the end of the whole transaction, that some at least of the deepest moral problems might be solved by fraternity. He made no exorbitant demands upon my purse, and seemed to appreciate the way in which I had accepted him – adding an agreeable intimation of his own satisfaction at the delight I took in his delightfulness, and all this was expressed by him in a wholly manly way, although I could not help imagining what he might have undergone on previous occasions within the walls of that chamber, and thinking how mean and base any comradeship must be, built upon such foundations. We parted the best of friends, exchanging addresses; and while I was in London, I met him several times again, in public places, without a thought of vice.

This experience exercised a powerful effect upon my life. I learned from it – or I deluded myself into thinking I had learned – that the physical appetite of one male for another may be made the foundation of a solid friendship, when the man drawn by passion exhibits a proper respect for the man who draws. I also seemed to perceive that, within the sphere of the male brothel, even in that lawless godless place, permanent human relations – affections, reciprocal toleration, decencies of conduct, asking and yielding, concession and abstention – find their natural sphere: perhaps more than in the sexual relations consecrated by middle-class matrimony. So at least the manly and comradely attitude of the young soldier, who had sold his body to a stranger, and with whom I as a stranger fraternized, indicated. Was this a delusion? To this hour I do not know, though I have extended the same experience, with similar results, a hundredfold, never seeming to outrage any purely natural sentiments, but only colliding with the sense of law and the instincts of convention. I came away from the male brothel with a strong conviction that, although it was a far more decent place than I expected, *this* was not the proper ground in which to plant the seeds of irresistible emotion. It offered an initial difficulty – a false position – which had to be overcome. It raised disgust, and I left it shaking the dust and degradation of the locality off my feet. With just the same feeling of disgust, not more, not less, have I quitted female brothels. But there I never found the satisfaction which the soldier gave me. From him I learned that natural male beings in the world at large were capable of corresponding to my appreciation of them. A dangerous lesson, perhaps.

Meanwhile I was giving my lectures on Florence to the Royal Institution. Very dull lectures they were, for my soul was not in them; my soul throbbed for the soldier; and I had composed the lectures specially for what I most abhor, an audience of cultivated people. This is a paradoxical confession. I am nothing if not cultivated; or, at least, the world only expects culture from me. But, in my heart of hearts, I do not believe in culture except as an adjunct to life. Life is more than literature, I say. So I cannot, although I devote my time and energy to culture (even as a carpenter makes doors, or a carver carves edelweiss on walnut wood), regard it otherwise than in the light of pastime, decoration, service. Passion, nerve and sinew, eating and drinking, the stomach and the bowels, sex, action, even money-getting – the coarsest forms of activity – come, in my reckoning, before culture. The man, the man's the thing. And the man in me tumultuously throbbed for the escapements from that droning lecture desk into a larger, keener, more dignified, more actual existence. Little did I care what the gentlemen in frock coats and the ladies in bonnets thought of my lectures. I did not care what they thought, because I knew that the real arena for myself and the rest of them was not in that theatre of disputations, elucidations, and plausible explications of all sorts of theories. It lay outside, inside, in a world of things which each carries about with him, and into which each penetrates when the voice of the lecturer is no more heard in the theatre.

The theatre of the Royal Institution – that dismal pit in which a lecturer stands, under malign London light in February, with a cold draught pumped upon his shoulders – took its revenge upon me for the insolence I have declared and my indifference to culture. In short, I caught a bad cold in the lungs, while engaged in that husky task

255

of lecturing to drowsy folk on topics which they neither understood nor cared to be instructed in.

This cold developed into a sharp attack of bronchitis, when I returned to Clifton. I had a long and tedious illness; my good friend and doctor, John Beddoe, pronounced that the left lung was now at last seriously and dangerously compromised. He sent me off to Greece: I was to go there in the company of F. Tuckett of the Alpine Club. But I only got as far as Cannes upon the way. A certain δαιμόνιον [divine sign],[1] instinct of abstention – which attends all open-minded human beings when they have a choice between the possible and the impossible in practical circumstances – told me that I was unfit to risk a journey into Greece, and that it would be inflicting a too serious responsibility upon my travelling friends if I should do so. In other words, I felt too weak to go to Greece; and, without exactly knowing why, I determined to await a coming crisis in regions which were better known to me. Dr Beddoe, if he should read this, may perhaps say that I chose wrongly, because I did not trust to the recuperative force of nature. But he was not in my skin at the time when I abandoned Greece and turned to Lombardy.

It is only the man himself who knows (and he knows very indistinctly) with what forces he has to measure himself. Dr Beddoe knew nothing of what had passed between me and the brawny young soldier in the male brothel near the Regent's Park. I knew something about the new factor which had been introduced into my life by experiences in London, and what I knew taught me that I must wait and reckon with it. I could not fly from it. I had to face it. The solution was not yet found for moral difficulties which had begun to present themselves in different ways from what I had imagined. What was Greece, its monuments, its mountains, its transparent air, for a man at strife with his own soul – indifferent to antiquity for the moment, hungering after reality, careless of nature, acutely sensitive to life? Greece, for such a man, was only a wide field of experience in the solution of the now commanding problem – the problem of correlating his dominant passion with the facts of existence. And the man, I, did not possess physical strength enough to try the issues in so bewildering a region as Greece offers to a scholar and a nature-lover. The δαιμόνιον told me to draw in my sails. What little strength I had left must be reserved for the close battle with my passions; and my physical resources must be dedicated to the contest which could not longer be deferred.

So I pottered about Lombardy in the spring of 1877. I trailed the skirts of my physical and nervous unrest through those Italian cities, always alive to their monuments of art and history, always touching human nature at its crudest and coarsest points, and in no wise gaining satisfaction. The problem was not solved but protracted; and what the soul gained or lost in this process of experience was a levelling down until it touched the groundpan of 'pauvre humanité'. The lesson taught me by the soldier in London found its application here. And yet, so strong is custom, so imperious is education, I never condescended to a single act which the most virtuous could call reprehensible. I consorted with what are supposed to be the dregs of human nature; but I demanded nothing from these men and women but comradeship. What I discovered was that I could love and fraternize with the least and last and poorest, that I could call the meanest my friends, my brothers and sisters. But I had no gospel to preach to them. I only came to understand them and their integrity with myself.

On my way back from this spring journey, while I was diversifying these practical experiences with the study and translation of Campanella's sonnets, I fell ill at Turin. A night of acute physical disturbance and fever there warned me that I was upon the verge of a serious collapse. Summoning all my strength and courage, I travelled without stopping to Clifton. The day after I reached home, I was laid prostrate with a violent haemorrhage from the lungs. The storm in my petty region had broken out now. A great peace came over me, as I lay for weeks in bed (fed through the mouth by my wife, who acted as a ministering angel), forgetful of the conflict, slowly and painfully recovering a dram of strength. It was a blissful interlude in my life of passion, those weeks in which I lay resigned to death. But life returned; and though I was maimed and bruised, definitely convicted of acutal phthisis and of breaking-down of the lung tissue, I felt the call to live. When I got up at last from my sick-bed, I could hardly recognize myself as the same person. The struggle for mere life had now absorbed and superseded the struggle for what I sought in life. I seemed for the moment like a man new-born. I was a child in the hands of something divine, to which I responded with an infinite gratitude. So preoccupied was I with the difficulty of existing that I did not then think what further existence would imply – the recrudescence of my old pangs and pains and wounds, the resumption of the burden of my personality. I employed

myself to the best of my ability in setting my worldly affairs in order
(being conscious of impending death); and for the rest I exercised
my literary faculty in such light work as I could do – translating
the sonnets of Michelangelo Buonarroti and Tommaso Campanella,
which I had begun before my illness. Never have I felt happier in
the soul than during those weeks, when my life was hanging on a
thread, and when the sensuous faculties remained in abeyance – the
real man, the self which is immortal, being left open to only intellectual influences, and those pervading only a small portion of his total
sensibility.

It was impossible to think of remaining in England; and the doubt
was whither we should wend our way – whether to the Canaries or
Australia (for the sake of the sea journey) or to Egypt. I decided
against the sea journey after short deliberation. I knew too much
about its inconveniences from invalids who were better able to
endure them than I was.

We determined at last upon a winter in a Dahabeeyah. We were
to take Janet and Madge . . . with us, leaving Lotta and Katharine
under the charge of their nurse with our relations at Clifton and
Oxford. But before we made the move, I went up to London and
consulted Sir William Jenner. He told me very gravely that I must
not leave England without settling all my affairs, and that, in his
opinion, a fresh cold would render my recovery impossible. He also
recommended me to spend some weeks upon the way to Egypt in
the High Alps, in order, if possible, to gain a little strength. I had
every reason to trust in his judgement, for he knew the circumstances
of my family and had watched my sister Lady Strachey's case for
years. She had been suffering from chronic disease of the lungs like
me, but had already fallen into the condition of a regular invalid.
On my asking if he thought my state at all as serious as hers, he
replied, 'I have never seen Lady Strachey in anything like the same
danger of a rapid and irretrievable breaking up of the lungs. You
must not allow yourself to think that you can take the same liberties
with yourself as I should permit her.' This answer surprised me, for
I had always been accustomed to regard my poor sister as less
favoured than myself to a marked degree. It made me sober, and
prepared me for beginning a manful battle with my treacherous foe.

My youngest sister, Mrs. T. H. Green, and her husband happened
at this time to be staying at Davos Platz. They wrote a very favour-

able account of the place – it was the first time I heard of it – the doctors, appliances for illness, air, hotels and so forth. This induced me to prefer Davos to the Engadine, especially as I should have her company there.

Accordingly I arrived, more dead than alive after the fatigues of the hot journey, at Davos on 7 August 1877. As the valley opened before me from the height of Wolfgang, veiled in melancholy cloud, toward the close of a weary day, I thought that I had rarely seen a less attractive place to live in. Everything looked so bleak and bare; and though I loved the Alps, I discerned little of their charm in Davos. What should I have thought, had I then been told that twelve years afterwards, on the anniversary of that day, I should be penning these lines in a house built for my habitation here? That I should have spent by far the larger part of those intervening years in ever-growing and abiding love for Davos, in strenuous literary work, and in the enjoyment of a society singularly congenial to my peculiar nature? On 7 August 1889, while I am writing in the open air, under the shadow of my *Wandelbahn* or ambulatory, I look back with a curious mixed sense of gratitude, surprise and self-abasement over those twelve years past. Janet, our first-born, who was then as beautiful as an angel, as wise as Hypatia, as lithe as a young antelope, is dead. My sister Lady Strachey has been dead some years. My brother-in-law, T. H. Green, died long ago. . . . And I, who least deserved perhaps to live, who had so little prospect then of living, am yet here. God forgive me and assist me; God grant I may not arrive at wishing that the day which brought me to this valley had been my last! I cannot, indeed, in any circumstances do *that*. Whatever happens, I shall remember that these years of my chequered, confused and morally perturbed existence have been the best, the healthiest and the most active of the whole. I may have to say with Job, '*Quare de vulva me eduxisti?*' But I shall not say, '*Quare me ad Davosias duxisti, Domine?*' ['Wherefore did you bring me forth out of the womb?' 'Wherefore did you bring me to Davos, O Lord?']²

Dr Ruedi, when he came to inspect me the morning after my arrival, pronounced it a grave case, and said that the left lung had begun to form a cavity a little way below the nipple. He gave me directions which I scrupulously followed. The first three weeks were spent in sitting all day long in the open air upon a gravel terrace in part of the Hotel Belvedere. Then I was allowed to go into the wood. My manservant took me up in a little carriage, hung a hammock between two pine trees, carried and placed me in the hammock, and when the sun came near to setting fetched me again in the carriage.

Whenever I pass the place where they used to sling my hammock, a curious sense of reverence comes over me, a feeling of the mystery surrounding human life. Then I seemed so surely marked out for gradual declension that my thoughts assumed the grey and quiet tone of resignation. I lay watching the squirrels leap from pine to pine above my head, and the clouds sail through the quiet spaces of the sky – listening to my wife's reading of Boswell's *Johnson* – noticing the children play, turning now and then a couplet in my Michelangelo translation. I was not fit for work. Nature went healthily to sleep in me; and the first sign of convalescence was a slow dim sense of reawakening mental energy, very different from the feverish and fretful activity of the past years. This found its expression one day soon after noon – I remember the hour, the place, the aspect of the sky and valley well – when I felt impelled to write that series of my sonnets which are called 'Sonnets on the Thought of Death'.[3]

Fortunately we were favoured with a wonderfully fine autumn. About the beginning of September I was permitted to walk a little, and to take drives. Then I began to explore the beauties of Davos; climbing by slow degrees higher and higher up the Schatzalp, which I finally surmounted in November; driving with my wife into Sertig Thal, Dischma Thal and the Züge. I saw that Davos could be lived in, and felt myself so well here that I resolved to give up Egypt and complete my winter under Dr Ruedi's care. I wrote on the subject to Sir Wm Jenner, who replied that he must bid me pause and reflect before I determined 'to give my vile body to the Davos doctors'. Not intimidated by this, because I knew that I was thriving, and greatly dreaded change, I stuck to my plan, put aside our Nile outfit and sent to England for clothes and furs suited to an Alpine winter.

Meanwhile, with the gradual return of vitality, the sense of beauty returned; and I wrote some sonnets on the problem of man's irrepressible desire, which grazed the surface of my life's wound. The pain of that incurable wound slumbered, however, and I fondly dreamed that it would never recrudesce.

I ought here to mention that it had become an article in my creed of social duty that men and women convicted of hereditary disease, phthisis or insanity, ought to refrain from procreation. Acting upon this principle I separated from my wife with her approval. She gave it readily; for the sexual side of marriage had never been for her more than a trouble. She disliked childbirth, and had, I think, no constitutional difficulties to overcome. In truth our married life had long been ill-arranged upon the ordinary basis of cohabitation. We had taken precautions against pregnancy; and our intercourse in this respect was principally determined by the need I felt of sexual outlet. This outlet was now definitely closed; and with reviving energy, the need became imperious. I suffered a period of painful and exhausting erethism, attended with profuse seminal losses. Still I stuck to my decision, mainly because I judged, and judged rightly, that this return of sexual appetite was the sign of returning vigour. Even now I do not repent of the line we took. It placed me upon a sound and true relation to my wife – that of pure and faithful friendship, which from the commencement had been the real basis of our union. It delivered us both from sordid cares and preoccupations, and left her, on the verge of middle life, in full possession of her physical faculties. Still it had serious drawbacks for a man of my temperament. I began to feel morally irresponsible toward the woman who had willingly sanctioned the solution of the sexual bond between us. This state of things has lasted now for twelve years, during which we have rarely shared the same bedroom, and never the same bed.

A slight incident, late in the autumn of 1877, occurred, which warned me that the slumbering wound was still unhealed. Sitting upon the terrace of the Belvedere Hotel one afternoon, a young man passed before my eyes and stopped at no great distance to obey a natural call. He was, I think, a Tyrolese pedlar, dressed in short jacket and knee-breeches of brown velveteen: a handsome fellow with a bold bright gaze and the loose free lounge of a born mountaineer. He had probably taken too much wine, and there was licence in his gait. Desire for the *Bursch* [youth] shot through me with a sudden stab. I followed him with my eyes until he passed behind a haystall; and I thought – if only I could follow him, and catch him there, and pass this afternoon with him upon the sweet new hay! Then I turned to my Campanella's sonnets, and told myself that these things were for ever over.

Dr Ruedi ordered me to drink as much Valtelline wine as I could without disturbing my digestion. I followed his advice, and found it suited me admirably. The wine, rather distasteful at first to an uneducated palate, acted like a powerful tonic, and in combination with the mountain air, regular exercise, simple habits and sound sleep, effected a cure.

All that winter, 1877–8, I remained of course very weak, suffering from frequent relapses, enduring long tiresome hours of inactivity, but still on the whole making slow progress. I attribute my gradual recovery in no small measure to the fact that I resolutely refused to give up study. Some hours of every day were devoted to literature; and thus I succeeded in printing and publishing two books (*Sonnets of Michelangelo and Campanella* and *Many Moods*), together with several articles for the *Cornhill* and the *Academy*, before the spring.

A young man called Christian Buol used occasionally to drive me out in sledges on the snow. He belonged to a very ancient noble family of Graubünden. The first Buol settled at Davos at the end of the thirteenth century. The pedigree records several lines of counts and barons of the empire. One of them, a Graf von Buol-Schauenstein, was known in England as Austrian ambassador during the Crimean war, and finds a place in Browning's poems. The armorial bearings of the Buols, 'party per pale azure and argent, a dame attired in medieval German costume holding in her dexter hand a rose, counterchanged', will be found in churches and on old manorial houses all about the valleys which descend upon the Rhine. Here in Davos they have preserved the simplicity of patriarchal manners, though always conscious of their noble ancestry; and, what seems very strange to English folk, they are so identified now with the Swiss democracy that they do their own work in the woods and fields, keep an inn, and speculate commercially. Christian's eldest brother was the doctor at Thusis, another was the owner of a hotel, a third was studying medicine, two were in America, and there were several more. I think his mother had borne sixteen children to his father, the Landamtmann of Davos.

Christian was the youngest of this family – just nineteen when I first knew him; and one of the finest specimens of robust, handsome, intelligent and gentle adolescence I have ever met with. Possessed of enormous muscular strength, he had the quiet temperate manners, and the subdued speech, of a well-trained gentleman. I soon began to love him: shyly at first, struck with the wonder of discovering anyone so new to my experience, so dignified, so courteous, so comradely, realizing at one and the same time for me all that I had dreamed of the democratic ideal and all that I desired in radiant manhood. When he came towards me, standing erect upon an empty wood-sledge, and driving four stout horses at a brisk trot down a snow slope, I seemed to see an ancient Greek of the Homeric age, perfect in σωφροσύνη and unassuming power. 'That is a man,' I felt within myself. And I also felt obscurely that my ruling passion had reached a new and better stage, devoid of sentimentality, devoid of sordid appetite, free from the sense of sin. It was indeed impossible to think of Christian Buol and of sin in the same moment. Of this twelve years of intimate friendship with him have amply assured me.

Anyhow, I made up my mind to bid for his friendship. On a dull cold day, between Christmas and the New Year, I saw him standing at the door of a cow stable belonging to the Buols. This stable has now been removed, and the house of Christian's brother, Dr Florian Buol, occupies the site. I had a new meerschaum pipe in my pocket – a pretty bauble in a morocco case, sent me from Paris. I went up to him, and asked him if he would accept this as a New Year's gift from me. He took it with kindness, showing, I thought, just a touch of surprise. Nothing more passed. But he has afterwards told me that the surprise I noticed was due to the fact that no *Cur-gast*, or winter-invalid at Davos, had shown the same personal interest in him before. In fact he liked it, though, with the stately repose of a Bündner, he made no demonstration of his liking. I was left with the uncomfortable doubt, which is one of the pleasant pangs of incipient affection, whether I had not committed a *gaucherie*.

Nothing was said or done on either side, after this incident, to alter our relations. But little by little I perceived that they were growing closer, and that in his own calm way Christian appreciated the very slight advances I made toward him. Through the next three months we grew in intimacy and discussed a variety of topics in our drives. I asked him to dine in my private room at the Belvedere, and he invited me on his birthday (22 March) to a family party in the old house of the Buols. I well remember that room panelled with Cembra planks – the first of so many Bündner rooms into which I afterwards gained entrance as a welcomed honoured guest – the grave faces of his brothers, and the grand bearing of his old mother, born Ursula Sprecher von Bernegg. It was like a scene out of one of Whitman's poems, filling me with the acutest sense of a new and beautiful life, to partake in which I was invited by a friend. I only feared that I should not be fit to play my part among these people.

They seemed to me essentially superior in some points of breeding and in general human dignity to what I had hitherto known in any of the numerous circles I had visited. Nor was this an illusion. After many illusions have been rubbed away by intercourse with the people of Graubünden, I retain my sense of their noble, because absolutely natural, breeding. It springs, I think, from the self-respect of free men, for centuries unqualified by caste, who have always lived plainly, battled with a stepmotherly nature, and submitted to the discipline of patriarchal authority and severe social criticism in small communities.

An accident informed me about this time that Christian's brother, the owner of Hotel Buol, was involved in serious financial difficulties. Like so many Swiss people of good means, he had engaged in a speculation for which he was not fitted by previous experience. In short, he was not born to be an innkeeper, and to compete with Dutch and German men of business. These persons, I heard, were buying up his debts, and meant to force him to a sale of property – by which he would have been declared bankrupt. It was a word dropped out of vulgar elation by a German innkeeper, which informed me of the projected transaction. Concealing my indignation at the baseness of the scheme, I resolved to ascertain the facts of the case, and, if I judged the undertaking not too perilous, I proposed to supply the Buols with enough capital to help them out of their embarrassments.

Christian, when I asked him, told me plainly what he knew about the situation; and I saw that a round sum of £1000 would suffice to avert ruin from his brother's head. Accordingly, I said that I had cash to that amount at my disposal – it was, in fact, just what I had meant to spend upon my now finally abandoned Dahabeeyah. If his brother Caspar liked, we might do business. So I lent the money upon the best security which the Buols could give; and the only difficulties I met with in the transaction arose from my astonishment at the simplicity of Swiss law respecting mortgage, the absence of any lawyer in Davos who might have helped me, and the sensitive pride of the Buol family. I have had no cause to regret a step which was prompted by friendship for Christian and by indignation against commercial conspirators. Nor do I regret having advanced a further sum of £2000 to the family upon a subsequent occasion. They have dealt loyally with me on all points; and their property rising greatly in value owing to the prosperity of Davos, has given me the amplest security for my loan, a large part of which is now paid off.

This incident I record chiefly because it illustrates to what good results a love which most people regard as abominable and unnatural may lead. Love for Christian Buol, respectful but ardent, induced me thus to help his family at a shrewd pinch. Had it not been that I, an English stranger, had been attracted by the splendid youth who drove me, the Buols would certainly be now in a very different position to that which they occupy — involved like the Brosis of Klosters and the Sprechers of Davos in inextricable financial difficulties. And here I must add that my wife, acquainted at every point with the details of the transaction, and not ignorant of my affection for Christian, gave her unhesitating assent to my plan for their salvation. Generous and noble wife, born of a noble stock, and gifted with the noblest natural sentiments!

The friendship which sprang up between me and Christian Buol was cemented by this act of confidence on my part. I do not think we either of us attached great importance to it. My feeling for him rested on quite a different ground from that of money relations. And he was not the man to give anything whatever of himself in return for pecuniary considerations. He understood, however, that I had conceived a real and disinterested liking for his family; and he knew that I had given substantial proof of my attachment. We were thus brought into closer rapport than that of a mere casual intimacy.

When I proposed to take him with me on a journey into Italy, which I projected for the spring, he was delighted. He had not travelled further than to Chur, Tirano in the Valtelline, Vico Soprano in the Val Bregaglia. The prospect of visiting the lake of Como, Milan, Venice, Genoa, and other places which he came to see in April and May, was attractive to the vigorous young fellow.

We made a most delightful journey together; and in the course of it, he showed that he was ready, out of sympathy and liking for me, to concede many innocent delights of privacy, which cost him nothing and which filled me with ineffable satisfaction. In his company I seemed to realize what my nature had been blindly seeking for through many tedious years — a loyal comradeship, to which my friend's physical beauty added for me the charm of sensuous romance. We often slept together in the same bed; and he was not shy of allowing me to view, as men may view the idols of their gods, the naked splendour of his perfect body. But neither in act nor deed, far less in words, did the least shadow of lust cloud the serenity of that masculine communion. He gave what honour and affection prompted him to concede, I took what passion and my reverence for the generous youth allowed me to enjoy. I did not want more indeed than the blameless proximity of his pure person. Odd and unnatural as this may seem to those who cannot understand a man's love for a man, or to those who have made their minds up that such love must be brutal, I declare that this is the fact. Anyone who has enjoyed the privilege of Christian's acquaintance will know that he could not have yielded a base pleasure to me, and that I could not have dared to demand it. If the soldier whom I met in the London brothel taught me the rudiments of comradeship, Christian made me perceive its higher, more delightful issues. I have never enjoyed a more sense-soothing and more elevated pleasure than I had with him – sex being nowhere – drowned and absorbed in love, which was itself so spiritually sensual that the needs of the body disappeared and were forgotten. Words fail me when I try to describe a relation which had much of hazardous, but which the respective natures of the men concerned made natural and right. A spy might have looked through cracks in doors upon us; and the spy would have seen nothing reprehensible. So we continued to respect each other; and when he told me that his heart was set upon a girl, whom he had learned to love in the school at Thusis, and whom he subsequently married, our relations remained unaltered. He accepted me for what I was; and I asked nothing except his proximity. It was enough for me to be with him.

Alas, while writing this, I must perforce lay the pen aside, and think how desolate are the conditions under which men constituted like me live and love. Into comradeship itself does not our abnormal nature introduce an element of instability, even as it distorts marriage? Something remains amiss, unsatisfied, ill-correlated in each case. The utmost we dare expect is tolerance, acceptance, concession to our inclinations, gratitude for our goodwill and benefits, respect for our courtesy and self-control. The best we obtain is friendship grounded on the intimate acquaintance with our character derived from long experience in extraordinary circumstances. Love for love we cannot get; and our better nature shrinks from the vision of what a love aroused in the beloved (corresponding to our love for him) would inevitably involve. We are therefore too often goaded into insane acts by the mere discord between our desires and their dearly beloved object – between our cruelly repelled senses and our sustained ideal – by the impossible cul-de-sac into which nature has driven our sexual instincts, and the rebellion of the aspiring spirit, finding itself in 'a waste of shame' or in the desert of unfulfilled longings. I have veiled some aspects of this pitiable situation in my sonnets on 'Intellectual Isolation' and 'L'Amour de l'Impossible'.[4] But it would need the pen of the all-revealer, the truth-dictator, the Word, to express the whole of this dire agony. . . .

I left the Hotel Belvedere and settled with my family in Hotel Buol, which through my influence was immediately converted into a flourishing hotel for English people; and so it has continued for the last eleven years. The Buols, in fact, have to thank the *beaux yeux* of Christian, and the affection he inspired in me, not only for salvation from financial ruin but also for prolonged prosperity. This I set down not in self-praise, but as a testimony to that Erôs whom the world misjudges and conceives incapable of good.

Christian used always to travel with us in Italy until his duties on the farm at Davos kept him at home. And then I took his nephew Christian Palmy, a young man of nearly the same age and almost equally attractive, though in a different way.*

By my friendship with these people I was introduced to Graubünd-eners of all kinds and sorts. Without dwelling further on the topic, I will only say that I now count scores of men among my intimate acquaintances – peasants of every description, postillions, drivers, carters, conductors of the *diligence*, carpenters, doctors, parsons, schoolmasters, porters in hotels, herdsmen on the alps, masons, hunters, woodmen, guides, hotelkeepers, shopkeepers, stableboys, artizans. In my personal relations to them I have never met with one who shared my own abnormal tastes; but upon this point I have invariably received from them a frank compliant correspondence when I sought it. This has happened frequently; for I am unable to dissociate in certain cases my friendly feeling for a man from the plastic admiration of his beauty. I have driven with them across all

---

*Those who have read my *Italian Byways* will now see why the book is dedicated to the two Christians. – J. A. S.

the mountain roads in summer and winter, gone to their balls and village theatricals, smoked and drunk with them in taverns, invited them freely to my house, slept with them in their own cottages on lonely hillsides, joined their clubs, and shared their pastimes. Entering thus into their lives, I have brought, as I confessed above, my passions with me; and often have I enjoyed the sweetest fruits of privacy, with no back thoughts except such as must be always given to law and custom. It would astonish an Englishman who knows nothing of the Swiss to hear that during the whole course of this careless and promiscuous intimacy, I have never heard low talk or witnessed a single unbecoming action on the part of my acquaintances. In heart and nature I found this people of Grau-bünden essentially pure and gentle. From those who had been sophis-ticated by residence in foreign cities I kept more aloof; for contact with the bourgeoisie does not improve the manners, though it may not contaminate the morals, of mountaineers. I cannot speak from wide experience of the Swiss outside this canton; and some things lead me to suspect that the Graubündeners, owing to their peculiar history, have a higher average of manliness and manners than will be found at large in Switzerland. Be that as it may, I have enjoyed in this society privileges of which I had not dreamed before I settled at Davos.

For a student and a man of letters what I learned from these sturdy children of nature has been invaluable. They have confirmed my belief in democracy, and proved to me that high thinking and loyal feeling can be combined with the plainest living. Nor are they in any true sense of the word uneducated or stupid. The general excellence of Swiss primary schools, the exercise of equal political rights, the discharge of public duties, the absence of class distinctions and caste privileges, the common service in the army, the habit of reading newspapers, the conversation of the tavern to which men of every quality and all professions go to exchange thoughts and hear news, the mixture in every family of peasants, merchants, magis-trates, artizans and doctors of the liberal sciences (each member choosing his own line) – all these conditions of a life exceedingly unlike our own in England raise the average intelligence and cultiva-tion of the male population to a high level. I know one clergyman of great distinction whose son is in training for a butcher; a porter in a Chur hotel one of whose uncles was bishop of Chur, while the other was a *diligence* conductor; a doctor of civil law whose brothers are poor peasants and chamois-hunters; a family two of whose members are working carpenters, while the other two are partners in a firm at Palermo clearing above £3000 a year.

I might run on *ad infinitum*, extending the list of apparent social anomalies. But when one sees the system in working order, there is nothing to surprise. All seems natural. You go to consult the *Landammann*, or supreme magistrate of the *Landschaft*, upon some knotty point of law or some difficulty regarding the introduction of a railway. His secretary in the Rathaus informs you that he is carrying hay, and will be found at home for dinner at 11 a.m. Strolling across the meadows to his wooden house, you meet him helping to load his stalwart son with a heavy burden; and as you walk slowly to the humble roof, he gives a lucid explanation of the point at issue, displaying native shrewdness, fortified with an exact calculation of financial circumstances, complete knowledge of the legal aspects of the case, and a sagacious insight into the characters of the men who have to be considered. Maybe, if you are a friend, he invites you to share the midday meal. This consists of bread, dried meat, sausages and cheese, all of good quality, and is partaken of by the family and their farm servants sitting round one table in their shirtsleeves. After a while, I repeat, there is nothing surprising in this state of things. It comes to be recognized as beautifully, ideally natural – as what ought to be, and may possibly be universal at some future period of history. No doubt the absence of overwhelming wealth and the contentment with comparative poverty, which are marked features of Swiss society, help to facilitate this simplicity of life. And something is due to the fact that few families are destitute of landed property, while each man is a member of some commune, where he can vote on public business, exercise influence by speaking, and to which in the last resort he can appeal for maintenance – unless he have temporarily lost his rights by misconduct.

Finally, it need not be remarked that, here as elsewhere, human nature has its seamy side, and that the mountaineers of whom I have been speaking are distinguished by some repellent qualities. They are close in money matters, hard at driving bargains, phlegmatic, slow to move, prosaic in their aims and aspirations, unimaginative and indifferent to ideas. These characteristics, however, do not render them unprofitable companions for one who, like myself, possesses faults of quite the opposite description. In truth I have

269

learned from them more than I can say. Their society has been to me a constant source of relief in my solitary life of literary industry. It would be an ideal condition of existence were I as free from dread of human law and custom as I am conscience-free before God and nature in the matter of my passions.

Much of our time, during these years of Davos residence, have been spent in Italy; and I now occupy the entresol of my friend H. F. Brown upon the Zattere at Venice under a lease from him. These Italian journeys brought me acquainted with a certain number of Italian young men, some of whom I managed to treat in the same way as I treat my comrades in Graubünden. That is to say, I have formed permanent friendships into which an element of passionate desire has entered upon my side, while my comrade gave freely and frankly what I asked for. The relation thus established varies in each new case, being infinitely elastic and capable of subtle modifications according to the disposition of the comrade. In order to base a friendship of this kind on solid foundations, it is needful that the seeker or the lover should conform to the instincts and respect the feelings of the sought and loved. Acting thus he may expect a moderate degree of satisfaction. I will give an instance.

Chapter Seventeen

Angelo Fusato

In the spring of 1881 I was staying for a few days at Venice. I had rooms in the Casa Alberti on the Fondamenta Venier, S. Vio, and it was late in the month of May.

One afternoon I chanced to be sitting with my friend Horatio Brown in a little backyard to the wineshop of Fighetti at S. Elisabetta on the Lido. Gondoliers patronize this place, because Fighetti, a muscular giant, is a hero among them. He has won I do not know how many flags in their regattas. While we were drinking our wine Brown pointed out to me two men in white gondolier uniform, with the enormously broad black hat which was then fashionable. They were servants of a General de Horsey; and one of them was strikingly handsome. The following description of him, written a few days after our first meeting, represents with fidelity the impression he made on my imagination.

He was tall and sinewy, but very slender – for these Venetian gondoliers are rarely massive in their strength. Each part of the man is equally developed by the exercise of rowing; and their bodies are elastically supple, with free sway from the hips and a Mercurial poise upon the ankle. Angelo showed these qualities almost in exaggeration. Moreover, he was rarely in repose, but moved with a singular brusque grace. – Black broad-brimmed hat thrown back upon his matted *zazzera* of dark hair. – Great fiery grey eyes, gazing intensely, with compulsive effluence of electricity – the wild glance of a Triton. – Short blond moustache; dazzling teeth; skin bronzed, but showing white and delicate through open front and sleeves of lilac shirt. – The dashing sparkle of this splendour, who looked to me as though the sea waves and the sun had made him in some hour of secret and

271

unquiet rapture, was somehow emphasized by a curious dint dividing his square chin – a cleft that harmonized with smile on lips and steady fire in eyes. – By the way, I do not know what effect it would have upon a reader to compare eyes to opals. Yet Angelo's eyes, as I met them, had the flame and vitreous intensity of opals, as though the quintessential colour of Venetian waters were vitalized in them and fed from inner founts of passion. – This marvellous being had a rough hoarse voice which, to develop the simile of a sea-god, might have screamed in storm or whispered raucous messages from crests of tossing waves. He fixed and fascinated me.

Angelo Fusato at that date was hardly twenty-four years of age. He had just served his three years in the Genio,[1] and returned to Venice.

This love at first sight for Angelo Fusato was an affair not merely of desire and instinct but also of imagination. He took hold of me by a hundred subtle threads of feeling, in which the powerful and radiant manhood of the splendid animal was intertwined with sentiment for Venice, a keen delight in the landscape of the lagoons, and something penetrative and pathetic in the man.

How sharp this mixed fascination was at the moment when I first saw Angelo, and how durable it afterwards became through the moral struggles of our earlier intimacy, will be understood by anyone who reads the sonnets written about him in my published volumes. These are 'A Portrait' and 'Angelo Ribello' (*Vagabunduli Libellus*, 1884, pages 119, 120); together with the whole of the following series of sonnets: *Animi Figura*, 'L'Amour de l'Impossible', i, ii, iii, iv, v, vi; *Vagabunduli Libellus*, 'Stella Maris', i, ii, iii, xii, xiii, xvii, xviii, xix, xx, xxi, xxii, xxiii, xxiv, xxv, xxxv, xLi, xLiii, xLiv, xLv, xLvi, xLvii, xLviii, xLix, L, Li, Lii, Liii, Liv, Lv, Lvi, Lvii, Lviii, Lix, Lx, Lxi, Lxii; *Animi Figura*, 'Self-Condemnation', i–vii, 'O Si! O Si!', 'Amends', i–iv. Taken in the order I have indicated, and detached from the artificial context framed to render publication possible,* these sonnets faithfully describe the varying moods, perplexities and conflicts of my passion before it settled into a comparatively wholesome comradeship.

Eight years have elapsed since that first meeting at the Lido. A steady friendship has grown up between the two men brought by accident together under conditions so unpromising. But before I speak of this – the happy product of a fine and manly nature on his

---

*Many of these sonnets were mutilated in order to adapt them to the female sex.

side and of fidelity and constant effort on my own – I must revert to those May days in 1881.

The image of the marvellous being I had seen for those few minutes on the Lido burned itself into my brain and kept me waking all the next night. I did not even know his name; but I knew where his master lived. In the morning I rose from my bed unrefreshed, haunted by the vision which seemed to grow in definiteness and to coruscate with phosphorescent fire. A trifle which occurred that day made me feel that my fate could not be resisted, and also allowed me to suspect that the man himself was not unapproachable. Another night of storm and longing followed. I kept wrestling with the anguish of unutterable things, in the deep darkness of the valley of vain desire – soothing my smarting sense of the impossible with idle pictures of what it would be to share the life of this superb being in some lawful and simple fashion:

$$\phi\alpha\acute{\imath}\nu\epsilon\tau\alpha\acute{\imath} \mu o\iota \kappa\hat{\eta}\nu o\varsigma \acute{\imath}\sigma o\varsigma \theta\acute{\epsilon}o\iota\sigma\iota\nu$$
$$\acute{\epsilon}\mu\mu\epsilon\nu' \acute{\omega}\nu\eta\varrho \acute{o}\tau\tau\iota\varsigma \acute{\epsilon}\nu\acute{\alpha}\nu\tau\iota\acute{o}\varsigma \tau o\iota$$
$$\acute{\imath}\zeta\acute{\alpha}\nu\epsilon\iota$$

['He seems to me to be the equal of the gods, that man who sits across from you . . .']² In these waking dreams I was at one time a woman whom he loved, at another a companion in his trade – always somebody and something utterly different from myself; and as each distracting fancy faded in the void of fact and desert of reality, I writhed in the clutches of chimaera, thirsted before the tempting phantasmagoria of Maya.* My good sense rebelled, and told me that I was morally a fool and legally a criminal. But the love of the impossible rises victorious after each fall given it by sober sense. Man must be a demigod of volition, a very Hercules, to crush the life out of that Antaeus, lifting it aloft from the soil of instinct and of appetite which eternally creates it new in his primeval nature.

Next morning I went to seek out Angelo, learned his name, and made an appointment with him for that evening on the Zattere. We were to meet at nine by the Church of the Gesuati. True to time he came, swinging along with military step, head erect and eager, broad chest thrown out, the tall strong form and pliant limbs in action like a creature of the young world's prime. All day I had been

*The key to all the phrases I have used above, 'unutterable things', 'valley of vain desire', 'the impossible', 'Chimaera', 'Maya', will be found by those who read my poems. Each phrase has its specific significance.

wondering how it was that a man of this sort could yield himself so lightly to the solicitation of a stranger. And that is a puzzle which still remains unsolved. I had been told that he was called *il matto*, or the madcap, by his friends; and I gathered that he was both poor and extravagant. But this did not appear sufficient to explain his recklessness – the stooping to what seemed so vile an act. I am now inclined, however, to imagine that the key to the riddle lay in a few simple facts. He was careless by nature, poor by circumstance, determined to have money, indifferent to how he got it. Besides, I know from what he has since told me that the gondoliers of Venice are so accustomed to these demands that they think little of gratifying the caprice of ephemeral lovers – within certain limits, accurately fixed according to a conventional but rigid code of honour in such matters. There are certain things to which a self-respecting man will not condescend, and any attempt to overstep the line is met by firm resistance.

Well: I took him back to Casa Alberti; and what followed shall be told in the ensuing sonnet, which is strictly accurate – for it was written with the first impression of the meeting strong upon me.

I am not dreaming. He was surely here
　And sat beside me on this hard low bed;
　For we had wine before us, and I said –
'Take gold: 'twill furnish forth some better cheer.'
He was all clothed in white; a gondolier;
　White trousers, white straw hat upon his head,
　A cream-white shirt loose-buttoned, a silk thread
Slung with a charm about his throat so clear.
Yes, he was here. Our four hands, laughing, made
　Brief havoc of his belt, shirt, trousers, shoes:
　Till, mother-naked, white as lilies, laid
There on the counterpane, he bade me use
　Even as I willed his body. But Love forbade –
　Love cried, 'Less than Love's best thou shalt refuse!'

Next morning, feeling that I could not stand the strain of this attraction and repulsion – the intolerable desire and the repudiation of mere fleshly satisfaction – I left Venice for Monte Generoso. There, and afterwards at Davos through the summer, I thought and wrote incessantly about Angelo. The series of sonnets entitled 'The

Sea Calls', and a great many of those indicated above were produced at this time.

In the autumn I returned alone to Venice having resolved to establish this now firmly rooted passion upon some solid basis. I lived in the Casa Barbier. Angelo was still in the service of General de Horsey. But we often met at night in my rooms; and I gradually strove to persuade him that I was no mere light-o-love, but a man on whom he could rely – whose honour, though rooted in dishonour, might be trusted. I gave him a gondola and a good deal of money. He seemed to be greedy, and I was mortified by noticing that he spent his cash in what I thought a foolish way – on dress and trinkets and so forth. He told me something about his history: how he had served three years in the Genio at Venice, Ferrara and Verona. Released from the army, he came home to find his mother dead in the madhouse at S. Clemente, his elder brother Carlo dead of sorrow and a fever after three weeks' illness, his father prostrated with grief and ruined, and his only remaining brother Vittorio doing the work of a baker's boy. The more I got to know the man, the more I liked him. Yet there were almost insurmountable obstacles to be overcome. These arose mainly from the false position in which we found ourselves from the beginning. He not unnaturally classed me with those other men to whose caprices he had sold his beauty. He could not comprehend that I meant to be his friend, to serve and help him in all reasonable ways according to my power. Seeing me come and go on short flights, he felt convinced that one day or other my will would change and I should abandon him. A just instinct led him to calculate that our friendship, originating in my illicit appetite and his compliance, could not be expected to develop a sound and vigorous growth. The time must come, he reasoned, when this sickly plant would die and be forgotten. And then there was always between us the liaison of shame; for it is not to be supposed that I confined myself to sitting opposite the man and gazing into his fierce eyes of fiery opal. At the back of his mind the predominant thought, I fancy, was to this effect: 'Had I not better get what I can out of the strange Englishman, who talks so much about his intentions and his friendship, but whose actual grasp upon my life is so uncertain?' I really do not think that he was wrong. But it made my task very difficult.

I discovered that he was living with a girl by whom he had two boys. They were too poor to marry. I told him that it was his duty to make her an honest woman, not being at that time fully aware how frequent and how binding such connections are in Venice. However, the pecuniary assistance I gave him enabled the couple to set up house; and little by little I had the satisfaction of perceiving that he was not only gaining confidence in me but also beginning to love me as an honest well-wisher.

I need not describe in detail the several stages by which this liaison between myself and Angelo assumed its present form. At last he entered my service as gondolier at fixed wages, with a certain allowance of food and fuel. He took many journeys with me, and visited me at Davos. We grew to understand each other and to conceal nothing. Everything I learned about him made me forget the suspicions which had clouded the beginning of our acquaintance, and closed my eyes to the anomaly of a comradeship which retained so much of passion on my part and of indulgence on his. I found him manly in the truest sense, with the manliness of a soldier and warm soft heart of an exceptionally kindly nature – proud and sensitive, wayward as a child, ungrudging in his service, willing and good-tempered, though somewhat indolent at the same time and subject to explosions of passion. He is truthful and sincere, frank in telling me what he thinks wrong about my conduct, attentive to my wants, perfect in his manners and behaviour – due allowance made for his madcap temperament, hoarse voice and wild impulsive freedom.

I can now look back with satisfaction on this intimacy. Though it began in folly and crime, according to the constitution of society, it has benefited him and proved a source of comfort and instruction to myself. Had it not been for my abnormal desire, I could never have learned to know and appreciate a human being so far removed from me in position, education, national quality and physique. I long thought it hopeless to lift him into something like prosperity – really because it took both of us so long to gain confidence in the stability of our respective intentions and to understand each other's character. At last, by constant regard on my side to his interests, by loyalty and growing affection on his side for me, the end has been attained. His father and brother have profited; for the one now plies his trade in greater comfort, and the other has a situation in the P & O service, which I got for him, and which enables him to marry. And all this good, good for both Angelo and myself, has its tap-root in what at first was nothing better than a misdemeanour, punishable by the law and revolting to the majority of human beings. The situation is so anomalous that I still shudder when I think of it, knowing how impossible it is to bring forth good things out of evil, and how little I have done to eradicate my inborn insanity. Angelo's own theory about liaisons of this sort is that they do not signify, if they are monogamous and carefully protected by the prudence of both parties. Then they remain matters for the soul of each in sight of God – 'Our Lord above', as he says, pointing to the skies. On the other hand a man who goes from love to love – with Jack today and Tom tomorrow – sinks deep into the mire, loses respect, and ends in degradation. While discoursing on this topic, he instanced Marzials and Lord Ronald Gower.[3]

My belief is that the Venetians understand the link between Angelo and myself, but that they accept it after becoming convinced of its permanence and freedom from the vices of *volgivaga Venus* ['love that prowls at large'].[4]

They then say what has been put into monumental words by a man of the gondolier class: '*Quando viene il desiderio, none' è mai troppo*' ['When desire comes it is never excessive'].

In my connections of this sort with men – and they have been very numerous – I can say with truth that I always aimed at comradeship, and never treated my companion as a mere instrument of lust or pleasure. This has given a healthy tone to my feelings about masculine love, and it has also introduced an element of serious responsibility into the matter. I do not deny that I have taken occasional liberties with strangers – soldiers on the streets, sailors, folk who offered themselves in foreign cities, professional male prostitutes, and casual acquaintances. But these adventures gave me little pleasure, and left me with a strong disgust, except in the case of some good fellow who took the moment in the sense I did. To pay a man to go to bed with me, to get an hour's gratification out of him at such a price, and then never to see him again, was always abhorrent to my nature. I have tried the method, and have found that it yielded no satisfaction – less even than similar arrangements which I have made with women in brothels. The sexual relation between man and man seems to me less capable of being reduced to frank sensuality than the sexual relation between man and woman. An element of intimacy is demanded, out of which the sexual indulgence springs like a peculiar plant, which has its root in something real, which does no injury to either party, which leads to no result of fruitage in the flesh of either, and which therefore exists only as the sign on both sides of particular affection. When a young man whom I loved has become aware that I desired this pledge of comradeship, this satisfaction of my want, he never refused it, never showed that he disliked it. But I have not sought it, except in the occasional instances mentioned above, unless I was aware that the man knew I was a friend and meant to hold by him. At that point, he gave what I desired, as a token of friendliness. It cost him nothing, and he saw that I took pleasure in it. Without altering his own instincts and appetites for the female, it enlarged his experience and was, in many cases I think, not without its pleasure for himself. At all events it bloomed up, like a spontaneous flower, from the conditions of our intercourse as comrades.

This kind of thing seems to me innocuous and quite outside the region of immorality. I can also defend, on what appears to me sufficient grounds, a large amount of promiscuity. In the very nature of the sexual contact between two males there inheres an element of instability. No children come of the connection. There can be no marriage ceremonies, no marriage settlements, no married life in common. Therefore, the parties are left free, and the sexual flower of comradeship may spring afresh for each of them wherever favourable soil is found. Viewed in this way, viewed as the final expression of mutual love and liking, I see no harm to society or character in sensual enjoyment between man and man. Something is asked on one side, conceded on the other, which leaves both as it found them, and which binds neither except as it is a pledge of their affection. Vice only comes into the matter when the man who seeks allows himself to be the creature of mere lust; or when the man who gives does so for the sake of gain. It is the same as with wine. There is no evil in moderate indulgence. The dedication of the higher self to lust or drunkenness, the immersion of the personality in either pursuit, is ruinous.

Of course the responsibilities connected with this passion, in the way I understand them, tax a man's resources. In many cases he must be prepared to support his friend with money or with influence. In all cases he must be ready to yield him yeoman's service in the battle of life. But this is what we are supposed to do for friends. The mere fact that sexual connection has taken place does not alter the conditions. It certainly makes the friendship more personal, more intimate. Those, therefore, who invite this final flower to grow upon the soil of friendship cannot neglect its corresponding consequences. They are linked to the man whom they have loved, who has suffered them to love, or has corresponded to their love, in a way which introduces strict relations. I have hitherto found that this duty, correlative to the pleasure of absolute intimacy, becomes a means of binding the two men together firmly – if both are honest, and the duty is honourably discharged. It does not break their love. On the contrary, their love is cemented by the introduction into it of daily-life affairs.

An opponent might observe that all this comes to money in the long run. I do not know what does not come to money in the long run: women, horses, houses, do so. Besides, there is much which is not money whereby a friend can help a friend he loves.

Angelo is an episode, a very important episode, in the history of my life during the Davos period. Like Ariosto's epic, the poem of my existence has been made up of episodes, connected by slender threads with the main theme. This peculiarity in it is due to the abnormal nature of my desires, which never find the rest of perfect reciprocity.

I have nearly done the work of self-delineation. It remains to describe with a few brief touches what the tenour of our life has been here. We have lived as an united family, and I think my wife and children will combine in saying that I have played the part of husband and of father to them well. We have shared numerous pleasures of all sorts together, and have suffered one great sorrow in the long illness and death of my dear eldest daughter. My deepest cares and interests have always been for them; and it is only the thought of them that adds a pang to those passions on which I have dwelt so much, with a deliberate purpose, in this autobiography.

The leisure of the mountains has enabled me to do much work since I settled at Davos. In order that it should not appear that my intellectual activity has been diminished by other preoccupations, I will repeat, by way of catalogue, what I have published during the last twelve years.

History

Four volumes of the *Renaissance In Italy*
Italian Literature
Catholic Reaction

Poetry

Sonnets of Michelangelo and Campanella
Many Moods
New and Old
Animi Figuri
Poems and Translations (in preparation)

Descriptions of travel

Sketches and Studies in Italy
Our Life in the Swiss Highlands
Italian Byways

Biography

Shelley ('English Men of Letters' series)
Sidney ('English Men of Letters' series).
Life of Michelangelo Buonarroti
Ben Jonson ('English Worthies' series)

Criticism and translation

Wine Women and Song

Translation

Benvenuto Cellini
Count Carlo Gozzi

Articles for the Encyclopaedia Britannica

Machiavelli
Petrarch
The Renaissance
Tasso
Italian history, etc. etc.

English literature

Shakespeare's Predecessors in the Elizabethan Drama

Introductions

General introduction to the Mermaid Series
Heywood (Mermaid Series)
Tourneur and Webster (Mermaid Series)
Ben Jonson

Religio Medici (Camelot Classics)
The Decameron (unpublished)

Criticism

Twenty Essays, Speculative and Suggestive

Miscellaneous

This autobiography; *A Problem in Modern Ethics*; Scattered articles in the *Quarterly, Fortnightly, Cornhill, Macmillan, Pall Mall Gazette, Academy*, etc.

This, I submit, is a large amount of work to accomplish in fourteen years; for I may fairly carry the whole to the account of this period, seeing that, although the larger part of *Many Moods* and *New and Old*, together with some of the descriptive pieces in *Sketches and Studies*, were produced before I came to Davos, I have in manuscript at least as much belonging to my time at Davos.

So then, working steadily at what I take to be an average of six hours *per diem*, walking on the hills, sharing the occupations of my wife and daughters, enjoying the society of my peasant friends with a keen relish, I have passed this period in greater health upon the whole and with more serenity of mind than fell to my lot in earlier youth and manhood.

And yet I carry within me the seeds of what I know to be an incurable malady – not merely the disease of the lungs, which is always ready to reappear – but that more deeply rooted perversion of the sexual instincts (uncontrollable, ineradicable, amounting to monomania) to expose which in its relation to my whole nature has been the principal object of these memoirs.

It is a singular life history; and yet, for aught I know, it may be commoner than I imagine.* A town-bred boy, burdened with physical ailments, shy and sensitive, above the average in mental faculty, but ill-adapted to the ordinary course of English education. Emotion wakes in him; and just when the first faint stirrings of sex before the age of puberty are felt, he discerns the masterful attraction

---

*When I wrote the above, I had not yet read the autobiographies of *Urnings* printed in Casper-Liman's *Handbuch der Gerichtlichen Medicin*, in Ulrichs' 'Numa Humantius' various tracts, notably in *Memnon*, and in Prof. Krafft-Ebing's *Psychopathia Sexualis*. I have recently done so, and am now aware that my history is only one out of a thousand.

of the male. He feels it dimly and grotesquely at the commencement, then distinctly, overpoweringly, in dreams and waking fancies. It connects itself with the impressions he derives from art, from poetry, from nature. Remaining a timid, reserved, refined child, he goes to a great public school, is ailing there, incapable of joining his comrades in their games, inferior to the best of them in scholarship. His life passes like a turbid vision of the night. The vicious habits of the boys around him repel him with a keen repugnance, He is poisoned by discovering the secret of his headmaster. Plato's paiderastic dialogues bring a sudden revelation, and he devotes himself to the study of Greek love. All this while he forms himself surely, blindly, into a literary being with an absorbing passion for persons of his own sex. He falls in love shyly, purely, imaginatively, with a boy of little less than his own age. This leads to nothing but the torture of caressed emotion, the thrilling of some coarser chords which he resolutely masters. He goes to Oxford, begins to discover his mental force, dreams continually, carries off the usual academic prizes, but cares little for such success. At root he is love-laden, love-smitten, wounded. Suffering comes to him, through his own fault in part, but more through the malice of a treacherous friend. Determined to trample down his abnormal inclinations, he marries a woman for whom he feels the strongest admiration and the firmest friendship, but not the right quality of sexual passion. Soon afterwards he falls ill, and is pronounced consumptive. Incapable of following a profession, he spends years in seeking health, with his wife, with children growing up. At length, when he has reached the age of twenty-nine, he yields to the attraction of the male. And this is the strange point about the man, that now for the first time he attains to self-mastery and self-control. Contemporaneously with his first indulged passion, he begins to write books, and rapidly becomes an author of distinction. The indecision of the previous years is replaced by a firm volition and a consciousness of power. He can deal more effectively with men and women, is better company, learns to write with greater force. He seems to draw strength from the congenital malady which has now come to the surface. Upon the verge of fifty, this man is younger and wholesomer than when he went to Harrow at thirteen. He is easier to live with than when he married at twenty-four. He has to some extent surmounted his consumptive tendencies. He has made himself a name in literature. Altogether he is more of a man than when he repressed and pent within his soul those fatal and abnormal inclinations. Yet he belongs to a class abhorred by society and is, by English law, a criminal. What is the meaning, the lesson, the conclusion to be drawn from this biography?

NB: I am writing these passages in my study. At the window sits a young peasant, reading the old *Landbuch* (statutes) of Davos, by whose side I slept last night. Bewildering contradictions, tending to madness.

Few situations in life are more painful than this: that a man, gifted with strong intellectual capacity, and exercised in all the sleights of criticism, should sit down soberly to contemplate his own besetting vice. In pleasant moments, when instinct prevails over reason, when the broadway of sensual indulgence invites his footing, the man plucks primroses of frank untutored inclination. They have for him, then, only the fragrance of wayside flowers, blossoms upon the path of exquisite experience. But, when he comes to frigid reason's self again, when he tallies last night's deeds with today's knowledge of fact and moral ordinance, he awakes to the reality of a perpetual discord between spontaneous appetite and acquired respect for social law. By the light of his clear brain he condemns the natural action of his appetite; and what in moments of self-abandonment to impulse appeared a beauteous angel, stands revealed before him as a devil abhorred by the society he clings to. The agony of this struggle between self-yielding to desire and love, and self-scourging by a trained discipline of analytic reflection, breaks his nerve. The only exit for a soul thus plagued is suicide. Two factors, equally unconquerable, flesh and the reason, animal joy in living and mental perception that life is a duty, war in the wretched victim of their equipoise. While he obeys the flesh, he is conscious of no wrongdoing. When he awakes from the hypnotism of the flesh, he sees his own misdoing not in the glass of truth to his nature, but in the mirror of convention. He would fain have less of sense or less of intellect. Why was he not born a savage or a normal citizen? The quarrel drives him into blowing his brains out, or into idiocy.

Appendix One

Case XVII in *Sexual Inversion* by Havelock Ellis (1897)[1]

A was the son of a physician. Father's family robust, vigorous, healthy and prolific. They had been Puritans since the middle of 16th century. Mother's family tainted with both insanity and phthisis. A's maternal grandmother and one aunt died of phthisis. The two eldest children of A's parents were girls: one of these died of phthisis at the age of 42. Next came male twins, born dead. Next a boy, who died of hydrocephalic inflammation at the age of three to four. A was born in 1840, and had a sickly childhood, suffering from night-terrors, somnambulism, excessive shyness, religious disquietude. The last of the family was a girl, who has grown up into a healthy and intellectually robust woman.

A has communicated these facts concerning the development of his sexual instincts.

(1)   In early childhood, and up to the age of 13 he had frequent opportunities of closely inspecting the genital organs of both boys and girls, his playfellows. The smell of the female parts affected him disagreeably. The sight of the male organ did not arouse any particular sensation. He is, however, of opinion that, living with sisters, he felt more curious about his own sex as being more remote from him. He showed no effeminacy in his preference for games or work.

(2)   About the age of 8, if not before, he became subject to singular half-waking dreams. He fancied himself seated on the floor among several adult and naked sailors, whose genitals and buttocks he contemplated and handled with relish. He called himself the 'dirty pig' of these men, and felt that they were in some way his masters, ordering him to do uncleanly services to their bodies. He cannot remember ever having seen a naked man at that time; and nothing in his memory explains why the men of his dreams were supposed to be sailors.

(3)   At the same period, his attention was directed to his own penis. His

284

nurse, out walking one day, said to him, 'When little boys grow up, their p's fall off.' The nursery-maid sniggered. He felt that there must be something peculiar about the penis. He suffered from irritability of the prepuce; and the nurse powdered it before he went to sleep. There was no transition thence to onanism.

(4) At the same period, he casually heard that a man used to come and expose his person before the window of a room where the maids sat. This troubled him vaguely.

(5) Between the age of 8 and 11 he twice took the penis of a cousin into his mouth in the morning, after they had slept together; the feeling of the penis pleased him.

(6) When sleeping with another cousin, they used to lie with hands outstretched to cover each other's *penes* or *nates*. A preferred the *nates*, but his cousin the *penes*. Neither cousin, just mentioned, was homosexual; and there was no attempt at mutual masturbation.

(7) He was in the habit of playing with five male cousins. One of these boys was unpopular with the others, and they invented a method of punishing him for supposed offences. They sat round the room on chairs together, each with his penis exposed. The boy went round on his knees and took each penis into his mouth in turn. This was supposed to humiliate him. It did not lead to masturbation.

(8) He accidentally observed a boy who sat next him in school, playing with his penis and caressing it. This gave him a powerful uneasy sensation.

With regard to all these points, A observes that none of the other boys with whom he was connected at that period, and who were exposed to precisely the same influences, became homosexual. He also remarks that most boys thrown together will have the fact of the penis brought frequently before their notice.

(9) One of the very first events in his life which he can recall is the following. A male cousin of about 22 was reclining on an armchair, with legs spread out. A jumped upon his lap, and felt his hand fall upon a soft yielding thing in the young man's trousers. A perceived that his cousin shrank together with pain, and wondered what this meant.

(10) A was mentally precocious. When he began to read books, he felt particularly attracted to certain male characters: the Adonis of Shakespeare's poems (he wished he had been Venus), Anzoleto in George Sand's *Consuelo*,[2] Hermes in Homer. He was very curious to know why the Emperors kept boys as well as girls in their seraglios, and what the male gods did with the youths they loved.

(11)   While at public school, he never practised onanism with other boys, though they often tempted him, and he frequently saw the act in process. It inspired him with a disagreeable sense of indecency. Still in his 15th year, puberty commenced with nocturnal pollutions and occasional masturbation. His thoughts were not directed to males while masturbating, nor to females. A spoke to his father about these signs of puberty; and on his father's recommendation, he entirely abandoned onanism.

Footnote. He reckons that he may have practised self-abuse about once a week during a period of from six to seven months.

(12)   The nocturnal pollutions became very frequent and exhausting. They were medically treated by tonics – quinine and strychnine. A thinks this treatment exasperated his neurosis. All this while, no kind of sexual feeling for girls made itself felt. With the exception of a comradely liking for his younger sister and her Swiss governess, he was perfectly indifferent to them. He could not understand what his school fellows found in women, or the stories they told about wantonness and the delights of coitus.

(13)   His old dreams about the sailors disappeared. But now he enjoyed visions of beautiful young men and exquisite Greek statues. Occasionally he saw in sleep the erect organs of powerful grooms or peasants. The gross visions offended his taste and hurt him; he took a strange poetic pleasure in the ideal forms. But the seminal losses which attended both kinds, were a perpetual source of misery to him. There is no doubt that at this time, i.e. between the 15th and 17th years, a homosexual diathesis had become established in A.

(14)   It was in his 18th year that an event which A regards as decisive in his development occurred. He read the *Phaedrus* and *Symposium* of Plato. A new world opened, and he felt that his own nature had been revealed. Next year he formed a passionate but pure friendship with a boy of 15. Personal contact with the boy caused erections, extreme agitation, and aching pleasure: not ejaculation however. Through 4 years of intimacy A never saw him naked, or touched him pruriently. Only twice he kissed him. A says that those two kisses were the most perfect joys he ever felt.

(15)   A's father became seriously anxious both about his health and reputation. He warned him of the social and legal dangers attending his temperament. Yet he did not encourage A to try coitus with women. A's own sense of danger would, he thinks, have made this method successful: at least, the bait of intercourse with females would have lessened his neurosis and diverted his mind to some extent from homosexual thoughts.

(16)   Now opened a period of great pain and anxiety for A. It is true that at the University he made very brilliant studies, and won for himself a distinguished reputation. As poet and prose-writer he was already known in

his 22nd year. Still his neurasthenia increased. He suffered from insomnia, obscure cerebral discomfort, stammering, chronic conjunctivitis, inability to concentrate attention, and dejection. It must be added that, when he was 25, a chronic disease of the lungs declared itself, which forced him to winter out of England.

(17) Meanwhile A's homosexual emotions strengthened and assumed a more sensual aspect. Yet he abstained from indulging them, as also from onanism. Fear of infection prevented him from seeking relief in ordinary coitus. Having no passion for women, it was easy to avoid them. And yet they inspired him with no exact horror. He used to dream of finding an exit from his painful situation by cohabitation with some coarse, boyish girl of the people. But his dread of syphilis stood in the way.

(18) A now felt that he must conquer himself by efforts of will and by persistent direction of his thoughts to heterosexual images. He sought the society of distinguished women. Once he coaxed up a romantic affection for a Bernese maiden. But this came to nothing, probably because the girl felt a want of absolute passion in A's wooing.

(19) He was now strongly advised to marry by his father and other physicians. He did so when he was exactly 24 years and 1 month old. Then he found that he was potent. But to his disappointment he also found that he only cohabited with his wife *faute de mieux*. He still dreamed of men, desired them, even began to desire soldiers. He begat in all 4 children, females. His wife, the member of a noble family, disliked sexual connection and hated pregnancy. This was a great misfortune for A. His wife's temperament led to long intervals of separation *a toro*. During those months, this physical, mental and moral discomfort was acute. At last, unable to bear it any longer, he indulged his passion with a young man of 19. This took place when he was 30 years of age. Soon afterwards he wholly abandoned matrimonial connections. He did this with the full approval of his wife, to whom the step brought relief. The reason assigned was that his pulmonary disease made slow but sure advances, rendering the further procreation of children morally wrong.

(20) When A had once begun to indulge his inborn homosexual instincts, he rapidly recovered his health. The neurotic disturbances subsided; the phthisis – which had progressed as far as profuse hemorrhage and formation of cavity – was arrested. By the age of 50, that is during the next 20 years, he made himself one of the leaders of English literature.

(21) A has not informed me what form of homosexual intercourse he practises. He is certainly not simply passive and shows no sign of *effeminatio*. He likes sound and vigorous young men of a lower rank from the

age of 20 to 25. I gather from his conversation that the mode of pleasure is indifferent to his tastes.

(22)   A believes firmly that his homosexual appetite was inborn and developed in exactly the same way and by the same exciting causes as the heterosexual appetite in normal persons. He is persuaded that, having in boyhood frequented the society of boys and girls alike, he leaned toward the suggestions of the male because there was in him a congenital bias of sex in that direction. He has no moral sense of doing wrong, and is quite certain that he suffers or benefits in health of mind and body according as he abstains from or indulges in moderate homosexual pleasure. He feels the intolerable injustice of his social position, and considers the criminal codes of modern nations, in so far as they touch his case, to be iniquitous. As an artist and man of letters he regrets the fate which has forced him to conceal his true emotions, and thereby to lose the most genial channels of self-expression.

Appendix Two

Extract from a letter to H. F. Brown

H.F.B. Davos re Autobiography Dec. 29. 91

It [the autobiography] was so passionately, unconventionally set on paper. Yet I think it a very singular book – perhaps unique, nay certainly unique, in the disclosure of a type of man who has not yet been classified. I am anxious therefore that this document should not perish. It is doubtful when or whether anyone who has shown so much to the world on ordinary ways as I have done, will be found to speak so frankly about his inner self. I want to save it from destruction after my death, and yet to reserve its publication for a period when it will not be injurious to my family. I do not just now know how to meet the difficulty. And when you come here, I should like to discuss it. You will inherit my mss. if you survive me. But you take them freely, to deal with them as you like, under my will. I have sketched my wish out that this autobiography should not be destroyed. Still, I see the necessity for caution in its publication. Give the matter a thought. If I could do so, I should like to except it as a thing apart, together with other documents from my general literary bequest; so as to make no friend, or person, responsible for the matter, to which I attach a particular value apart from life's relations. . . .

    God bless you.

           J.A.S.

Appendix Three

Symonds's quarrel with Rutson

This is the history of the Rutson affair.

I was abroad with him in the autumn of 1863. He then at Leipzig told me he was desirous of marrying my sister Charlotte. Again at Rome soon after Xmas in that year on the eve of his leaving for England he repeated this desire with energy, so as to make me think that he really wished to marry her but that he prudently sought some further acquaintance with her. He talked much about the solidity which this step would add to *our* friendship.

Just before I met Rutson in Germany in 1863 I made acquaintance with the Norths in Switzerland, at Mürren. There I made up my mind that Catherine was the only woman whom I should ever care to marry; and I wrote to my sister to tell her that she had narrowly escaped having a sister-in-law brought home: I have this letter.

After Rutson left Rome in January 1864 he met Catherine with the Ewarts and went twice to the play with her and met her once at dinner at Mrs Brassey's. I returned from Italy in April 1864 and in May went to live in the same house with Rutson in London. I then told him that if he was still anxious of seeing more of Charlotte with a view to marriage, I should have to tell my father, which I did. Rutson did not much like this at first; but he only objected to it because it seemed to make his views too definite.

Both my father and I felt, and told him, that we would rather have him than any other man for my sister's husband. But my father called in question the health of Rutson's family. He has two mad uncles; his mother is strange; his elder brother is so deficient in intellect as to have made his father unwilling to have him for his heir; two of his cousins are odd. On deliberation my father decided that it would not be prudent for the marriage to take place. Rutson then insisted and showed the utmost eagerness to have it prosecuted. My father being anxious to strain a point in favour of a man for whom he had so great a regard, then said that we might take the opinion of the chief doctors in London. We did so and went to several, stating the case. They all took my father's view. Rutson with great reluctance and much sense of the hardness of my father, was thus obliged to relinquish his plan.

This took place in May. I became very ill about that period. In the midst of my illness I told Rutson that I had seen Catherine North in Switzerland and thought that I should like to marry her. He said that he had met her and thought her very nice; but not the least suspicion crossed my mind that he cared for her. I asked whether his cousin Mary Ewart would give me an introduction to them; for, though the Norths had asked me to come and see them in London, I hardly liked to act upon this general invitation. He said Mary would certainly be glad to do so.

I went to dinner at the Norths'; and called after it one Sunday afternoon, when I found Calene [Catherine?] and looked at her drawings and had a long talk with her. That same evening I met Rutson and walked in Richmond Park with him, and told him how much I was getting to like Catherine. Something in his look or manner seemed to me odd; and I turned round and said, 'Why, you do not care for her, do you? Because we had better understand ourselves.' He at once said, no, no! He had hardly seen her; he did not care for her. And I remember thinking it had been half ungenerous and indelicate of me to have this momentary suspicion, seeing that he had professed himself so fond of my sister and had been seeking to be accepted as her suitor by my father. I explained to myself the sudden thought by the natural suspiciousness of a lover.

Rutson showed the greatest interest in my courtship; and I am absolutely certain that whatever he may then have said, he never said anything which reached my intelligence at all implying that he loved Catherine. Had it been so, had he put anything like a sacrifice before me, I was in a humour then to do anything rather than *accept* his sacrifice. I should have told him clearly that a man ought not to make, far less to accept, such sacrifices; but that two friends ought to run fair in such a race. Yet there was no appearance of his making a sacrifice. He had hardly seen Catherine. I had seen her first and had prosecuted her acquaintance while he remained quite idle about her; and while he was professing a love for my sister which induced him to go about to all these doctors and to press my father to accept him as a suitor.

I went abroad and soon was engaged to Catherine. Rutson wrote me constant kind letters full of the most warm affection. I supposed all this while that he was expressing his love and care for me, and felt very grateful.

Until one day at Poschiavo after our engagement, on 26 August, a combination of circumstances – my own gloomy temper, Mr North's warnings, Catherine's irritability, and a dread of the fixed state of marriage – made me satirical and vicious. His rose-coloured letters flowed in, and I wrote him a bitter jaundiced one which ought never to have gone. For this letter, which he kept and sent to my father, I gave him afterwards the fullest apology I could. I owed him an apology for the terms in which I spoke of his friendship for me – but for nothing else. If he disliked any other parts of the letter, they still did not wrong *him*, however much they might have been unworthy of *me*.

We came home and often saw Rutson. But in the spring of 1865 he began to tell me he was very ill, to hint at uneasiness about me and my state of mind; and at last said that I had accepted a sacrifice from him before my marriage, that he had relinquished Catherine to me, and that I was in some way ungrateful. The thing appeared to me absolutely monstrous – mad – most disgusting. I told him (i) that I had never known of any sacrifice, (ii) that such a sacrifice, if made, ought never to have been mentioned, (iii) that he could not have made such a sacrifice, since he hardly knew C. and had no right to her as he was professing an attachment to my sister. He answered in these extraordinary words: 'My love for your sister was a calculation, for C. an inspiration.' I did not know how to treat him, but I suspected his sanity. He still leanèd on me very much and he was dreadfully ill.

About this time he asked me to go to his father and tell him he wanted money to marry upon or go into the house. I did not know his family; but I offered to go at once to Newby Wiske and see him. R. then said his mother could not have visitors in the house – I must write to his sister. I said I would rather speak than write. He urged me to write, and I said I would do so as he wished it. I wrote to his sister and told her how ill I thought he was, how much he needed distraction and the like. I sent the letter. He rushed off, unknown to me, to his home; found his sister before she got the letter, asked her for it, received it sealed, and then, instead of destroying it at once, *read* it and returned in a fury abusing me for my 'damnable dishonourable' letter.

I pacified him. I began to think him quite deluded. His cousin Mary Ewart wrote to tell me she believed his notion about C. a pure hallucination – that she had seen him much in the summer of 1863 and had noticed none of it. He continued to lean on me and I did all I could to help him. We used to talk for five or six hours a day about the past, about his wretchedness etc. He used to beg me and C. to help him to find a wife. But at the same time he would now and then get into violent states of anger and pain and make me over and over again express my sorrow for the two offensive letters: I always retracted the whole of the Poschiavo letter and expressed my *sorrow* that the letter to his sister had been written; but I could not say that I had been guilty of anything but want of tact in the manner of writing it, while I told him that the way in which he had got possession of it and the use he had made of it was (at least) most unjustifiable.

About this time, I think it was, R. wished to correspond with Catherine and to enter into a 'sisterly' relation with her. He used this phrase, and again mentioned the *sacrifice* he supposed himself to have made as giving him some right to lean on her. I knew what a source of pain and anxiety he had been to me. And for this reason, and because he wounded my taste, and because I thought that such an intimacy would be bad for us all three and be (after his declarations) compromising to me, I would not allow it. I then told C. the *whole*. She was very much disgusted and of her own accord repudiated the notion of any special intimacy being allowed.

In the autumn of 1865 he went abroad. After his return the old distressing scenes recommenced. We constantly met and raked up the whole matter but to no effect. I could not and would not lie that I had accepted a sacrifice.

Next he appealed to my father who went into the whole matter and could not find me wrong in it, but believed R. to be deluded. R. broke with him upon this.

I was much abroad in the spring of 1866. When I came back the same sort of correspondences continued, but I have forgotten their coherence. I only remember of this period that I made several declarations of my willingness to believe in his statement that he had *intended* to express to me his regard for C. in 1864 and that it was owing to my own stupidity that it had not reached my intelligence; but I could not say I had ever guessed it till he told me of it in the spring of 1865.

In that autumn he abused my father to me so that I nearly broke with him. We, however, came to terms. His rancour against my father was such that when *his* father died and mine wrote to condole he never noticed the letter.

The correspondence dropped now; but it began again in the spring and summer of 1867, when C. and I saw him for the last time in July (I think) and told him, both of us, *for the first time severely* how selfish and absurd we thought his conduct had been. C. attributed much of my illness (both head and lungs) to my over-attention to his wearying communications.

In this statement I have hitherto confined myself, as far as possible, to a narrative of events. I have a few things to say now about my own feeling. Rutson sought my friendship; I did not seek his. He regarded me with admiration, and credited me with a nobleness of character of which he had but small means of judging. He tried to do whatever I did, to like my likings etc: so much so that Green once said, 'R. likes you too much – it is all nonsense his taking to these aesthetics – he does no good with them and they only spoil him.' He helped me very much in a disagreeable affair I had at Magdalen, and I have always been most grateful to him for this.

This attachment to me was always foremost in his speech and in my thought, so that when he seemed anxious to marry my sister, it had the appearance of an extension from me to her of lively regard. And when he talked about his love for C. after my marriage I regarded this as another transference of his affection for me to an object which I had set my heart on. It was *thus* that I explained his hallucination; and Mary Ewart arrived at the same explanation by her own observation. It was this affection that made him seek to find his wife through me *after* my marriage.

In the early stages of this matter I suffered appallingly from his suffering. It seemed like a hideous dream – this story of a sacrifice, this burden of a life devoted to me, thrust upon me. The tragedy cast a horrible light on my own marriage. It required all my force to remind myself that he was deluded, that there had been no such crime. At times I almost felt, under the smart of his accusations and despairs, as if I wished I had gone to the dogs instead of being married.

My respect for his character made me attribute much weight to what were mere ravings. I scrutinized my own feelings. I tested my own memory. I probed my conscience to see if there were any self-deception on my part. But I always found the same report – that I had entered simply, honourably and straightforwardly into my marriage – that I had accepted no sacrifice and incurred no debt of gratitude to R. except such a debt as comes from great love and great exertion to help me when I was in trouble at college. This debt I tried to pay by giving him my time and attention and care, by exposing my health in every way for his sake, by restraining my temper, by forgetting his insulting words spoken in anger, by bearing with him in short as I should have borne with no one else.

I have written all this trusting to my memory and with the full persuasion that the whole of it is substantially correct. I have in no place or way altered, hidden or slurred over anything.

J. A. Symonds
Hastings
November 1868

Appendix Four

Norman's Letter to Symonds

6 Northcote Road
Clifton
26 November 1886

My dear Johnnie,

Your question is not I think a very easy one to answer – chiefly because people do not talk about their experiences in this line much. I think one may say without fear or contradiction that a very large proportion of the 'unnatural vice' which they say is so prevalent in public schools has nothing whatever to do with the reading of the classics – and I should doubt much whether ever any one at school was first put upon the track of it by his classical studies. – for (1) boys have been initiated into the mysteries of παιδεραστία [homosexual love] unofficially long before their reading of the classics has any effect on their conduct, some purely, some impurely – 'spooning' to use a school boy term comes so naturally to a large number of boys, and the spooning may be quite harmless, innocent of any desire tending to ὕβρις [pride] or of course may be quite animal and find its only satisfaction in ὕβρις, in one form or another. I should much doubt whether Lyttleton[3] is right in thinking that *all* 'dual vice' comes from 'solitary vice' – but I am quite sure that if you had a large boarding school compound of young Jesus Christs even, spooning would not be unknown. E.g., T. E. Brown has told me that he had a passion for a boyfriend, and this was absolutely pure, and it seems inconceivable that T. E. B. was ever guilty of the 'solitary vice' or that his juices were ever in anything but a thoroughly hearty and healthy condition. (2) The classics that the boys read at school are not as a rule those that contain allusions to παιδεραστία. They read the *Iliad* of course but it does not I think occur to them that there was anything between Achilles and Patroclus, nor I think do they attach much meaning to the friendships of Orestes and Pylades, Theseus and Pirithous and co. Theocritus they read, but the idylls they read are not the paiderastic ones, and the edition they are provided with is probably expurgated. They never read as school subjects at all events the *Phaedrus* and *Symposium* – and I much doubt whether they read them as πάρεργα [hobbies, sidelines] – a very very few only do so, if any. I *can* tell you of a single instance that has come within my own experience of a boy who got a twist that way. He went up from us as a scholar to Balliol, and before he had been long at Oxford he declared himself a paederast, and went so far as to publish or at all events write and get printed an ''Απολογία περὶ παιδεραστίας' ['an apologia for homosexual love'] – which contained a defence of the habit, i.e. of the ideal παιδεραστία – the purely spiritual views. I do not think that he for a moment contemplated any such co-habitation as the Greeks permitted themselves under certain conditions – it was all up in the clouds as the love of the beautiful. This youth was sent down from Balliol, and sent on a voyage round the world, much as one sends an invalid round the world to get rid of a disease. This boy was 'hurt'.

My own idea, founded more or less on experience, is that it is not the scholars as a rule who take to spooning and sometimes debauching beautiful choirboys etc. but far more fleshly people. Those who have really studied Greek literature are so far from being injured in any way, rather kept straight and narrow on the ideal lines – they appreciate the ugliness of ὕβρις.

The end of all this is that I do not believe the evils Lyttleton combats are in any way due to a study of the classics. The study of the classics may give a sanction to some few for παιδεραστία but does not put them upon vices – the love of boys for boys is I believe inevitable in our public schools to which we point as our national glory – and not only is it inevitable, but I would go so far as to say it is desirable if it can be kept in an absolutely pure region. The beastly form of it is I am afraid also almost inevitable – the best safeguards against it are a well-filled routine of work and play – hard play, tiring and exciting. I don't believe you'll touch the thing by religion – neither do I think you'll do much by telling boys at a certain age all about the reproductive organs etc. You'll rouse curiosity in more than you will allay it in. I dare say if you get them thoroughly well frightened as to the effects on their bodily health, you might do much that way – a thorough knowledge of the laws of health would be very advantageous, but I don't see how you are to get it. The pedagogue as we know him is not very well qualified to give it.

I don't know whether I have given you anything in answer to your questions. I have been obliged to write in great haste and at odd moments. My own case in this matter was not perhaps an isolated one. Corrupted at a very early age by a Harrow eleven boy who came over to Ashborne to play in a cricket match, and invited to his house by him where I stayed two or three days, nights were more to the point, and by him introduced to a sense of what one was made of, for years I never could throw off a perfect lust for being spooned. I regarded every big boy as a possible admirer – and when I got a bit older myself, I regarded every small boy as a possible spoon. A most pandemic state. The combined influence of Percival and yourself did something to cure me of this – but here you see is another case where the paiderastic instinct (if it can be so far dignified as to be called paiderastic) was not in any way caused by the reading of Gk lit., but was rather chastened and directed by a literary education. I dare say I have told you all this before, but it seems to me a case which Lyttleton might be glad to get hold of, if he could, – but God forbid he ever should – and then mangle many other poor little boys who are got hold of in this way by some great lustful beast, fat, soft and sleeky. He was a very good cricketer . . . .

I must write no more now. Goodbye. Of course all this is very private. I should like one of the pamphlets, unless you dislike letting one out of your hands. What an enterprising compositor![4] Will he proclaim you for it?

Yours aff.
                    Norman Moor

References

1. Childhood, 1840–51, 7 Berkeley Square, Bristol

1. This seems to have been an earlier version of *Daily Food – A text and a verse for every day in the year* (The Religious Tract Society, London, 1884).
2. 'Quires and places where they sing', from the Rubric after the Third Collect, *Book of Common Prayer*.
3. Lady Lucie Duff Gordon (1821–69). Her most frequently published work was *Mary Schweidler, the Amber Witch* (translated from the German, 1844). *The Story Without an End* is by Sarah Austin from the German of Friedrich Wilhelm Carové (1789–1852) and was first issued in London in 1834.
4. Daniel Maclise (1806–70) illustrated many works.
5. Symonds must be confusing Cruikshank with John Leech's famous illustration of Marley's ghost.
6. Chambers's *Cyclopoedia or an Universal Dictionary of Arts and Sciences* (first edition 1728).
7. Paul Johann Anselm Feuerbach (1775–1833) was famous for his work in criminal law reform. Possibly the work referred to is *Merkwürdige Criminalfälle*, 1808–11 (*Remarkable Criminal Cases*, translated by Lucie Duff Gordon, 1846).
8. Emily Taylor, *The Boy and the Birds* (London, 1835), illustrated by Landseer.
9. The Plymouth Brethren were a Christian fellowship which disregarded denominational barriers in order to recapture the simplicity of the Apostolic Church. They received their name from Plymouth, England, where their first congregation was held in 1831.
10. Chadband was the fat and hypocritical minister in Dickens's *Bleak House*, published in monthly numbers, 1852–3.
11. Judges IV, V; Acts IX 36.
12. 2 Kings II 5–15.

13. George Müller who preached at Bethesda was joint pastor at Bethesda Chapel, the leader of the Open Brethren Church (a division of the Plymouth Brethren).

14. Samuel Prout (1783–1852), English water colourist, whose drawings first familiarized Ruskin with French architecture.

15. John Sterling (1806–44), friend of Carlyle; founder of the literary group, the Sterling Club.

16. John Thomas Abdy (1822–99) became Regius Professor of Civil Law in 1854. Symonds is mistaken: in 1889 Abdy was Professor of Civil Law at Gresham College. ·

17. Symonds was distantly related to Byron through his mother's side of the family. His grandfather's sister married Richard Byron, Rear Admiral in the Royal Navy, who was grandson to the fourth Lord Byron and first cousin to the poet's father.

18. Mortmain Act: in law the generic term used to describe various statutes imposing restrictions upon the donation of property by will to churches or charitable institutions.

19. Francis Galton (1822–1911), celebrated author of *Hereditary Genius, its Laws and Consequences* (1869).

20. Bastille Day dinners were established as an annual event by radical Dissenters during the French Revolution. See Claire Tomalin, *The Life and Death of Mary Wollstonecraft* (Harcourt Brace Jovanovich, New York and London, 1974), page 93. This is apparently the first such event.

21. Rammohun Roy (1774–1833), religious leader and social reformer, sometimes called the father of modern India, died in Bristol.

22. Non-jurors were the beneficed clergy who refused in 1669 to take the oath of allegiance to William and Mary.

23. William Leonard Addington Sidmouth (1794–1864).

24.
> He who bends to himself a Joy
> Doth the winged life destroy;
> But he who kisses the Joy as it flies
> Lives in Eternity's sunrise.
>
> (William Blake, *Gnomic Verses*, xvii.1)

25. The Clarenceux King of Arms is one of the three Kings of Arms who exercise supreme authority in English heraldry.

26. Ovid, *Metamorphoses* II. 137. The advice (unheeded) from the Sungod to his son Phaethon before the latter set out on his fateful journey across the heavens in his father's chariot.

27. Probably *A Practical Introduction to Latin Prose Composition* by Thomas Kerchever Arnold, London, 1839.

28. Pindar, *Pythian* VIII 95–6; one of the more famous examples of Greek pessimism.

2. Containing material which none but students of psychology and ethics need peruse

1. Paul Moreau, *Des aberrations du sens genetique* (Paris, 1887). B. Tarnowsky, *Die krankhaften Erscheinungen de Geschlechtssinnes* (1887). Richard von Krafft-Ebing, *Psychopathia sexualis* (1886).
2. Carl Heinrich Ulrichs (1825–95). His specialties were jurisprudence and theology but under the pseudonym 'Numo Numantius' he wrote pamphlets on homosexuality.
3. The 'neuropathic grandmother'. According to Steven Marcus, 'The word neuropathic was a generic term of the period and referred to anyone who had or had had a psychiatric illness. At the time they thought all such illnesses were literally located in the nerves (i.e. the neurons, etc.) – hence the term neuropathic. It covered everything from hysterics to neurasthenia to psychotic states. In other words, it was a "scientific" term covering vast areas of ignorance, as so many medical terms continue to do.'
4. Cesare Lombroso (1836–1906), Italian physician and criminologist who pioneered efforts towards rehabilitation of criminals. Lombroso's *Man of Genius* (1891) supported Moreau's contention that genius is essentially a neurosis.
5. John Ferbuson Nisbit (1851–99). In *Insanity of Genius* (1891) he argues that genius and insanity are but different phases of a morbid susceptibility or a want of balance in the cerebro-spinal system.

3. First period of boyhood, 1851–4, Clifton Hill House

1. 'Miss Kilmansegg and Her Precious Leg, a Golden Legend', a tragi-comic poem by Thomas Hood was published in the *New Monthly Magazine* (1841–3).
2. 'The unimaginable touch of time'; Wordsworth, *Ecclesiastical Sonnets*, III. xxviv 'Mutability'. 'From High to Low'.
3. The Tinnevelly Station is an important missionary station in southern Madras, India.
4. William Warburton, *Divine Legation of Moses Demonstrated*, 2 volumes (1737–41).
5. Homer, *Iliad* xxiv. 347–8. The context is of the god Hermes, disguised as a youth, coming to meet King Priam on his way to reclaim from Achilles the body of Hector.
6. Andromache, wife of Hector, mother of Astyanax who had been killed by the Greeks.
7. Euripides, *Hippolytos* 612.
8. Apollo was forced to serve as Admetus' herdsman after angering Zeus by killing the Cyclops. Admetus treated him kindly and when Admetus was later in trouble Apollo tried to help him.

9. Praxiteles, Athenian mid-fourth-century sculptor. Symonds is quoting from his poem 'The Genius of the Vatican' in *Many Moods*.
10. Hebe, daughter of Zeus and Hera, and wife of Heracles, was renowned for her beauty.
11. *Apoxyomenos* is a statue of an athlete scraping himself with the strigil, by the fourth-century sculptor Lysippus (Vatican Museum).
12. Raffaelo Sanzio (1483–1520), painter; John Flaxman (1755–1826), English sculptor; Friedrich August Moritz Retzsche (1779–1857), German engraver.
13. Carlo Lasinio (1759–1838), printer and engraver, curator of Campo Santo at Pisa, published *Pitture e affresco del C. S. di Pisa* (1810).

    Sir William Hamilton (1730–1803), the diplomat and archaeologist, while envoy extraordinary at Naples purchased a remarkable collection of Greek vases belonging to the Porcinari family. He sold it to the British Museum in 1772.

    In 1816 Ferdinand I donated his collection of antiquities to the Museo Borbonico in Naples. In 1860 it became the property of the Italian state and was renamed the Museo Nationale.

    The Society of Dilettanti was founded in 1732 as a dining club for dissolute grand-tourists. Within a hundred years the society had completely transformed the study of Greek antiquities. It published a number of finely illustrated works. (See L. Cust and S. Colvin, *History of the Society of Dilettanti*, London, 1898, and J. Mordaunt Crook, *The Greek Revival*, London, 1872.)
14. Robert MacPherson (1811–72). Originally a surgeon in Edinburgh, he settled in Rome where in the early 1850s he turned to photography and became the leading architectural photographer in Italy. The reference is to Signorelli's frescoes in the Duomo (see Helmut Gernsheim, *History of Photography*, page 283 and plates 157, 159).
15. Richard Duppa (1779–1831), *A Selection of Twelve Heads from the Last Judgment of Michael Angelo* (1801).
16. Paolo Toschi (1788–1854). In 1837 Toschi was commissioned to carry out the reproduction of Correggio's (and Parmiagianino's) injured frescoes in the churches of San Giovanni Evangelista and the Madonna della Steccata at Parma, in watercolour and engraving. The results were published in forty-eight plates (see Bryan's *Dictionary of Painters*).
17. Colgnaghi Company, the print publishers and print sellers, was founded in 1790 and is still in existence as art dealers in London.
18. The painting of Symonds by Stanhouse Vigor is now in the possession of Bristol University. Sidbury Manor was the home of Charles Cave, Symonds's brother-in-law.
19. Frederick Maurice (1805–92) was a renowned Christian socialist.
    Frederic Myers (1811–51) was curate of St John's Parish, Keswick,

from 1838 until his death. See Bernard M. G. Reardon, *From Coleridge to Gore: A Century of Religious Thought in Britain* (London, 1971), pages 216–19.

Lord Lansdowne (1816–66) was Home Secretary 1827–8. He remained in the Cabinet without office until 1858.

The others were: Henry Hallam (1777–1859), historian; Benjamin Jowett (1817–93), classical scholar, liberal theologian, Master of Balliol College; Thomas Spring-Rice Monteagle, first Baron (1770–1866); James Daird Forbes (1809–68), man of science, in 1859 appointed principal of United College, St Andrew's; Henry Austin Bruce Aberdare, first Baron (1815–95); Lady Dufferin (1807–67), one of the daughters of Thomas Sheridan; Very Rev. Gilbert Eliot, Dean of Bristol 1850–91; Sir Edward Strachey, husband of Symonds's sister Maribella.

Alfred John Carpenter (1825–92) was elected Liberal MP for North Bristol in 1886. Sir William Montagu Scott McMurdo (1819–94) was a general.

4. Second period of boyhood, 1854–8, Harrow on the Hill

1. A form or class in the lower part of the school. The term 'Shell' originated at Westminster School in the eighteenth century where a form of younger boys used to be taught in an alcove which had a shell-shaped roof.
2. William Mure, *A Critical history of the language and literature of antient Greece*, 5 volumes (1850–7).
3. Henry Yates Thompson later became proprietor of the *Pall Mall Gazette*.
4. Alfred Pretor later edited classical works. He died in 1908.
5. A reference to the debilitating effect that the luxury of Capua had on Hannibal's troops over the winter of 216–5 BC (see Livy 23. 18; 23–54.)
6. Gustavus Bosanquet (1840–1932) became a clergyman after leaving Cambridge.
7. Simonides – Greek patronymic (cf. Heraclides, son of Heracles).
8. Nones and complines are two of the traditional offices of the Church, revived by the High Church group in the nineteenth century.

5. Painful circumstances connected with the last year of my life at Harrow

1. Juvenal II. 10 – from a bitter satire upon homosexual behaviour. the full quotation reads, 'How can you criticize immorality, when you are the most infamous trench among the Socratic buggers?'
2. Symonds is probably thinking of Clough's *Dipsychus*, representing the

conflict between a tender conscience and the world. The reference is to 'dipsychos', a rare Greek word meaning 'twin-souled'.

3. There is probably a confusion here. Henry Cary (1804–70) translated Herodotus and Plato in 1848–9. The well-known crib man was W. B. Kelly who produced a series of *Kelly's Keys* to the classics from 1848 onwards.

4. The term 'exeat' is used for any occasion when boys leave the school premises.

5. Theokritos XII. 15–16. Most modern scholars read πάλιν for πάλαι which would be rendered, 'Men are back in the Golden Age, when the beloved boy has returned one's love.'

6. Unable to trace.

7. Harpocrates (Egyptian Horus), youthful sun born afresh each morning, represented as sitting with his finger in his mouth, symbolic of childhood. The Greeks and Romans called him the god of silence.

8. Theognis – Greek elegiac poet of the late sixth or early fifth century BC. Two volumes of his poetry survive. Book II and some of Book I contain pederastic overtones.

9. *The Anthology* – Greek epigrams begun by Meleager in first century BC. The original title, *Garden Anthology*, means a garland or collection of flowers.

10. Anacreon – c. 570 BC, was a lyric poet writing in Ionic dialect. Ibycus was a sixth-century lyric poet, while Pindar, writing in the fifth century, was a great choral lyricist.

6. Adolescence, life at Oxford, and the painful incidents of my first year there

1. Edwin Palmer (1824–95) was Archdeacon of Oxford from 1878. Robinson Ellis (1834–1913) was Corpus Professor of Latin Literature at Oxford from 1893. John Conington (1825–69) was elected to the chair of Latin language and literature at Oxford in 1854. Goldwin Smith (1823–1916) was Regius Professor of Modern History at Oxford between 1858 and 1866. Charles Parker (1829–1910), a Fellow of University College 1854–69, later became an MP for Perthshire.

   The others referred to are: Charles Henry Pearson (1830–94), colonial minister and historian; Arthur Penrhyn Stanley (1815–81), Dean of Westminster 1864–81; Albert Dicey, a noted jurist, appointed Vinerian Professor of English Law at Oxford in 1882; Thomas Hill Green (1836–82), appointed White's professor of moral philosophy in 1878; Mark Pattison (1813–84), Rector of Lincoln College; Francis Otter (1832–95), a liberal politician; and Albert Osliff Rutson (1836–90), a barrister and active in public life.

2. William Johnson (later Cory), author of *Jonica* (1858); his pupil was Charles Wood, later Viscount Halifax.
3. Francis Du Boulay (1810–92), chaplain to Bishop Philpotts of Exeter.
4. A *testamur* is a certificate from the examiners that a candidate has satisfied them.
5. Charles Elton (1839–1900), lawyer and antiquary.
6. Moderations are the first public examination for the degree of BA, taken at the end of the undergraduate's second year.
7. Herodotos I.66; from the Oracle of Apollo given to the Spartans asking for success in their planned campaign against Arkadia.
8. A Latin version of a Greek saying: Σπάρτην ἔλαχες, ταύτην κόσμει (Euripides fr. 7323, from the lost play *Telephos*), also cited in Greek by Cicero (*ad Atticum* 4.6.2).
9. *Alton Locke* (1850), a novel by Charles Kingsley.
10. Henry Montagu Butler succeeded Vaughan as headmaster at Harrow, 1859–85.
11. It is curious that Dalrymple later contributed a chapter on Dr Vaughan for Howson and Warner's *Harrow School*. Symonds continued late in life to refer affectionately to him in his letters.
12. In 1859 the Archbishop of Canterbury was John Bird Sumner. In June 1859, the Prime Minister, Lord Derby, was succeeded by Lord Palmerston.
13. Dr Vaughan did not die until 1897.
14. F. W. H. Myers (1843–1901), son of Myers of Keswick, became an inspector under the education department. A poet, he was also one of the founders of the Society for Psychical Research.
15. Henry Hart Milman (1791–1868), historian and poet, first Professor of Poetry at Oxford, was later Dean of St Paul's. Mrs Higford Burr, *née* A. Margaretta Scobell, was married to the politician, Daniel Higford Burr.
16. W. R. W. Stephens was Dean of Winchester, 1894–1902.

7. An important episode in my Oxford life: Alfred Brooke

1. The first line of the Latin version of Psalm Forty-two.

8. End of my Oxford life, wanderings in Switzerland, Rosa Engel and Catherine North, Italy

1. The Hon. L. S. Stanley, who succeeded to the title of Lord Stanley in 1909, became involved in various forms of social work. Albert Sidney Chavasse, also at Balliol, later became a barrister and eventually a proctor of the university in 1880. James McCall Marshall later became a master at Dulwich College, 1865–84, and headmaster of Durham School, 1884.

2. The first line is a version of the first line of the Latin of Psalm Eighty-four: 'How lovely are thy temples O Lord of hosts!'

3. Richard Congreve (1818–99) was an ardent disciple of Comte's positivism.

4. Hon. and Rev. W. Fremantle (1831–1916) was Dean of Ripon 1895–1915.

5. Lord Pembroke (1850–95) was the thirteenth earl.

6. G. A. Simcox became a distinguished classical scholar but even more distinguished as an eccentric. In 1905 he disappeared mysteriously during a walking tour in Ireland.

7. John Fisher (1809–96) was bursar of Magdalen.

8. After rigorous resistance the terms of the Oxford University Bill were accepted by Magdalen's new president, Frederic Bulley, in 1854. This complicated struggle is described in Charles E. Mallet's *A History of the University of Oxford* (London, 1927) and H. A. Wilson's *Magdalen College* (London, 1899).

9. W. R. W. Stephens was Dean of Winchester 1894–1902.

10. Mrs Josephine Butler (1828–1906) was an energetic social reformer.

11. Diotima, a priestess, was reputed to be the teacher of Socrates, referred to in the *Symposium*.

    Egeria, according to Roman legend, was the counsellor and wife of King Numa who, in order that he might commend laws to the people, declared that they were previously sanctified and approved by her.

12. Possibly a relative of Christian Charles de Bunsen, German Ambassador in London 1841–54.

13. John Rickards Mozley (1840–1931) was for a time a school inspector and from 1865–85 Professor of Pure Mathematics at Owens College, Manchester.

    Oscar Browning (1837–1923), an author, was Master at Eton 1860–75. See *Memories of Sixty Years at Eton, Cambridge and Elsewhere* (1910).

    Arthur Sidgwick (1840–1920), brother of Henry Sidgwick, was assistant master at Rugby 1864–79 and a Fellow of Corpus Christi College, Oxford, from 1882 to 1902.

14. A. B. Webb (1839–1907) became colonial bishop of Bloemfontein, Orange Free State, 1870–86.

15. Henry Graham Dakyns (1838–1911) was a master at Clifton College.

16. Jean Paul Richter (1763–1825) the German novelist.

17. Aristophanes, *Frogs* 84, referring to the poet Agathon who had left Athens for the court of Macedon.

305

9. Life in London, marriage, first attack of lung disease

1. In Symonds's own copy of *Leaves of Grass* (1860) opposite section 41 of 'Calamus' ('I meant that you should discover me so, by my faint indirections') he has written, 'This is the true method w*h* I have failed in.'
2. Sir William Bowman (1816–92) was a leading ophthalmic surgeon in London.
3. Dr William Acton (1814–75) wrote *A practical treatise on diseases of the urinary and generative organs* (1841).
4. Anton Gregor Rubinstein, pianist (1830–94), Alfredo Carlo Piatti, cellist (1822–1901), Joseph Joachim, violinist (1831–1907), Zelia Trebelli, mezzo-soprano (1838–92), Therese Titiens, soprano (1831–77), Antonio Giuglini, tenor (1827–65), Adelina Patti, soprano (1843–1919), Pauline Lucca, soprano (1841–1908).
5. Mrs Clough was the widow of Arthur Hugh Clough. In 1869 Symonds and Mrs Clough brought out a two-volume edition of Clough's poetry. Thomas Neville Abdy (1810–77) was MP for Lyme Regis, 1847–52. He was created a baronet in 1850.
6. Sir Spencer Wells (1818–97) was surgeon to the Queen's household.
7. Mary Ewart (born 1830) had previously known Symonds through relatives living in Clifton and Bath. She later became keenly interested in women's education.
8. Lucretius IV. 1134.
9. The son of his old schoolmaster in Clifton.
10. William John Vane, third Duke of Cleveland (1792–1864).
11. Untraced.
12. George Miller (1835–1909), a former Harrovian, later assistant in the National Education Department.
13. Thomas Woolner (1825–92), Pre-Raphaelite sculptor. The bust of Dr Symonds was displayed at the Royal Academy in 1872.
14. Lady Kay Shuttleworth, Catherine's half-sister, was the wife of the famous educational reformer, Sir James Phillips Kay Shuttleworth.

10. Early years of marriage: a tour of Normandy, peregrinations of all sorts, interrupted literary labour

1. 'Diego' (no date) published in the pamphlet *The Lotos Garland of Antinous* (Babington, page 23). The others cannot be located.
2. Theognis 1335–6.
3. *Anthologia Palatina* XII. 125, a homosexual love poem by Meleagros (100 BC); the first three lines run: 'Love brought beneath my mantle one night a sweet dream about an eighteen-year-old boy still wearing the *chlamys*.'

   [A *chlamys* was a long cloak worn by boys in their late teens. In the

306

ms., J.A.S. reads ὀκτωκαιδεκάτος whereas the correct reading should be ὀκτωκαιδεκετους.
4. Based on Catullus 5.
5. Dante, *Inferno* xv. 114.
6. Semnai Theai – the Eumenides, the kindly goddesses.

11. Peregrinations continued – Switzerland, Provence, the Riviera – settlement at Clifton, autumn 1868

1. See Jonah IV 6–10.
2. Adapted from Persius III. 38 which runs; *virtutem videant intabescant relicta* ('May they behold virtue, and having abandoned her, may they perish').
3. Dante, *Inferno* VII. 121–3. Actually this does not describe the slothful, but members of the three classes of the wrathful defined by St Augustine following Aristotle: the choleric; the bitter or sullen; and the ill-tempered or vengeful.
4. Dakyns Collection.
5. These poems seem to have disappeared.

12. Emotional development

1. In *A Problem in Modern Ethics*, Symonds lists the following among the works consulted: J. L. Casper and Carl Liman, *Handbuch der Gerichtlichen Medicin* (Berlin, 1889); Richard von Krafft-Ebing, *Psychopathia sexualis* (1889). He also read, during the sixties, a series of pamphlets intended to alter the stringent laws against homosexuality in Germany written by Carl Heinrich Ulrichs under the pseudonym 'Numa Numantius'. He visited Ulrichs in L'Aquila in 1891.
2. Themis, goddess of divine law, order, and justice.
3. The innocent lovers in Book II of Longus' prose romance *Daphnis and Chloe* know nothing about sexual love until a farmer's wife, Lucaenion, initiates Daphnis into the mysteries of sex (III. 12–14, 17–21).
4. Sir John Seeley's *Ecce Homo* (1865) was a survey of the life of Christ as one of the great religious reformers.
5. 'The Amateur Casual' by James Greenwood was published in the *Pall Mall Gazette* on 12, 13 and 15 January 1866. It was published as a book in 1877.
6. These poems seem to have disappeared.
7. Section 8 of the 1860 edition of *Leaves of Grass*. See *Leaves of Grass*, ed. Harold W. Blodgett and Sculley Bradley (New York University, 1965), page 595.
8. Roden Noel (1834–94), a minor poet, was a son of the Earl of

Gainsborough. Claude Delaval Cobham (1842–1917) became a translator and editor of materials about Cyprus.

9. *Weibling* was the term Ulrichs gave to one type of *Uranian*, or homosexual, the type who is attracted to strong and masculine men.

13. Norman

1. Theokritos. From the *Anakreontea*, a body of love poems (frequently homosexual) written 100 BC to 200 AD.

2. *Anthologia Palatina* XII. 219 – a verse from a poem by Straton (second century AD), whose poetry is exclusively homosexual, in which the poet argues the superiority of intercourse with a boy.

3. The theories of Max-Müller (1823–1900), though now mostly obsolete, during the nineteenth century exercised considerable influence on philology.

4. Eros, Storge and Agape (passion, affection and spiritual love) are 'the three falls' – a wrestling term to denote the three falls needed to win a bout. Used in an erotic context by Plato at *Phaidrus* 256 b.

5. Butler's 'Sermon on Self-deceit' is the tenth of the *Fifteen Sermons*.

6. Pindar, fragment 123.8.

7. Applied to the sight of one's beloved by Plato at *Phaidrus* 254 b.

8. Seems to have been written by Symonds himself.

9. Francis Newman, brother of John Henry Newman, was teaching classics at Bristol College at this time. W. J. Courthope was Professor of Poetry at Oxford 1895–1900.

10. His daughters' governess.

11. *Anthologia Palatina* XII.125.

12. Untraced.

13. Edward A. Sothern (1826–81) was a well-known actor.

14. Probably by Symonds.

15. J. E. Pearson (1850–1931) later became a master at Clifton. A. Nash (1851–1913) later became a barrister in Sydney, Australia. C. W. Boyle (1853–1900) was utterly undistinguished (apart from Dakyns's infatuation for him). He was killed in action in South Africa.

   Thomas Herbert Warren (1853–1930) later became president of Magdalen College (1885–1928). A. R. Cluer (1852–1942) became a leading London judge and police magistrate. H. F. Brown (1854–1926) edited and published *Calendar of State Papers, Venetian* (1891–1905). He was appointed Symonds's literary editor.

16. Probably by Symonds.

17. John Nichol was Professor of English Language and Literature at Glasgow 1862–89.

18. Rev. Henry Hayman (1823–1904) had been headmaster of St Andrew's College, Bradfield.

19. Probably by Symonds.
20. Probably by Symonds.
21. From Plato, *Republic* 474 e (as a love-term between homosexual lovers).

14. Intellectual and literary evolution

1. Symonds is referring to Matthew Arnold's famous description of the poet Thomas Gray.
2. A common Aristotelian phrase for a pastime, an adjunct to one's profession.
3. The reference is to the 10,000-year captivity of Prometheus, about whom it could be said that he had too much free time.
4. E. T. Cook (1857–1919) became editor of the *Pall Mall Gazette* in 1890. He resigned in 1892 when the paper was sold to Mr Astor.
5. Mark Pattison (1813–84) was Rector of Lincoln. A formidable scholar, he is thought to have provided George Eliot with the model of Casaubon in *Middlemarch*.
6. Horace, *Ars Poetica* 373.
7. See note 3.
8. A Stoic and Aristotelian term.
9. Farinata degli Uberti, a noble Florentine, leader of the Chibelline faction, was driven from his country in 1250 by the Guelphs whom he defeated ten years later. Dante in his *Inferno* represents him as lying in a fiery tomb which was not to be closed until the Last Judgment Day. The relevant line appears in Canto X, line 36: '*com' avesse l'inferno a gran dispitto*'.
10. Jean Charles Leonard Simonde de Sismondi's sixteen volumes of the *History of the Italian Republics of the Middle Ages* were published between 1807 and 1818. Lodovico Muratori (1672–1750) was an Italian historian.
11. William Mure, *A critical history of the language and literature of antient Greece*, 5 volumes, 1850–57.
12. Vergil II. 428. Used by Vergil of all the most virtuous of the Trojans who for all his piety and virtue, nevertheless perished in the sack of Troy. It became proverbial for events which seemed to occur contrary to any human criteria.
13. Symonds had been persuaded to run but had to withdraw because of health. Principal Shairp of St Andrew's was the successful candidate.
14. Hall Caine's review of *Vagabunduli Libellus* appeared in the *Academy*, 29 November 1884.

15. Religious development

1. Christopher Cholmeley Puller (1840–1902) was at Balliol. Charles Parker (1829–1910) served on commissions for public schools. James Bryce (1839–1922) was a jurist, historian and statesman. Edwin Palmer was Corpus Professor of Latin Literature at Oxford, 1870–78.
2. From a famous prayer by Kleanthes, Stoic philosopher of the third century, BC.
3. Symonds is quoting from his poem 'To the Praxitelean Statue Called the Genius of the Vatican' (*Many Moods*).

16. The transition to Davos Platz, and life there

1. The famous 'divine sign' of Socrates which would prevent him from doing any action that he ought not to do.
2. The first line is based on the lament of Job.
3. 'Sonnets on the Thought of Death' are in *Many Moods* (1878).
4. These poems are included in *Animi Figura* (1882).

17. Angelo Fusato

1. The Army Corps of Engineers.
2. Sappho 31. 'Equal to the gods' means that Sappho is admiring the man's strength in being able to sit so close to the person whose very sight drives Sappho wild.
3. Theo Marzials (1850–1920) was a clerk in the British Museum and also a composer of popular songs. Lord Ronald Charles Sutherland-Gower (1845–1911) was a well-known sculptor. His *Old Diaries 1881–1892* (1902) contain several references to Symonds.
4. Lucretius IV.1071.

Appendices

1. Case XVIII is the case history of Symonds himself.
2. *Consuelo* (1842).
3. The Rev. the Hon. Edward Lyttelton, headmaster of Eton. In 1877 he privately printed a pamphlet *The Causes and Prevention of Immorality in Schools*.
4. See page 232.

Index